The Best of
"THE PUBLIC SQUARE"

The Best of "THE PUBLIC SQUARE"

BOOK THREE

Richard John Neuhaus

With an Introduction by

Joseph Bottum

William B. Eerdmans Publishing Company
Grand Rapids, Michigan / Cambridge, U.K.

Published 2007 by
Wm. B. Eerdmans Publishing Co.
2140 Oak Industrial Drive N.E., Grand Rapids, Michigan 49505 /
P.O. Box 163, Cambridge CB3 9PU U.K.

Printed in the United States of America

12 11 10 09 08 07 7 6 5 4 3 2 1

Library of Congress Cataloging-in-Publication Data

Neuhaus, Richard John.
[Public square. Selections. 2007]
The best of "The Public square". Book three / Richard John Neuhaus; with an introduction by Joseph Bottum.
p. cm.
ISBN 978-0-8028-2720-3 (pbk.: alk. paper)
1. United States — Religion — 1960- 2. Christianity — 20th century. 3. Religion and politics — United States. 4. Religion and sociology — United States. 5. Religion and politics. 6. Religion and sociology. I. Title.

BL2525.N483 2007
261.0973 — dc22

2007009963

www.eerdmans.com

Contents

Introduction

Richard Starr, the managing editor of the *Weekly Standard,* once remarked that if there were any justice in the world, the production of "The Public Square" would be recognized as one of the great feats of journalism in our time. Since 1990, in a monthly column of ten to twenty thousand words, Father Richard John Neuhaus has covered a range of topics nearly impossible to believe. The prose is sharp and crisp, the tone is both serious and witty, and the effect has been a grand commentary on the great religious and cultural arguments of our time.

Starr's line seems right — and yet, perhaps "The Public Square" succeeds so well as journalism precisely because it isn't journalism, at least not in the way the word is commonly used. Take any of the newspaper columnists you admire and sit down with a book-length collection of their columns. You will quickly discover that their work seems to have changed to something much less enjoyable. Part of it, of course, is that the topics of such op-ed columns grow quickly dated, but another part is this: The pieces of writing you admired so much at eight hundred words a day start to cloy when strung together at fifty thousand words. The writer's tricks show through a little too clearly, the unchanging voice starts to bore, and the compression that was pleasant in a newspaper column begins to seem annoying in a book.

It is not the least of his triumphs as a writer that Richard John Neuhaus has managed to escape much of the cloyingness and datedness that dogs journalists' opinion writing. The popular blogger Andrew Sullivan detests much of the analysis contained in "The Public Square," and yet he, along with many others, has credited "The Public Square" with being the *ur*-blog — forming, as it were, the gestalt in which the best Internet writing would later come to dwell. That, too, seems right: Particularly with the smaller items, the "While We're At Its" in the second half of each "Public Square," Fr. Neuhaus defined the quick, bite-sized notes that writing for the Web would use. But it also seems to miss the central accomplishment of "The Public Square." If you find a book-length collection of newspaper columns hard slogging, you ain't seen nothing yet. Wait till book-length collections of blog items start to appear.

No, what Richard John Neuhaus has accomplished in his monthly column for the journal *First Things* is a surprising combination of the timely and the timeless — a voice that can move easily from one to the other, of course, but also a willingness to combine them: using the timely as an occasion to apply the lessons of the timeless. Just in this collection of items from "The Public Square," you'll find, for instance, the publication of a book on vegetarianism used as an occasion for thinking deeply about the human relation to God's creation, about the keeping of pets, and about a nature that is somehow a reflection of its Creator's glory and at the same time red in tooth and claw.

A passing comment from the editor of *Sacred Architecture* becomes an opportunity to think our way through the reason for buildings, their relation to human beings, and their striving for beauty. The appearance of a small biography of Martin Luther King Jr. offers a chance to remember the civil rights movement, the role of friendship, and the costs and benefits of a prophetic stand in politics. The completion of the definitive biography of Fyodor Dostoevsky allows contemplation of the importance of religion for literature, the successes and failures of fiction in conveying truth, and the problems of the nonreligious in writing of the religious. On and on the examples go — one of the great journalistic feats of our time, most of all because it is something more than journalism.

The best way to get to know "The Public Square" is to subscribe to the journal *First Things*. It's there that you can read, month after month, the work of Richard John Neuhaus. Born in Canada, Fr. Neuhaus is a graduate of Concordia Theological Seminary, St Louis, Missouri. In 1991, he was ordained a priest in the archdiocese of New York.

One of the leading authorities on the role of religion in the contemporary world, Fr. Neuhaus is the editor in chief of the journal, a monthly magazine of religion, culture, and public life. Among his best known books are *Freedom for Ministry; The Naked Public Square: Religion and Democracy in America; The Catholic Moment: The Paradox of the Church in the Postmodern World;* and, with Rabbi Leon Klenicki, *Believing Today: Jew and Christian in Conversation.* In 1995, he edited with Charles Colson *Evangelicals & Catholics Together: Toward a Common Mission.* His most popular books include *Death on a Friday Afternoon: Meditations on the Last Words of Jesus from the Cross* and *As I Lay Dying: Meditations upon Returning.* His most recent work is *Catholic Matters: Confusion, Controversy, and the Splendor of Truth,* published by Basic Books in February 2006.

As a Lutheran clergyman, he was for seventeen years senior pastor of a low-income black parish in Brooklyn, New York. A leader in organizations dealing with civil rights, international justice, and ecumenism, Fr. Neuhaus has been the subject of feature articles in popular and scholarly publications both here and abroad, and he has been the recipient of numerous honors from universities and other institutions, including the John Paul II Award for Religious Freedom. He has held presidential appointments in the Carter, Reagan, and first Bush administrations. In a survey of national leadership, *U.S. News & World Report* named Fr. Neuhaus one of the thirty-two "most influential intellectuals in America." *Time* magazine, in a 2005 cover story, named Fr. Neuhaus one of the most influential religious figures in America.

It is a measure of the success of "The Public Square" that this marks the third book-length collection drawn from the monthly column. The junior fellows and assistant editors who have worked at *First Things* have done the work of extracting and collecting the items for this volume, and they each deserve thanks: John Rose, Jordan Hylden, Ryan T. Anderson, and Vincent Druding.

The items have been arranged to form, chapter by chapter, a reading roughly the size and range of a typical month's worth of "The Public Square": a set of essay-length discussions (the title pieces, as we call them in the office), followed by a number of smaller items that come under the heading "While We're At It." If you find you need more, you should subscribe to the journal *First Things* (online at *www.firstthings.com* or by phone, toll-free, at 877-905-9920), where you will find not only "The Public Square" but also articles, poems, and reviews from many of America's best writers on religion, culture, and public life.

Joseph Bottum
New York, New York

I

The Wisdom of the Elders

It was that time of year again, and thousands of commencement speakers hoped that millions of graduates would remember their words better than the speakers remember what was said when they commenced. At the University of Rochester, James O. Freedman, former President of Dartmouth, held forth. "Someone once asked Woodrow Wilson when he was President of Princeton University what the function of a liberal education ought to be. And Wilson replied, 'To make a person as unlike his father as possible.'" So much for education as the transmission of a heritage. I don't know if Wilson actually said that, but, if so, it would be a kindness to his memory to forget it. A liberal education, Freedman went on to say, "ought to make a person independent of mind, skeptical of authority and received views, prepared to forge an identity for himself or herself, and capable of becoming an individual not bent upon copying other persons — even persons as persuasive and influential as one's father." There you have it: independence, skepticism, individualism, forging a unique identity — I wannabe Me! One does hope the students were skeptical of the authority of their commencement speaker.

At the Fashion Institute of Technology in New York City, the actor Alec Baldwin dispensed wisdom. Mr. Baldwin, it may be recalled, raised hopes when he said he would leave the country if George W. Bush became President, but then reneged on his promise. Baldwin told the students of fashion that "billions of people around the world" buy all kinds of things in order to "make a statement to the best of their ability, and within the boundaries of their own tastes and budgets, about who they are." The problem is that "most of them are not creative people. They just don't have that gene. They haven't developed that muscle. So the uncreative people of the world rely on the creative people of the world to help them." There you have it: a perfect match of creative speaker and creative graduates, locked in mutual admiration. None dare call it elitism.

Julian Bond of the NAACP did the honors at Susquehanna University, a putatively Lutheran school in Pennsylvania. He quoted someone who had escaped from the World Trade Center on September 11 who said, "If you'd seen what it was like in that stairway, you'd be proud. There was no gender, no race, no religion. It was everyone helping each other." To which Mr. Bond commented, "But away from that stairway — in America's streets — there is gender, there is race, there is religion." Mr. Bond has, over his many years, done his bit to get rid of gender and religion, even as he has made his living by race, the difference that, one might suggest, should make the least difference.

Then there was Anna Quindlen at Sarah Lawrence College. "When I quit the *New York Times* to be a full-time mother, the voices of the world said I was nuts," she declared. Think of that. From Hamburg to Bangladesh, from Stockholm to Shanghai, from Honduras to the remotest reaches of Siberia, the voices of the world joined in declaring, "Anna Quindlen is nuts!" Ms. Quindlen exhorted the students to be radical individualists, following her example. "Each of you is as different as your fingertips. Why should you march to any lockstep? Our love of lockstep is our greatest curse, the source of all that bedevils us. It is the source of homophobia, xenophobia, racism, sexism, terrorism, bigotry of every variety and hue, because it tells us there is one right way to do things, to look, to behave, to feel, when the only right way is to feel your heart hammering inside you and to listen to what its timpani is saying."

One imagines a graduate of independent mind in the audience whose timpani was telling her that Anna Quindlen is the quintessential representative of the self-flattering feminism that has turned the lives of so many women into a misery. Ms. Quindlen would, in no uncertain terms, let such a student know that that is the wrong response and she had better get back in step with folks like her who repudiate marching in lockstep. That's the logic that has always prevailed among the herd of independent minds.

In hope of relief from the deluge of commencement bullfeathers, I turned to the famously conservative novelist Tom Wolfe, who spoke at Duke University. He's interested in neuroscience and said, "Let's not kid ourselves. We're all concatenations of molecules containing DNA, hard wired into a chemical analog computer known as the human brain, which as software has a certain genetic code. And your idea that you have a soul or even a self, much less free will, is just an illusion."

There you have it: the elders offering final counsel to the successor generation, the beneficiaries of the greatest educational system in the world, the bearers of civilization's legacy across new frontiers of human aspiration and achievement. Another generation of Ralph Waldo Emerson's children, exhorted to preen themselves on their individualistic conformism, remembering always, of course, that none of it is true. *(August/September 2002)*

The Soul of Steven Pinker

It is not entirely a straw man that he is attacking. For a long time now, especially among educators, there has, in fact, been an influential school of thought at war with the very idea of human nature. Everything is determined by nurture, environment, and social conditioning, they say. Then there is the reaction launched by Edward O. Wilson with his 1975 book *Sociobiology,* arguing along with such as Richard Dawkins, author of *The Selfish Gene,* that nature is trump. Pushed out of the argument because it is so impossibly incorrect is *The Bell Curve* by Richard Herrnstein and Charles Murray, which argued that IQ and other factors crucial to social success are genetically determined and are unequally distributed among racial groups. But the opponents of natural determinism lump Wilson, Dawkins, and Herrnstein and Murray together as the enemies of equality and the commitment to make the world a much better place by the achievement of social justice.

Now comes along Steven Pinker, a psychologist of language at M.I.T., with a new book, *The Blank Slate: The Modern Denial of Human Nature* (Viking). Pinker is telegenic and articulate — some say facile — and *Maclean's,* the magazine of Canadian identity, describes him as "endearingly Canadian; polite, soft-spoken, attentive to what others say." Pinker, who comes down on the side of Wilson and Co., says, quite rightly, that proponents of the blank slate approach are sometimes prone to implicitly totalitarian plans of social engineering aimed at imposing equality. Equality, he says, is a moral and political idea, not a scientific reality, and again he is right about that. Human beings, and especially human minds, are not equal; they come with innate, genetically formed abilities and behavioral tendencies. The conclusion drawn by Professor Pinker is that a child's life is shaped by natural endowments (genes), family experience, peer groups, and chance happenings. That seems a rather modest payoff for so much ratiocination and scientific huffing and puffing.

What all the major parties to this academic contest have in common is that they are thoroughgoing materialists. Prof. Pinker, for instance, may be "polite, soft-spoken, and attentive to what others say," except when it comes to others —

from Plato to Aquinas and from Kierkegaard to Polanyi — who think that human beings are more than matter. The suggestion of anything beyond the reach of his neuroscience — the soul, for instance — is derisively dismissed as the myth of "the Ghost in the machine," a myth abandoned by all but "the religious right." It is, in fact, such dogmatic and vulgar materialism that requires a blind leap of faith. Both the blank slatists and the nature determinists typically assume that those unwilling to make that leap are beyond the pale of rational discourse.

A Different Fundamentalism

Of course, they do not really believe that their ideas are exhaustively explained either by neurological synapses or by environmental conditioning. They write books, give lectures, and appear on talk shows contending that they really do have ideas that are, well, true — just as though there is reason, or soul, or even a ghost in the machine. When asked why we should take their ideas seriously if they are no more than the predetermined products of genes or conditioning, they are inclined to respond, "It is an interesting paradox, isn't it?" No, it isn't. It is simply the incoherent nonsense that follows from a fundamentalist leap of faith into dogmatic materialism.

This does not mean there is nothing to learn from reading books such as *The Blank Slate.* There is much that is useful to know about both natural endowments and environmental influences. We are, after all, embodied souls or, as some prefer, ensouled bodies, and are created for society. We may be instructed by a skilled anatomist who dissects the sexual organs or the brain, while politely declining to believe him when he asserts that that is all there is to sex or to thinking. Likewise, we may be grateful for insights into environmental influences without believing that they adequately explain our lives as we know our lives by living.

To understand ourselves as creatures rather than products, as persons possessed of reason and related to the infinite, simply makes more sense of more things that we cannot help but know are true. Among the problems with materialist fundamentalism, apart from its implausibility, is that it is so very boring. That being said, prepare to see Steven Pinker on a forthcoming talk show, responding when challenged (if he is challenged) with, "It is an interesting paradox, isn't it?" At which point you may say to the screen, ever so politely, "No, Prof. Pinker. It is neither interesting nor a paradox." You might want to follow that with a prayer for the soul that his belief system prevents him from recognizing that he has. *(December 2002)*

Wild Moralists in the Animal Kingdom

Prejudice gets a very bad press, but one cannot live without it. On numerous questions, we have all made judgments that are "pre" our present encounter with the question. "No, thank you, I do not care for broccoli; and no, I'm not interested in revisiting the question." Not all such questions are as important as broccoli. It has been brought to my attention that some readers think vegetarianism is so manifestly and self-evidently wrongheaded that, after rejecting it upon first encounter, one would be a moral idiot to give it a second thought. The occasion for such outbursts is my essay in *National Review* (December 31, 2002) on Matthew Scully's recent book, *Dominion: The Power of Man, the Suffering of Animals, and the Call to Mercy*. Why, I am asked, do I even take the time to read such a book, never mind write an essay on it? Vegetarians, fruitarians, animal rightists, tree huggers. Don't I know they're a company of crazies, cranks, and puling adolescents of all ages who major in moral minors in order to divert attention from what in their lives they really *should* feel guilty about? Well, not quite.

It is true that I'm a paid-up subscriber to the robust and emphatically embodied view of life. With Chesterton, I think it not sacrilegious but persuasive analogy to envision the end of life's journey in terms of an eternal convivium, with a thick steak, a pint of ale, and a good cigar in a particularly comfortable country inn, and with the best of friends, of course. With due respect to the saints who are, an ascetic like the desert fathers I am not. Moreover, I have to work at containing my impatience with people who are not content with the perpetual monitoring of their moral pulse, but are eager to help me out by monitoring mine as well. More sensitive than thee or me, they can be counted upon to rain their distress upon the threatening appearance of almost any happiness — other than theirs in winning the self-bestowed prize for superior scrupulosity. Such people are simply too sensitive for decent company. I do not say we should go out of our way to offend their sensibilities, but a little tweaking is sometimes in order.

So why, then, did I treat Mr. Scully's book with such respect? The answer is that it is, for the most part, a book that makes serious arguments. Too many arguments, no doubt. It is unfortunate that his editor was on vacation, leaving the text to go chasing after every forensic hare in excurses that run over the tops and around the bends of subjects sometimes remotely related to the case he wants to make. The best part of the book, which is written from an expressly Christian and conservative way of looking at the world, is his contention that the morality of the humane treatment of animals rests not — as the "animal rights" theorists such as Peter Singer would have it — on animals being equal to human beings but precisely on their being unequal and therefore so very dependent and vulnerable. That's why the subtitle speaks of "the call to mercy" rather than "the call to justice," although Scully does, against his better instincts, end up entangling himself in some of the esoterica of the animal rights theorizing. Most pertinent to public policy is his polemic against industrial, or containment, farming. He visited some huge pig plants in North Carolina and what he reports is unpleasant in the extreme. "If you could walk all of humanity through one of these places," he writes, "90 percent would never touch meat again." That's hyperbolic, but in a cause deserving of notice.

Conversations with Sammy

In terms of the egregious infliction of pain, it would seem that present practices in industrial farming constitute cruelty to animals and beg for regulative attention. Scully makes a persuasive case that the same must be said of many laboratory experiments with animals. Egregious means unnecessary, but, in the view of Scully and those of like mind, all raising of animals for food is egregious, since it is not absolutely necessary to eat meat. Most everybody understands what is meant by the infliction of pain. If that is the question, then the discussion turns to if and in what ways animals experience pain, and from there it can move to finding less painful, or even painless, methods of using animals for food. But cruelty is only one part of the argument. Another is the "deprivation" experienced by animals who are denied the living out of their natural propensities. Here the argument gets very wobbly, appealing to sentimentality and anthropomorphisms by which we are asked to imagine how we would feel if people did to us what people do to those pigs and Frank Perdue's chickens. I, for one, wouldn't like it at all. But I am inclined to doubt that pigs or chickens or, for that matter, mosquitoes have a life plan that anybody is frustrating.

I take second place to nobody when it comes to sentimentality about animals. Well, about some animals. My dog Sammy the Second, for instance. (Sammy the First died some years ago.) She has a pleasantly inflated view of my virtues, and she gives abundant evidence of sensations for which I cannot help but use words such as pleasure, fear, devotion, guilt, and hunger. Mainly hunger — for food and for affirmation, in that order. I have been caught in the act of discussing with her subjects both mundane and recondite. For example, the consciousness of animals. I am not embarrassed to say that I find these discussions with Sammy very rewarding, although, admittedly, I supply the best lines. I would not think of having her for dinner, and anybody who threatens her harm will have to deal with both of us, although more ominously with her. Neither would I think of extrapolating from my playfully and unabashedly embroidered relationship with Sammy to construct moral imperatives for humanity's responsibility toward the animal kingdom. There's not much more to be said about it than that she's a lucky dog. I'm happy with the arrangement, and, so far as I can tell, she is brimming over with happiness in her doggy mode of being.

There are deeper dimensions worth exploring, of course. It is spiritually salutary to be reminded that we, along with Sammy and all the other animals, are creatures. Which is another way of saying that we are not God. Consider this fine passage from St. Augustine's *Confessions:*

> "And what is this God?" I asked the earth and it answered: "I am not He," and all the things that are on the earth confessed the same answer. I asked the sea and the deeps and the creeping things with living souls, and they replied, "We are not your God. Look above us." I asked the blowing breezes, and the universal air with all its inhabitants answered: "I am not God." I asked the heaven, the sun, the moon, the stars, and "No," they said, "we are not the God for whom you are looking." And I said to all those things which stand about the gates of my senses: "Tell me something about my God, you who are not He. Tell me some-

thing about Him." And they cried out in a loud voice: "He made us."

He made all of us animals, and to us human animals he gave a most particular charge, as we read in the first chapter of Genesis: "Then God said, 'Let us make man in our image, after our likeness; and let them have dominion over the fish of the sea, and over the birds of the air, and over the cattle, and over all the earth, and over every creeping thing that creeps upon the earth.'" There are some intriguing discussions among the rabbis and early teachers of the Church as to whether Adam and Eve were vegetarians before the Fall. Or maybe everybody was vegetarian up until Noah and his family came out of the ark and, as we read in Genesis 9, the mandate assumed a darker hue: "The fear and the dread of you shall be upon every beast of the earth, and upon every bird of the air, upon everything that creeps on the ground and all the fish of the sea; into your hand they are delivered. Every moving thing that lives shall be food for you; and as I gave you the green plants, I give you everything."

Escaping Complicity

They all cry out, "He made us." And we cry in response, "He made us too." But why and for what? Among other things, he made them for food. Or so it would seem. St. Augustine was not a vegetarian. As was St. Francis of Assisi — who is reputed to have understood most deeply the mysterious connections between ourselves and our fellow animals — not a vegetarian. Many people today are vegetarians, or vegans, as those of the strict observance commonly call themselves. There is no agreement on how many, but it is said the number is growing. If by vegetarian is meant someone who *never* eats meat or fish or fowl, it's probably one or two percent of the American population. That number is cut very sharply if vegetarianism includes a prohibition of animal products such as milk, cheese, and eggs. And, of course, leather and fur.

One cannot fault the consistency of those who, determined to escape complicity in the slaughter, put their dogs and cats on a vegetarian diet. There is much debate about this in vegan circles. The conclusion seems to be that it makes some owners feel better about themselves, and their pets very sick. The quest for absolute purity is a relentless master, and the doctrinal disputes and distinctions embroiling the vegan world are like the infightings of a religious sect, which in some ways it is. I see there are also websites run by ex-vegans, apostates as it were, who left the fold chiefly for health reasons. There are even not very good ex-vegan jokes. For instance, **Q:** How many vegans does it take to screw in a light bulb? **A:** Three; one to do the work and two to anguish over how many animals are killed by the habitat destruction necessary for extracting the minerals required to manufacture a light bulb.

The temptation to mock the hyper-sensitive, while not completely resistible, should be indulged within limits. I would seriously question the moral curiosity, if not intelligence, of anyone who has not given some thought to the rightness of our raising and hunting animals for food. When it came to butchering time on Rud Biesenthal's farm and Big Jack, the prize hog, was whacked on the head with a sledgehammer and then hung upside down by a chain pulley to have his throat slit and be bled before he was lowered into a boiling cauldron to scald off the hair, this twelve-year-old had deep thoughts about our right to pork chops and bacon. Such reactions are not to be brushed aside as juvenile squeamishness but should be thought through with care. The purpose of thinking something through is to arrive at a judgment. A judgment is subject to change in the face of convincing argument or evidence, but it is a judgment. Which means it is the alternative to crippling and guilt-ridden indecision.

To be well adjusted to the world as it is is not an indication of moral or spiritual health. A friend who agrees that vegan ideology cannot be lived consistently and is not a practicable means for alleviating the sorry state of the world nonetheless follows a fairly rigorous vegetarian diet. It is, she says, a matter of witness to a future promise. Remember the Peaceable Kingdom envisioned by Isaiah:

> For behold, I create new heavens and a new earth;
> and the former things shall not be remembered
> or come to mind. . . .
> The wolf and the lamb shall feed together,
> the lion shall eat straw like the ox.
> They shall not hurt or destroy in all my holy mountain,
> says the Lord.

My friend's vegetarianism is not a program of action but a testament of hope and is, I think, to be honored as such. Her purpose is not to lay a guilt trip on others nor to assert her superior sensibilities, but to remind us, and herself first of all, that in a fallen world we are to be yearning for a reality rightly ordered, as in "new heavens and a new earth." She is not discouraged by the knowledge that her witness runs counter to the way things are. That's the point of witness. She knows and can appreciate the story about the zookeeper who was famous for having trained a lion and a lamb to live peacefully together. "How do you do it?" asked an admirer. "It's simple," said the zookeeper. "Every morning a fresh lamb."

Vegetarianism in its myriad versions will not, and I think should not, become the rule. Not an inch can be given to the nastier elements in the animal rights movements that employ violence against people to enforce gentleness toward other creatures. We human beings will, to put it bluntly, continue to kill. We will continue to raise and hunt animals for food, and continue to cull deer and Canada geese that invade our living spaces. The Humane Society and the National Audubon Society, the cat people and the bird people, will continue to go to court on opposing sides over what is to be done about the 100 million cats (including strays) who kill billions of birds and other life forms each year. Few will develop qualms about exterminating rats, and even fewer will fret, as did the reviewer of Scully's book in the *New York Times Book Review,* about the pain we inflict upon the vegetables we eat. Most people are aware of the ways in which many animals are dependent upon human beings, and the huge role that the domestication of animals, also for food, plays in our history and theirs. There are, I am told, fifty million dogs in America while wolves are numbered in the thousands. If, as some urge, we adopted a more natural approach and let dogs be dogs and wolves be wolves, I expect those numbers would be fairly quickly reversed. It is not evident that this would be to anybody's benefit, except maybe for the wolves.

Red in Tooth and Claw

If we stopped eating meat, entire species would quickly become extinct. For instance, almost nobody raises pigs for the pleasure of their company. Moreover, if left on their own, millions upon millions of animals would die more brutal deaths at the hands of a nature red in tooth and claw. There is an element of sadness in the death of a deer shot by a hunter. It is not quite the horror of a deer ripped apart by a pack of coyotes. Many hunters — and this may go back to our primordial roots — practice little rituals of respect for the life that is taken. In a similar vein, it is not entirely whimsical that at table we acknowledge with thanks the animal and vegetable life that makes possible our meal. "He made us," they might well have said, and we readily agree. He made them to be Sunday dinner, and we are grateful.

Consideration should be given also to the countless small field animals that would be killed in order to cultivate enough grain to feed a nation, never mind a world, of vegans. The toll would be, some estimate, much greater than the number of lives now taken for meat. He made those field animals, too. Nor can we dismiss as trivial the part that gastronomy and other social conventions associated with feasting play in the civilizing of the human animal. True, our vegan friends boast of culinary developments with meatless delicacies, but I am inclined to be skeptical. And, because I am unpersuaded by their moral arguments, I feel no need to work at overcoming my skepticism.

There is undoubtedly a shadow of sadness over the complex patterns of cooperation, competition, and conflict in the animal kingdom for which we, of all the animals, have been commissioned to care. We — along with snails, cockroaches, rodents, leopards, cats, tuna, and mosquitoes — are caught up in a web of creaturely life marked by deprivation and bounded by inevitable death. We alone, however, can be, and are called to be, humane. That capacity and that call require, as noted above, a closer look at the practices of industrial farming as described by Scully and many others.

Lacrimae rerum. The tears of things. Karl Barth, the most influential Protestant theologian of the past century, wrote that those who dismiss empathy with our fellow animals as childish or sentimental "are themselves subjects for tears." He went on to say:

> The world of animals and plants forms the indispensable living background to the living space divinely allotted to man and placed under his control. As they live, so can he. He is not set up as lord over the earth, but as lord on the earth which is already furnished with these creatures. Animals and plants do not belong to him; they and the whole earth can belong only to God. But he takes precedence over them. They are provided for his use. They are his "means of life." The meaning of the basis of this distinction

> consists in the fact that he is the animal creature to whom God reveals, entrusts, and binds Himself within the rest of creation, with whom He makes common cause in the course of a particular history which is neither that of an animal nor a plant, in whose life-activity He expects a conscious and deliberate recognition of His honor, mercy, and power. Hence the higher necessity of his life, and his right to that lordship and control. He can exercise it only in the responsibility thus conferred upon him.

Barth offers this caution, however: "If we try to bring animal and vegetable life too close to human, or even class them together, we can hardly avoid the danger of regarding and treating human life, even when we really want to help, from the aspect of the animal and vegetable, and therefore in a way which is not really apposite." And, of course, that is exactly what happens with animal rightists such as Peter Singer who condemn as "speciesism" our insistence upon the singular dignity of the human. The hope for a more humane world, including the more humane treatment of animals, is premised upon what is denied by Singer and his like. Barth's point is nicely caught in Abraham Joshua Heschel's statement, "Man is both the cantor and the caretaker of the creation."

Life Feeding on Life

Lacrimae rerum. There is much to weep about. But it is a sin to permit our tears to drown out our song of gratitude and joy in the gift of creation. Yet it is true that — whether at the level of the animal, vegetable, or microbiological — the order of creation is that life feeds on life. That rule is universal and immutable. The most we can do by changing our habits is to decide not to feed on some forms of life, which decisions will always have about them an element of arbitrariness, producing the guilt-tripping and sectarian disputes that mark communities of disordered scrupulosity. Whether life fed on life before that unfortunate afternoon in the Garden of Eden, I do not know, but I cannot imagine how it could have been any other way. The same must be said of whether the universal rule will hold in the New Jerusalem. The revealed indicators are that things will be radically different, so radically different as to elude our wildest imaginings. We will, please God, find out in due course. Meanwhile, we are creatures in a creation caught up in a perpetual dance of life with death, and of death with life.

Vegetarianism and related moral impulses go way back to belief systems very different from ours, most of which have a very different understanding of creation and of what it means to be a creature. And, it follows, very different understandings of the Creator. In the sixth century B.C., Pythagoras and his followers embraced the kinship of all animals, apparently believing in the transmigration of souls or a form of reincarnationalism along the lines affirmed by many Buddhists, Hindus, and Jains to this day. Some eighteenth-century Enlightenment figures, such as Voltaire, praised vegetarianism, as did Shelley, Thoreau, Tolstoy, and George Bernard Shaw. Seventh-day Adventists are strong proponents, as are the people who live in the strange afterglow of Madame Besant and Theosophy. Frequently their cause is joined to the campaign against alcohol and smoking, which is yet another indicator, in my judgment, of moral reasoning gone awry. At the risk of being provocative, one notes that the most prominent vegetarian, and enemy of smoking and drinking, in the twentieth century was Adolf Hitler. As best one can tell from his muddled remarks on the subject, it had to do with not compromising the genetic superiority of his bodily fluids.

According to the admirable eleventh edition of the *Encyclopaedia Britannica,* "Racial Improvement" was an important part of the vegetarian movement as typically promoted by, for instance, the Order of the Golden Age at the beginning of the twentieth century. The *Encyclopaedia* explains: "On the ground that the aim of every prosperous community should be to have a large proportion of hardy country yeomen, and that horticulture and agriculture demand such a high ratio of labor, as compared with feeding and breeding cattle . . . the country population would be greatly increased by the substitution of a fruit and vegetable for an animal dietary." That seems terribly dated a century later when agricultural technology has made farming anything but labor intensive. On the other hand, authors such as Scully suggest it is a reasonable compromise to eat only animals who are raised in the old-fashioned way, commonly called "free farming," and, if that practice really caught on, one could imagine a revival of the racial improvement argument. Although it is likely that Mexican immigrants would be the chief beneficiaries of the improvement.

Rebels against Creaturehood

It is evident, then, that agitations over what we should and should not do with our fellow animals encompass a wide array of beliefs and concerns, from the transmigration of souls to eugenics to the preservation of species to questions of diet and health. If I believed in reincarnation and thought that this excellent broiled chicken may have been the temporary residence of Aunt Agatha, I wouldn't touch it. But I don't believe that. Nor do I share a belief, or call it a disposition, that is evident in people as various as Voltaire, Shaw, Tolstoy, Besant, and the members of the Order of the Golden Age. They have in common a disorder that, in the Christian tradition, has been called gnosticism or angelism. They are in rebellion against their creatureliness — in many cases because they have a big problem with being subject to the Creator. Angels are pure spirits, and gnostics are inclined to the view that the essential self is a divine spark only temporarily trapped in vulgar flesh. We are neither angels nor divine sparks.

There are revolutionary rebels against creaturehood who propose utopian schemes for achieving a higher level of existence. There are resigned rebels who stoically endure the unacceptable. Much more numerous are the guilt-ridden rebels, who apparently gain a measure of relief by making others feel guilty as well. To feel guilty about being a creature is a species of pride. All life feeds on life. Creatures have teeth and claws and instruments for grasping at one end and organs of excretion at the other. That, too, is what it means to be embodied. Our creaturely life is marked by sin, but it is no sin to be a creature. Knowing that we are creatures is the cause not of guilt but of gratitude. In Christ, God became one of us. Knowing that we are human creatures is also to know that we alone of all the animals are called to responsibility. We are to exercise dominion, to care and to take care. We will continue to deliberate and debate about what that requires in terms of public policy. For the living of their own lives, different people will make different decisions. And, please God, in our disagreements, both public and personal, over what it means to be humane toward nonhuman animals and other life forms, we will strive to be humane also toward one another. *(April 2003)*

While We're At It

❧ Why is so much contemporary art deliberately depraved, perverse, ugly, and determined to shock? Please be patient with me if I once again suggest that G. K. Chesterton put at least one part of the answer as well as it can be put. In *The Everlasting Man,* he discusses the decadence of Rome when, in the absence of true religion, the most creative minds indulged in a multitude of wildly conflicting mythologies "swarming like flies on a dung heap." He writes: "There comes an hour in the afternoon when the child is tired of 'pretending'; when he is weary of being a robber or a Red Indian. It is then that he torments the cat. There comes a time in the routine of an ordered civilization when the man is tired of playing at mythology and pretending that a tree is a maiden or that the moon made love to a man. The effect of this staleness is the same everywhere; it is seen in all drug-taking and dram-drinking and every form of the tendency to increase the dose. Men seek stranger sins or more startling obscenities as stimulants to their jaded sense. They seek after mad oriental religions for the same reason. They try to stab their nerves to life, if it were with the knives of the priests of Baal. They are walking in their sleep and try to wake themselves up with nightmares." There are other answers, to be sure, such as the dealers and collectors who control "the art world" and turn nightmares into cash. They are not so much jaded as cynical, capitalizing on depravity while enjoying a frisson of complicity in the artist's contempt for their safe and affluent lives. Having rejected the three transcendentals of the good, the true, and the beautiful, what is the alternative? *(August/September 2002)*

❦ When I was at seminary in St. Louis, I did some graduate work in philosophy at Washington University. The fellow who chiefly captured my attention, and, whatever his intentions, dissuaded me from viewing academic philosophy as a possible future, was a terribly clever young Ph.D. fresh out of Harvard, who, as an analyst of ordinary language, rejoiced in demonstrating that words do not mean what they purport to mean. He was very good at this. I had not thought about him in a long time until coming across this in Terry Eagleton's memoir *The Gatekeeper.* In his chapter on "Dons," he describes a "Dr. Greenway" who disillusioned him of the assumption that there is a connection between erudition and intelligence. Eagleton writes, "Greenway was certainly intelligent, but he had no more ideas in his head than a hamster.

Indeed, he was not only bereft of ideas but passionately opposed to them, which struck me as a little odd for a doctor of philosophy. He did not see the need for them, any more than he saw the need for wrapping his feet in asbestos or wearing a tutu. I soon discovered that his role as a teacher was to relieve me of my ideas, as the role of a burglar is to rifle your bedroom. I would stagger into a supervision clutching a huge, unwieldy armful of them, and he would cut them briskly down to size, toss them dismissively to each side, and pack me off poor but honest." To think of the dreary life of doing that to students year after year. I've long since lost contact with my Washington U. prof, but I hope he found a more honorable line of work. *(October 2002)*

❧ Sarah Lyall reports in the *New York Times* on a Turkish immigrant in Sweden who killed his twenty-six-year-old daughter because she "dishonored" the family by adapting to Swedish mores. Ms. Lyall observes that this is a "tragic emblem of a European society's failure to bridge the gap in attitudes between its own culture and those of its newer arrivals." Laws against murder are *so* ethnocentric. *(November 2002)*

❧ Professor David J. O'Brien of Holy Cross College in Worcester, Massachusetts, is not at all sure that groups such as Voice of the Faithful are really serious about, as they put it, "taking back our church." Writing in the *Boston Globe,* he asks, "Will they come up with the funds, $1 million to begin with, needed to turn a protest movement into an organization that can give the laity a genuine voice in the decisions that will shape the future of American Catholicism?" "Many Catholics," he writes, "are too poor, too busy, or too beset by life's trials to join a group. Those who have resources of time, money, and education have to act. . . . The future is, as it should be, in the hands of ordinary Catholics." The good news is that ordinary Catholics are not poor, busy, or beset by life's trials. *(November 2002)*

❧ George Lindbeck was an official Lutheran observer at the Second Vatican Council and he recalls a meeting with John XXIII when the Pope spoke on some of his favorite words from Scripture, "the mercies of the Lord are new every morning." The Pope said he had a hard time deciding what to do on any given day, but the Lord was merciful: He always told him every morning. Lindbeck thought he was referring to his convoking of the Council, which took everybody by surprise but which the Lord presumably told him to do. He adds: "John XXIII would repeat those words if he were with us now. He was basically a traditionalist rather like Mother Teresa, for example, and I suppose he would be appalled at much of the aftermath of the Council. Perhaps he would sometimes even wonder, as Luther did after the Reformation after a comparable lapse of time, whether it was really worth it. Yet the Lord's mercies are new every morning. What stops these words from being Pollyannish is their context: they come from Lamentations (3:22-23). Even in our day, cheerfulness keeps breaking through." *(February 2003)*

❧ The *New Republic* has Michael Sean Winters assaulting "George Weigel and his fellow neocons." The occasion is Weigel's book, *The Courage to Be Catholic,* and Winters is particularly offended that Weigel is not, as it is said, gay-friendly. "Weigel talks about the need for every Catholic to be more faithful. But he makes it sound so easy, nothing more complicated than keeping our pants zipped." Yet throughout the book, and beginning with the title, Weigel's argument is that faithfulness is a difficult but high adventure requiring courage, discipline, self-sacrifice, and sustaining grace. Winters does not see it that way. Weigel and the neocons are guilty of Pelagianism, intellectual pride, triumphalism, aversion to debate, and thinking they have all the answers. I, for one, plead innocent on the Pelagianism charge. *(February 2003)*

❧ I see that the Woodrow Wilson Center for Scholars in Washington, D.C., held a conference titled "Religion Returns to the Public Square: Faith and Politics in America." They had some fine speakers and I expect it was a worthwhile event, but I was a bit puzzled by this in the announcement: "Despite talk of a 'naked public square,' religion has never really lost its place in American public life." That is a truism that nobody — certainly not I — has denied. But, if in some important ways religion has not been absent, why was the conference called "Religion Returns to the Public Square"? Just asking. *(May 2003)*

❧ Apologetics — as in explaining, not apologizing for — has made a big comeback in recent years. Sara Maitland evaluates the twentieth-anniversary edition of Rosemary Radford Ruether's *Sexism and God-Talk,* which, she says, is an exercise in apologetics that has enabled many feminists, especially in the academy, to remain within a Christian framework, broadly defined. Along the way she describes how some folks, such as Ruether, do apologetics: "Take the bits of the faith you like, denounce the rest as 'cultural accretions,' apply some syncretic glue, and carry on regardless." Perfect. *(May 2003)*

❧ A priest writes that he just had dinner with ten of his parishioners. He describes them as "the best of Generation X." They are at Mass every Sunday, they are elite educated high-achievers, all under forty, involved in reading, sports, politics, and the rearing of their children. You get the idea. The priest writes: "I give you this background to help you appreciate the full force of this: these bright young Catholics have great contempt for the American episcopate. They expressed total incomprehension at the weakness and folly of the leadership being provided by the bishops, not just in the sexual abuse crisis but in the life of the Church generally. 'Do you know how hard it is to find a safe place to go to Mass when we're on the road, Father? Don't the bishops care that the liturgy has been hijacked by silliness?' 'Why doesn't the bishop do something about the sterilizations at the Catholic hospital?' And so on. Much of my time is spent with the very old, the very young, the very sick, or the very troubled, so to spend an evening with bright, engaged people who are seeking to follow Christ was a great delight. To discover that they are sorely disappointed in our bishops precisely because they hold that office in such high regard was a bit surprising; I suppose I had assumed that only priests and the cognoscenti fret over such things. These Gen X's are the agents of the New Evangelization; they deserve competent leadership they can respect." *(December 2003)*

❧ The "purification of memories" for which John Paul II has repeatedly called is catching on all over. In Fiji, in the tiny settlement of Nubutautau, villagers wept as they apologized to descendants of a British missionary, the Reverend Thomas Baker, whom their ancestors ate 136 years ago. The ceremony of reconciliation included the slaughter of a cow and the gift of 100 sperm whale teeth to the Rev. Baker's descendants. At the end of the ceremony, the village chief, Ratu Filimoni Nawawabalavu, embraced the British visitors. He is the descendant of the chief who cooked the missionary. I don't know if the Pope would approve of the slaughter of the cow, although it might be covered under the rubric of "the enculturation of the gospel." The save-the-whales people will probably not be so understanding about the teeth. The great question is: If the descendants of Thomas Baker can be reconciled with the Fijians whose ancestors had him for supper, why can't there be peace in the Middle East? Answer me that. *(February 2004)*

❧ Recall Snoopy of *Peanuts* fame sitting atop his doghouse typing out, "It was a dark and stormy night. . . ." San Jose State University in California has an annual "Bulwer-Lytton Fiction Contest," in which entrants (from all over the world) are challenged to compose the worst opening sentence of an imaginary novel. The first sentence of Baron Edward Bulwer-Lytton's 1830 novel *Paul Clifford* was this: "It was a dark and stormy night; the rain fell in torrents — except at occasional intervals, when it was checked by a violent gust of wind which swept up the streets (for it is in London that our scene lies), rattling along the housetops, and fiercely agitating the scanty flame of the lamps that struggled against the darkness." Michel Faber of Fearn Station House, Ross-shire, England, doesn't claim it's great but he protests that it is far from the worst opening sentence of a novel. "In truth," he writes, "if the opening sentence of the prelude to *Middlemarch* ("Who that cares much to know the history of man," etc.) had been subjected to the same sustained ridicule, the Bulwer-Lytton Fiction Contest might have been the George Eliot Fiction Contest instead." He has more than a point, and I can easily picture Snoopy typing, "Who that cares much to know the history of man. . . ." Imagine what fun Lucy would have had with that. *(March 2004)*

❧ I am told that Elaine Pagels' *Beyond Belief: The Secret Gospel of Thomas* is upsetting many Christians. No doubt, but I expect many others are aglow with Pagels' flattery of their unbelievably wonderful selves. The Gnostic message of Thomas teaches us that we all have this marvelous spark of divinity that Jesus, a really admirable human being, encouraged us to trust in seeking our own truth on the way to salvation. But then, don't you know, along came power-hungry bishops who, in cahoots with the likes of Emperor Constantine, exploited the Gospel of John — which had all those exclusive ideas about Jesus being God and the only way to salvation — in order to turn the ever-so-nice Jesus movement into an authoritarian religion with creeds that had to be believed (hence *Beyond Belief*). According to Gary A. Anderson of Notre Dame University, Pagels gets the Gnostics as wrong as she gets the early Christians. "If the White Queen bragged that she could believe six impossible things before breakfast," writes Anderson in the *Weekly Standard,* "the Gnostic adepts would need to multiply that by a factor of four, at least. Why Pagels happily swallows this camel while straining out the gnats of the creed is a mystery." If you're thinking about reading the book, Professor Anderson has some advice: "In sum, what we have in Elaine Pagels' *Beyond Belief* is a well-written account of why one educated woman finds herself unable to recite the creeds today — and why the Gnostics, rather than the orthodox early Christians, seem to her closer to the typical feelings of a twenty-first-century college professor. My own advice to the prospective reader would be to read a précis of the Gnostic myth and recite its cosmology six times before breakfast. If this sits well with you, then proceed deeper. Most, however, will find the challenge beyond belief." *(March 2004)*

❧ Medical concerns have been raised about the "morning after pill," but the *Christian Century* editorially opines that it's worth the risks. "The possible downside is offset by some distinct benefits. It seems to us a good idea to give women who wish to terminate a pregnancy the option of doing so at the very earliest — and morally preferable — stage rather than later. It's also a good idea to provide a method that reduces the total number of abortions." Unless, of course, terminating a pregnancy is morally indistinguishable from abortion. *(April 2004)*

❧ Tom and Ann Belser Brown write in the *Messenger,* a magazine of the Church of the Brethren: "We have had an END WAR license plate on our car since 1985 in Mississippi. When we moved to Indiana in 2001, we transferred that phrase to our new plate. A few months later, we joyfully found out that some good friends in Jackson took the END WAR for their Mississippi car tag. Unfortunately, war continues." Even after all that? *(April 2004)*

❧ Not to worry about all those people who say they believe in Jesus. Adam Kirsch, writing in the *New York Sun,* reviews Richard Wightman Fox's *Jesus in America: A History.* Says Mr. Kirsch, "If the omnipresence of Jesus in our ostensibly secular country is troubling, his malleability is reassuring: Americans seem less eager to do Jesus' bidding than to have him do theirs." Oh well, that's all right then. *(May 2004)*

❧ What would Jesus do about stem cell research? Michael Fitzgerald, who is a member of the Presbyterian Church USA, which he suggests is a good deal more enlightened than Catholics and other "conservatives," thinks he may have the answer. Writing in *Acumen,* a journal of business and science, Fitzgerald says researchers should not be distracted by legal and legislative questions. "Scientists should leave that fight to the lawyers and, instead, acknowledge something that most will find distasteful to contemplate — modern science is still playing catch-up to Jesus. Some of his miracles now seem less than awesome: Ordinary paramedics routinely bring people back to life. Artificial insemination matches virgin birth. Prozac and other drugs do a reasonable job of casting out demons." Many Christians, we are told, have qualms about creating embryos in order to use and destroy them, and progressive scientists need to meet those concerns head-on. "Scientists may doubt even the historicity of Jesus, let alone his putative divinity. But the most entrenched and effective opposition to stem cell research comes from people who buy into the New Testament hook, line, and sinker, and who may well doubt science itself. So the scientists must engage them on their own territory. In so doing, scientists may find that they've been ceding moral high ground unnecessarily." One has to wonder whether describing them as people who buy into the New Testament hook, line, and sinker is really the best way to persuade Christians who may be uneasy about Mr. Fitzgerald's suggestion that we must take over from God the process of creation. And, contra Fitzgerald, the argument that Jesus would support stem cell research because he violated the rules by healing on the Sabbath may strike some as less than conclusive. In addition to this latest specimen, *Acumen* has published some notably dumb attacks on the "sophistry" of the

President's Council on Bioethics for trying to draw lines with respect to what is distinctively human. But perhaps that is to be expected in a journal of business and science that treats science as a business. *(June/July 2004)*

❦ Several readers point out what they believe to be an egregious sign of the hubris of "the religious right." In a story on the annual convention of the National Association of Evangelicals held in Colorado Springs, the *New York Times* reports: "And the convention organizers were aware of their political clout. A slogan on the back of the convention program reads: 'What Can 30 Million Evangelicals Do For America? Anything We Want.'" Hubris? Not necessarily. Note that it says for America, not with America. Shouldn't we want people to want to do all they can for America? *(June/July 2004)*

❦ In Winslow Homer's 1899 painting *The Gulf Stream,* a black sailor is trapped on a sinking boat that is surrounded by sharks. The sharks encircle the boat, writes the noted art critic Nicolai Cikovsky, "with sinuous seductiveness." They "can be read as castrating temptresses, their mouths particularly resembling the *vagina dentata,* the toothed sexual organ that so forcefully expresses the male fear of female aggression." Reviewing Roger Kimball's *The Rape of the Masters* (Encounter), David Gelerntner writes: "Why would a critic write such stuff? Peer pressure, says Mr. Kimball: 'to ensure his own place as a "brilliant" "scholar" in a "great" contemporary university.'" But he provides the raw material for a deeper explanation. A century ago, professors could regard themselves as socially superior to artists and could afford to be generous and admiring without jeopardizing their own self-regard. But modern professors can no longer pull rank on anyone. Accordingly, two mammoth projects were launched. Since the early decades of the twentieth century, intellectuals have built a case that criticism can itself be a species of literature. There is something to that. But the educated public has continued to regard great artists as geniuses and great critics as critics. Hence the remarkable follow-on project of the past thirty-odd years: cutting the geniuses down to size. Mr. Kimball quotes Professor Keith Moxley, speaking for thousands of like-minded colleagues: "'Genius' is a socially-constructed category. Thus Michelangelo merely *appeared* to be a genius to the long-ago (pre-industrial, profoundly religious, all-but-incomprehensible) mind of sixteenth century Italy!" The title of Mr. Kimball's book will likely arouse critical theorists to further erotic frenzies, but his brief against intellectuals who write things that only other intellectuals could believe is not exaggerated. And Mr. Gelerntner's shot at a sociological explanation of what has brought us to our present pass is entirely plausible. "Many writers have discussed the death of authority; we ought to ponder the death of admiration too," says Gelerntner. When critics put "genius" in sneer quotes, they are really saying, "That was then, I am now. Don't look at what the 'genius' painted or wrote. Look at me!" It is not a pretty sight. *(November 2004)*

❧ I haven't seen all the reviews but have the impression that Mario Cuomo's book *Why Lincoln Matters: Today More Than Ever* is being almost unanimously panned, with criticism divided between the former New York governor's risible ignorance of Lincoln scholarship and his forced recruitment of Lincoln to today's Democratic Party. Not, however, in *Commonweal,* where Alan Wolfe of Boston College effusively praises the book and its author. It is really two books, he writes. "The one that appreciates Lincoln is as good as the one that lambasts Bush." As for the author, Wolfe writes that we should be grateful for anything that comes "from a man as admirable and thoughtful as this one." Then there is the final pitch: "Lincoln matters to us, among other reasons, because he matters to Mario Cuomo, and we should be indebted to the governor for bringing him once again to our attention." Ah yes, Lincoln. We had almost forgotten him. Thank you, Governor, for bringing him once again to our attention. And, by the way, a nice job on Bush. But then, we expect nothing less from a man as admirable and thoughtful as you. *(December 2004)*

❦ Duke University's Stanley Hauerwas has insisted over the years that Christian thinkers "must not do ethics for Caesar." In this view, doing ethics for Caesar (meaning the government) is an exercise of "statecraft" that constitutes formal cooperation with this oppressive liberal regime that is set against the lordship of Christ. Some might be surprised, therefore, to find Professor Hauerwas as an endorser of an advertisement in the *New York Times* sponsored by "Church Folks for a Better America," which is a project of "Peace Action Education Fund," which is a project of "Coalition for Peace Action." The ad condemns the Bush administration's policy in Iraq, declaring that "the time has come to bring this unjust and ill-considered war to an end." It goes on to make a number of positive recommendations, such as "a truly international peacekeeping force to be established by the United Nations." It does read very much like doing ethics for Caesar, and not very thoughtful ethics at that. The ad says, "We are Christians, from different communions. And citizens who span the political spectrum." Span: as in far left to liberal left. The ad appeared nine days before the presidential election. The radical call to costly discipleship prescribed by Hauerwas' mentor John Yoder and his *The Politics of Jesus* requires a bold and uncompromising commitment to defy what St. Paul calls the principalities and powers of the present time. With unflinching resolution, Hauerwas and friends courageously risk the wrath of the liberal academy and issue a clarion call for Christians to take up the cross and, despising the cost, prove their radical fidelity to the lordship of Jesus: Vote for John Kerry. Thus do the soaring flights of theological rhetoric make a crash landing in the thoroughly conventional moral posturings of partisan politics. *(January 2005)*

❧ Over the years, Gerard Bradley of Notre Dame and Robert P. George of Princeton have been among the most careful and persistent participants in civil debate over many questions, far from least of these being the question of abortion. During the notably nasty election season now past, they together published a piece explaining why that question should have priority in making a conscientious decision about the candidates. This elicited from a professor at Notre Dame a splenetic attack on Bradley and George as "Rambo Catholics" who are terrorizing souls, exploiting Catholic teaching for partisan purposes, leading an insurrection against the American constitutional order, and doing other very bad things. In the hope that the professor has since repented of such vicious slander, I do not mention the name. The reason for bringing the matter up is that one of the defenders of Bradley and George in the lively exchanges that followed the attack quoted a marvelous passage from George's *The Clash of Orthodoxies* on how to engage those with whom one disagrees on matters that really matter. The following is worth more than a moment's reflection: "They are not moral monsters. They are not Nazis or hatemongers. They are our colleagues and very often our friends. Many of them are doing their level best to think through the moral issues at the heart of our cultural struggle and arrive at conclusions that are right and just. They view themselves as partisans of a culture of freedom. In most cases, they carefully and honestly argue for those choices for death (as Dworkin himself calls them) whose moral worthiness they proclaim and whose legal permission and constitutional protection they defend. As a matter of reciprocity, it is, in my view, incumbent upon us, as their opponents, to engage them in debate, to answer their arguments, and to say why they are wrong. While we must oppose them with resolution and, indeed, determination to win, we cannot content ourselves merely to denounce them, as we would rightly denounce the moral monsters who created a different culture of death on the European continent in the 1930s and '40s." *(February 2005)*

Opus Dei plays a prominent part in the conspiracy theories propounded in Dan Brown's *The Da Vinci Code.* Learning that a company is running Da Vinci tours, Opus Dei decided to make lemonade out of lemons and invited the company to bring its clients to Opus Dei houses where they received a PowerPoint lecture on the truth about Opus Dei. Apparently the arrangement is working out to everyone's satisfaction, although possibly not to Dan Brown's. *The Tablet* reports that some Catholics are deeply troubled by the book. "We understand that members of one parish book club who read it were so troubled they sought an explanation from a priest." They sought an explanation from a priest! You can hardly get more troubled than that. *(February 2005)*

"Oh, not that old line again." Such is the frequent response when the claim is made that the demolition of the marriage-based family really began with the widespread acceptance of artificial contraception and its separation of sex from procreation. Now, however, "that old line" is getting new and more respectful attention. *Soft Patriarchs, New Men: How Christianity Shapes Fathers and Husbands* has been receiving well-deserved praise (see review, FT March 2005). The author is W. Bradford Wilcox, a sociologist at the University of Virginia, and he connects his argument to the question of contraception in an article in the ecumenical magazine *Touchstone,* "The Facts of Life and Marriage: Social Science and the Vindication of Christian Moral Teaching." He notes the well-orchestrated opposition to Paul VI's 1968 encyclical on human sexuality, *Humanae Vitae,* and contends that current scholarship debunks the opponents and underscores the prescience of the Pope in foreseeing the consequences of contraception. From the Bible through the *Didache* and the sixteenth-century Protestant Reformers, Christians were unanimous in affirming the integral relationship between love, sex, and openness to new life. The first break in the tradition came with the approval of contraception by the Church of England in 1930. All these years later, Wilcox is encouraged by a changing scholarly consensus on marriage and family, but also by a rethinking of contraception among Christians. "There is a new openness among Evangelical Protestant scholars and leaders to the truth and wisdom of the ancient Christian teaching against contraception. Among others, Albert Mohler, president of the Southern Baptist Seminary, Reformed Theological Seminary professor Harold O. J. Brown, and Evangelical theologian J. I. Packer have raised serious concerns about the moral permissibility and social consequences of contraception." He quotes Mohler who wrote in these pages: "Thirty years of sad experience demonstrate that *Humanae Vitae* [correctly] sounded the alarm, warning of a contraceptive mentality that would set loose immeasurable evil as modern birth control methods allowed seemingly risk-free sex outside the integrity of the marital bond. At the same time, it allowed married couples to completely sever the sex act from procreation, and God's design for the marital bond. . . . Standing against the spirit of the age, evangelicals and Roman Catholics must affirm that children are God's good gift and blessings to the marital bond. Further, we must affirm that marriage falls short of God's design when husband and wife are not open to the gift and stewardship of children." The radical destabilizing of sexual morality in recent decades, Wilcox notes, has had devastating consequences for the poor, for whom all of life, including family life, is precarious. This, he says, is the moment for Christian scholars and leaders of all kinds to take the lead in proposing a better way. "We must make it crystal clear that the church's commitment to the poor requires nothing less than a vigorous proclamation of the church's true and beautiful teaching about sex and marriage. In other words, we must make it clear that the preferential option for the poor begins in the home." *(April 2005)*

❦ A number of universities around the country are accommodating transgendered, transsexual, and otherwise ambiguously self-identified persons who protest the heteronormativity of restrooms designated for men and women. Matthew Rose, a doctoral student at the University of Chicago, former FT editorial assistant, and legendary football star of Wabash College, reports: "The University of Chicago has just supplied us with a number of bathrooms for those 'uncomfortable' about classifying themselves within the hegemonic taxonomies of bourgeois heteronormativity. The new bathrooms are private and much nicer than the bathrooms for those of us who have timidly accepted the social construction of our maleness or femaleness. They are so much nicer, in fact, that I use them regularly. When I was confronted about using the bathroom by a confused looking 'somebody,' I simply replied, 'I'm not comfortable calling myself a man on this campus.'" Heteronormativism. Add it to the list of things of which you are probably guilty. *(May 2005)*

II

Political Blasphemy

It lasted but a moment, but while it lasted it was political theater to be relished. The wondrously eccentric U.S. Court of Appeals for the Ninth Circuit — more precisely, two members of a three-member panel thereof — discovered that the phrase "under God" in the Pledge of Allegiance is *unconstitutional.* The judges sided with Michael Newdow, who had complained that his daughter is injured when forced to listen in public school to the assertion that there is a God. One story said that, in fact, the daughter regularly joined in the recitation of the pledge and was embarrassed by her father making a big stink about it. Never mind, the judges know the coercive establishment of religion when they see it.

Well, within hours the entire political order, from left to right and from dogcatcher to President, exploded in outrage at the Ninth Circuit's political blasphemy. In Washington, both houses promptly passed unanimous resolutions condemning the decision, after which our national leaders marched to the capitol steps to sing "God Bless America" and recite the Pledge of Allegiance, with voices raised to full-throated patriotic pitch at the words "under God." It took Jerry Falwell all of thirty minutes after the announcement of the court decision to declare that he was launching a campaign for a million signatures in protest against it. That seemed an exceedingly modest goal. A moral entrepreneur of greater imagination might have set a goal of 100 million signatures, with the assurance that the millions of contributions received would be spent in reaching the 180 million patriotic laggards. Sometimes nothing short of unanimity will do, or at least virtual unanimity, recognizing that the Ninth Circuit, Mr. Newdow, and Paul Kurtz's American Humanist Society are beyond hope.

Once our leaders had put on the record their wholehearted devotion to the proposition that ours is a nation under God — a proposition to which, judging by the public evidence, most of them had never before given a moment's thought — they felt much better about themselves and went back to business as usual, confident that the decision of the Ninth Circuit, which has a commanding lead in the judicial silliness sweepstakes, would, one way or another, be promptly negated. Political theater aside, the Ninth Circuit's provocation obviously struck a central nerve in the body politic, revealing the inchoate but powerful popular conviction that the phrase "under God" says something indispensable about the way Americans want to understand their country.

Above All That

Most Americans, that is. For a different take on the dust-up, representative of a certain sector of elite opinion, one goes — but of course — to the editorial board of the *New York Times.* Eschewing the vulgar atheism of the Newdow-Kurtz eccentrics, the *Times* is offended by the Ninth Circuit's lack of good manners. People of better breeding understand that public expressions such as "under God" are simply not to be taken seriously. They are but scraps of sanctimony tossed out to appease the gullible masses, while their enlightened masters get on with the running of a thoroughly secular society. The editors sniffingly observe that the words were added to the Pledge of Allegiance in 1954, "at the height of anti-Communist fervor." Anything approaching fervor in opposing communism has always been in bad taste at the *Times.* The editors continue, "It was a petty attempt to link patriotism with religious piety, to distinguish us from the godless Soviets." How petty can you get. If you're reading the editorial aloud, remember that "patriotism" is said with a supercilious raising of the eyebrow, and "religious piety" with a slight but sufficiently contemptuous snarl. The editors, or at least some of them, probably know that an officially atheistic totalitarian regime murdered millions of its people because of their religious faith, but that was long ago, and even at the time was no excuse for getting fervent.

"This is a well-meaning ruling," say the editors, "but it lacks common sense." Read: The court has been dangerously imprudent in upsetting the natives. "A generic two-word reference to God tucked inside a rote civic exercise is not a prayer." The grammar gets sticky here, but presumably the editors mean that the God referred to in "under God" is a generic deity. That is not quite the case, of course. Hinduism and Buddhism, for instance, do not propose a God whom one would be under in the way the pledge says we are "under God." Religio-cultural context, plus indisputable legislative intent, indicate that "under God" is meant to refer to the God of biblical religion, meaning Judaism, Christianity, and (although it was probably not in the legislative mind at the time) its latter-day expression in Islam. As interesting is the editorial claim that the phrase is not a prayer. It is, they say, a civic exercise; to which one might respond that any prayer in the public square is a civic exercise, which does not mean it is any less a prayer. But perhaps the key to the editors' meaning is that the Pledge of Allegiance is "rote" exercise. The word "rote" denotes something done routinely, mechanically, or unthinkingly. Maybe that is the way the editors of the *Times* say the Pledge of Allegiance, if they say it. They do not explain why they think less extraordinary Americans say it that way.

"We wish the words had not been added back in 1954," the editorial continues. "But just the way removing a well-lodged foreign body from an organism may sometimes be more damaging than letting it stay put, removing those words would cause more harm than leaving them in." The phrase "under God" is a foreign body, perhaps like a cancerous tumor, but it is safely contained and does not threaten to metastasize, so let it be. It would be nice to be rid of it, but surgery is dangerous. "The practical impact of the [Ninth Circuit] ruling is inviting a political backlash for a matter that does not rise to a constitutional violation." And even if it does, the editors want to save their powder. "Most important, the ruling trivializes the critical constitutional issue of separation of church and state. There are important battles to be fought over issues of prayer in school and use of government funds to support religious activities." The very next day, of course, the Supreme Court handed down the historic *Zelman* decision, declaring vouchers for religious schools to be constitutional. Now that, in the view of the *Times,* is a battle worth fighting, and the following day's editorial opposing *Zelman* was forceful; one might even say fervent. Fervor in the defense of secularism is no vice; aloofness in the battle for keeping the public square naked is no virtue.

I am glad that the words "under God" were added to the Pledge of Allegiance, and that they will almost certainly stay there. It is true that civic piety, like every other expression of piety, can be rote and empty. It can also be hypocritical. As I have said before, it used to be that hypocrisy was the tribute that vice paid to virtue, whereas now it is the charge that vice hurls at virtue. To say that ours is a nation under God is both a statement of theological fact and of moral aspiration. As a theological fact, it is true of all nations. As a moral aspiration, it is markedly — although perhaps not singularly — true of the United States of America. To say that we are a nation under God means, first of all, that we are under Divine judgment. It is also a prayer that we may be under Providential care. It is not a statement of patriotic pride, although many may think it is, but of patriotic humility. The reaction to the Ninth Circuit's decision was a salutary moment of public witness to the irrepressible popular intuition that, in the words of Lincoln, America is "an almost chosen nation." I do not expect the editors of the *Times* to understand any of this. To those of a certain mindset, the intolerable idea, the truly insufferable notion, is that they are under anything or anyone, even if that anything or anyone is no more than "a generic two-word reference." *(October 2002)*

Re-Evangelizing a "Post-Christian" World

Inveighing and evangelizing go hand-in-hand as Robert W. Jenson, a noted Lutheran theologian, responds to the question, "What Is a Post-Christian?" He begins with the counsel of Chesterton's Father Brown to a young secularist friend about his secularism: "It's drowning all your rationalism and skepticism, it's coming in like a sea; and the name of it is superstition. . . . It's the first effect of not believing in God that you lose your common sense and can't see things as they are. Anything that anybody talks about, and says there's a good deal in it, extends itself indefinitely like an endless vista in a nightmare."

Jenson started out many years ago being convinced by the "secularization theology" of Friedrich Gogarten (1887-1967), and Jenson is still convinced today, despite the ways in which that theological initiative has been distorted. Biblical truth does demythologize the world, says Jenson, but replaces the myth of beginnings, gods, and goddesses with the message of the promised Kingdom. "Thus the faith of Israel, and so of the Church, is eschatological, independently of particular passages of her Scripture or particular developments in her religious history. Scripture does not find the truth of things in what they have been and therefore are, but in what they will be beyond themselves, that is, in what they will be in God, for God is all there is beyond creatures."

Absent that eschatological hope, people embrace an "almost-nihilism," which is manifestly pseudo-nihilism in its eagerness to construct new gods. "The mark of almost-nihilism's religiosity is that it is made up, and known by its devotees to be made up. It is nihilistic religiosity in that its objects are known to be — nothing. To observe such arbitrary religious invention happening, you need only attend that remarkable caricature of the American religious scene, the annual national convention of the American Academy of Religion (AAR), most sessions of which will be devoted to considering what parts of what 'traditions' can be crafted together to make a religion satisfactory to some group and/or set of interests. All of what Fr. Brown calls the 'bestial gods of the beginning' are indeed inspected for what use we might make of them, i.e., what role they might play in our superstition, while the more conservative handle Christian 'symbols' and 'metaphors' and 'concerns' in just the same way. It is important to realize that these self-appointed religious founders-out-of-nothing are quite aware and deliberate about what they are doing. Or merely consider how the teachings and rites of our churches are often treated by their supposed members as a smorgasbord from which to assemble a religion to their taste, often enough making it quite explicit that this is what they are doing."

The general public rhapsodizes about "spirituality" while evangelical Protestant writers wax enthusiastic about "theism," as though Christianity is one of many species of a genus, all with interchangeable parts. So who is a post-Christian? Jenson answers: "Well — there are whole immense congregations, of all denominations or none, that are post-Christian at least in their public self-presentation.

Their theology is a collection of clichéd abstractions — 'love' and 'acceptance' and 'empowerment' and 'peace-and-justice' (one word), and so on — and they could easily make any hero or mythic figure at all be the loving or accepting or empowering one, or the guru of peace-and-justice, instead of Jesus, and sometimes do."

Christianity, on the other hand, is persistently particular: "Sherlock Holmes famously said that when you eliminate possibilities until finally only one is left, that is the solution no matter how improbable. That a first-century Palestinian Jew, precisely as the individual person he is, should be the structuring point of the universe, would not be the first guess of minds schooled by the great Greek thinkers. But the long experiment of Western Civilization has eliminated all the mediating possibilities, reducing them to superstition. We have left just the two: waiting for nothingness and waiting for Jesus. And since nihilism is demonstrably not an intelligible thought, waiting for Jesus is the rational choice."

I expect a good many readers will recognize what Jenson is getting at when he writes, "A great deal of our preaching and teaching is exactly backwards. So, for example, the preacher will say that what a text from one of the Gospels, about a miracle or parable, 'is really about is acceptance of people in all their diversity.' A true sermon would go just the other way: 'What our talk of acceptance and diversity etc. is really trying to get at is Jesus.'" The alternative to Christianity is superstition, which, as Fr. Brown knew, is an "endless vista." It is everything in general and nothing real or true in particular. Jenson's inveighing may be, as inveighing tends to be, exaggerated, but it is a salutary exaggeration. If the gospel were authentically preached and lived, he writes, "our churches will of course get much smaller than they are. It is all very well to denounce such theologians as Stanley Hauerwas for 'sectarianism,' but they have much the right of it against their critics."

I'm not sure at all. Presiding at the altar of Immaculate Conception on Fourteenth St. and First Ave., with hundreds and hundreds of ordinary Americans, I am consistently impressed by the intensity of the response to the particularity of Bible story, of bread and wine, of body and blood, of confession and absolution, of lively interaction with Mary and all the saints, and, yes, of miracles — and all this concentrated as concentrated can be on Jesus Christ incarnate, present, helping, judging, forgiving, and coming again. What Jenson says about the generalized and instrumental religiosity of AAR, of psychobabbled spiritualities, and of religion in the employ of sundry empowerments is all true enough. Today's task of re-evangelizing may be, in some sectors of our society, more difficult than was evangelizing in, say, the fourth century, mainly because in the West so many people think, mistakenly, that they know "the Christian thing."

Jenson writes: "When Constantine, speaking for a dying antiquity, called the Church to be the moral and intellectual restorer of late Mediterranean civilization, I do not see how the Church could have refused this service of love. But equally, as the West now defines itself against the faith, the Church only perverts herself when she tries to hang on to her Constantinian position, by bowing and scraping to the culture." I would suggest that the service of love, then and now, is to effectively proclaim the gospel, as in, "God so loved the world. . . ." The restoration of civilization may or may not be a consequence of such effective proclamation. The hoped-for public influence of the Christian message should not be derided as trying to hang on to a mythical "Constantinian position." Bowing and scraping is of course to be condemned, but alertness to the sensibilities of the culture is not bowing and scraping. It can be and should be understood as a necessary part of effective communication.

So I am ambivalent about Jenson's analysis. To be sure, the Church must be prepared to be countercultural, and when the crunch comes — as in the conflict between the culture of life and the culture of death — even *contra mundum.* But the driving force of evangelizing and re-evangelizing is love for the world, as God loves the world. When the Church is against the world, it is always against the world for the world. Admittedly, these are large and complicated questions, and I am keenly aware that also the faithful gathered at Immaculate Conception are often inwardly torn between Christian particularity and the superstitions and idolatries of the pseudo-nihilism in much of the surrounding culture. Yet the churches, however debilitated their proclamation and enervated their discipleship, are flourishing in America. Some may think it a sadness, but they are not likely to grow smaller in the foreseeable future. Whether it is a curse or blessing, we do not live in a post-Christian society but in an incorrigibly and confusedly Christian America.

Reflecting on related questions in the 1930s, T. S. Eliot contended that a society is not post-Christian until Christianity is formally rejected and replaced by another understanding of reality, something definite and with a name. That happened in the Soviet Union and Nazi Germany. It may be happening in Western Europe, although the replacement has not yet a name, except for "secularization," which denotes simply the decline of Christian faith and public influence. Those who are excessively impressed by the academy, the editorial page of the *New York Times,* and powers claiming to control what are called the commanding heights of culture may think America is post-Christian. It is not. It is, as it has always been, a maddeningly muddled Christian society. And perhaps becoming more so. Compared with accepting the responsibilities and addressing the problems that attend Christian America, coping with post-Christianity is a breeze. One can simply join up with a small and ever so much more satisfactory society of other true believers. As is the way with sectarianism. I do not think Jenson is proposing that.

Our circumstance is not all that new. To our individual

and communal circumstance St. Paul said what always needs saying, "Do not be conformed to this world, but be transformed by the renewal of your mind, that by testing you may discern what is the will of God, what is good and acceptable and perfect" (Romans 12). Whether in the first, fourth, or twenty-first centuries, Christians have never quite gotten the knack of distinguishing between transforming and conforming. Then too, America is not the world. The assumption of a post-Christian world offered by Jenson and others is very much attuned to our American situation and, to a lesser degree, to Western Europe. We Euro-Americans are a small, and becoming ever smaller, minority of the Christian movement. In Latin America, Asia, and Africa, the gospel — although alloyed, as always, with cultural counter-gospels — is exploding with the force of fresh discovery. Viewed on this larger screen, perhaps the Christian motto of the twenty-first century should be "Forward to Constantinianism!" It would be a very different Constantine and a very different Christendom than anything known in the past, but, like earlier times, it will be recognizable as yet another episode along the embattled, splendored, and stumbling way of the Church toward the historical vindication of the Jesus for whom we wait. *(February 2003)*

What Sacred Architecture Is For

Good. Somebody has said it and said it well. So, with no further ado, I will let Duncan Stroik, editor of *Sacred Architecture,* say it: "Everywhere I went in Italy last summer, save the eternal city, churches were asking an admission fee. The explanation was given that it costs a lot to maintain these buildings and keep them open and so it should be the responsibility of everyone who uses them to help pay for their upkeep. If this seems like a reasonable request, it is also a major contradiction with the purpose of a church. In Florence, charging for admissions started with the baptistery and the museum of the duomo — a nuisance that did not prevent visits or prayer in the church proper. Then it spread to the Brancacci chapel by Massacio, the New Sacristy by Michelangelo, and the burial chapel of the Medicis at the parish church of San Lorenzo. More recently San Lorenzo itself and the Dominican church of Santa Maria Novella have begun charging entrance fees. And while these churches only allow paying customers during the week, at the Franciscan church of Santa Croce an equally problematic attitude is exhibited: people are not allowed to enter on Sunday morning unless they are going to mass. These are churches which every tour group, pilgrimage group, art and architecture class should stop off to see, to draw, to visit, and to pray in. Now many will not make the visit, given time and money. Even worse, and more detrimental to the sacred character of the buildings, they will no longer be places for the faithful of the city. Without the love, care, and affection of the nonnas, the youth on their way to class, the workers on a break, and other faithful, these buildings will become simply museums. Florence, they say, is a city of museums and now ever more so.

"Venice also is so full of art and architecture and so lacking in permanent residents that tourists seem to take over. In Venice the Chorus foundation was formed by the Archdiocese in order to restore some of their magnificent churches and their sacred art. A worthwhile task, but it also means that fourteen of the major churches including the Frari and the Redentore are entrance by admission only. There are several benefits of this, of course: the buildings stay clean, unwanted beggars and graduate students are kept out, and all art lovers are protected from the distraction of people kneeling, praying, and lighting candles. Pay-per-view religion is a very contemporary idea and offers a new way to charge for indulgences. Now, it is also true that most of these churches are open for 'free' during one daily mass, and paid staff ensure that visitors participate in the liturgy and are prevented from looking at artwork or visiting side chapels. That should be done during normal business hours. We can be sure that Veronese, Bellini, Palladio, and Longhena would be surprised to know that Third Millennium Man believes he can separate faith and art. Other churches such as Santa Maria dei Miracoli, having lost their parishioners or religious congregations, have dispensed with the daily or weekly mass altogether and have become galleries of sacred art, with the occasional Vivaldi concert or upper-class wedding.

A Disconnect Between Faith and Art

"What a lost opportunity. Here are buildings constructed by the faithful and the finest artists and architects throughout the centuries, more beautiful than ever but not really serving their highest purpose: the praise of God and the bestowal of grace on men. Catholic art, along with the rich tradition of sacred music, continues to speak to people of differing cultural and religious backgrounds. Is this not an opportunity to be hospitable, to welcome the saint, the sinner, and the prodigal? Is not the cost of keeping our churches open, offering the liturgy, and reserving the Eucharist a price the Church can afford, no matter the monetary price?

"These developments bode poorly for the Church in Italy, and for Catholics everywhere. They signal the acceptance of the disconnection between faith and art for modern man, which during the past two centuries has been advocated by the avant garde. The separation of worship and devotion from beauty and art is schizophrenic for a Church that believes in the necessity of sacrament. I am sure that many tourists will get used to paying for church, while the faithful on pilgrimage or tour should be scandalized. 'But we only want to go in to pray at the tomb of Saint (Francis, Monica, Ignatius, Thérèse, etc.) or see the miraculous image.' 'I am sorry but you will have to either pay the admission price or come back on Sunday.'" (*Sacred Architecture* is published semiannually. Subscribe for $9.95 by writing P.O. Box 556, Notre Dame, Indiana 46556.) *(June/July 2003)*

Believing in Evolution

The angry dogmatism of its defenders such as Richard Dawkins and Daniel Dennett suggests that Darwinism as a comprehensive explanatory system is on the ropes. That doesn't mean that the arguments will not go on and on. They will. There is too much at stake. The arguments are not, finally, over scientific evidence in fields such as evolutionary biology. They are about the nature of reality and our place in it. Dawkins declares that Darwinism makes it possible to be an intellectually fulfilled atheist, and intellectual fulfillment, for an intellectual, is something like salvation. A good place to catch up on the state of the arguments to date is *Uncommon Dissent: Intellectuals Who Find Darwinism Unconvincing,* edited by William A. Dembski (ISI, 350 pp., $18 paper). Dembski has appeared in these pages and, along with Michael J. Behe, is credited (or blamed) for launching a school of thought that goes by the name of Intelligent Design.

In addition to Dembski and Behe, the book includes thirteen essays by a variety of scientists and philosophers who have been led to a position of skepticism toward, or outright rejection of, Darwinism. Of very particular interest is the essay "The Deniable Darwin" by mathematician and philosopher David Berlinski, which first appeared in *Commentary.* Berlinski offers a tour de force that is, variously, relentless in its logic, devastating in its studied understatement, and delightfully whimsical in exposing the incoherence of opposing arguments while never, unlike some of his opponents, being vicious. His essay and response to critics will come to be, I expect, a classic text in these debates.

Berlinski is assiduous in distancing himself from "creationists" or arguments claiming that manifest design logically requires a Designer. He contents himself with making the case that Darwinism is riddled with internal contradictions and simply does not explain what it claims to explain. While the more dogmatic proponents of Darwinist orthodoxy circle the wagons and fire imprecations at any and all who question the true faith, Berlinski does not accuse them of engaging in a conspiracy. "No conspiracy is required to explain the attachment of biologists to a doctrine that they find sustaining; all that is required is Freud's reminder that those in the grip of an illusion never recognize their affliction." As for the complexity of living systems, Berlinski says he entertains no "supernatural explanations." "The thing is a mystery, and if there is never to be a naturalistic explanation, I shall forever be content to keep on calling it a mystery." His purpose is limited to pointing out that Darwin's naturalistic explanation, turning on random variation and natural selection, is implausible, incoherent, and contrary to a great deal of scientific knowledge. Berlinski is especially effective in showing how Darwinists kick any idea of purpose, design, or teleology out the front door, only to smuggle such ideas in by the back door. Nature "selects" this or that, Nature "chooses," Nature "targets," and so forth. This Nature, whether upper or lower case, is a kind of deity in the details, ever invoked and ever denied.

One is sometimes asked whether one "believes in" evolution. More strident Darwinists adamantly insist that it is not a matter of faith; it is not a theory to be accepted or rejected; it is a fact to be acknowledged. But of course that is silly. It is precisely, and Darwin intended it precisely as, a theory to explain how the complexity of living systems came about. And there may be something to it in terms of micro-evolution, in possibly explaining how changes happen within particular species. As for macro-evolution — a general and all-encompassing explanation of how we and all other living things came to be — Darwinism is, in my considered judgment, preposterous. Berlinski is embraced by proponents of Intelligent Design for the persuasiveness and vigor of his arguments but also because he is an agnostic. It is odd but understandable that in our intellectual culture a critic of Darwinism is thought more credible if he is an agnostic or atheist. A scientist who believes in the Creator is suspected of cooking the evidence to support his belief. Whereas one who has made a commitment to agnosticism or, even better, atheism is thought to be neutral. This, too, is nonsense. There are devout and thoughtful Christians who accept Darwinism of one sort or another. The question before us is the evidence and proposed theories to explain the evidence. As the still-dominant theory — typically presented as a comprehensive belief system — Darwinism fails to explain too much that we know and claims to know much too much that we cannot know by reason and scientific evidence. As a belief system it suffers the distinct disability of being unbelievable. Of course there is much more to be said on these matters, and most of it is persuasively said in *Uncommon Dissent. (May 2004)*

America as a Religion

That America is guided by Providence is a belief deeply entrenched in the seventeenth-century beginnings, the constitutional period, Lincoln's ponderings on our greatest war, and Woodrow Wilson's convictions about the inseparable connections between freedom and American destiny. The belief has never been absent from American public life and discourse, although in the last half century many, and not least religious thinkers, have tried to discredit or marginalize it. In recent years, however, the idea of a providentially guided America has been making a comeback. One thinks, for instance, of Michael Novak's *On Two Wings*, which makes a strong case for the Founders' Hebraic understanding of history, as well as providing a marvelous florilegium of their statements about providential purpose (see review, FT May 2002). More recently, Steven Webb has provided an incisive and nuanced account of the history of the idea in *American Providence: A Nation with a Mission* (see review, FT February). Then there was and is the attention aroused by the controversy over "under God" in the Pledge of Allegiance, a phrase suggestive of both divine direction and judgment. Of greatest influence perhaps has been the harsh criticism of George W. Bush's employment of the idea of Providence in relation to the course of freedom in the world, even though his statements have generally been carefully honed and are unexceptionable in the context of presidential history.

Another important contributor to the new discussion is David Gelernter of Yale. I have earlier raised questions about his near-identification of Puritanism with Judaism in American history (see Public Square, FT January 2005). Now he has gone considerably farther with an essay in *Commentary*, "Americanism — and Its Enemies." Gelernter writes, "By Americanism I mean the set of beliefs that are thought to constitute America's essence and to set it apart; the beliefs that make Americans positive that their nation is superior to all others — *morally* superior, closer to God." He goes farther still: "Americanism is in fact a Judeo-Christian religion; a millenarian religion; a biblical religion. Unlike England's 'official' religion, embodied in the Anglican church, America's has been incorporated into all the Judeo-Christian religions in the nation." America is a religion that has been incorporated into other religions? The suggestion of syncretism is pronounced — or, as one reads on, the suspicion arises that

Americanism has in some way displaced the other religions. One wonders if this is a new version of "supersessionism," an idea excoriated in Jewish-Christian dialogue.

Gelernter writes: "I believe that Puritanism did *not* drop out of history. It transformed itself into Americanism. This new religion was the end-stage of Puritanism: Puritanism *realized* among God's self-proclaimed 'new' chosen people — or, in Abraham Lincoln's remarkable phrase, God's 'almost chosen people.'" Lincoln's is indeed a remarkable phrase, but the "almost" seems to get lost in Gelernter's account. In the nineteenth and early twentieth centuries, Reform Jews who rejected the Zionist idea of a Jewish state declared that "America is our Zion." Gelernter appears to have moved beyond that. "We can go further. To sum up Americanism's creed as freedom, equality, and democracy for all is to state only half the case. The other half deals with a promised land, a chosen people, and a universal, divinely ordained mission. This part of Americanism is the American version of biblical Zionism: in short, American Zionism." He says he is working on a "Thanksgiving Haggadah" that will recite the providential story of America including the "repeated reenactments of the Exodus that make up America's history." The Haggadah is, of course, the Passover retelling of God's liberation of the children of Israel, similar to the Anamnesis in the Eucharist that recites the saving deeds of God in Christ.

"And so," writes Gelernter, "we circle back to the beginnings of Protestantism, which begot Puritanism, which begot Americanism." There is no room for Catholicism in this telling of the story. "Papism" and Anglicanism's compromise with papism are the Pharaoh from which God delivered his Puritans who begot Americanism. That aspect of Gelernter's American religion is troubling, to put it delicately, but many will be even more troubled by the hubris of Americans being "positive that their nation is superior to all others — *morally* superior, closer to God," that America is "a promised land, a chosen people, and [has] a universal, divinely ordained mission." *The* promised land? *The* chosen people? More than all others? Presumably Gelernter, being a Jew, would not say so, although I am not sure.

Certainly, Christians *must* not say so. Christ and his body the Church is our first community, prior in time and prior in allegiance. Jews can speak to the Haggadah, but an American Anamnesis is, not to put too fine a point on it, idolatry. It is a welcome development of great importance that thinking about America and Providence is receiving renewed attention. The direction pointed by David Gelernter, however, ends up in conclusions that contributed to discrediting such thinking in the past. For a far more promising way of exploring these questions, I recommend Stephen Webb's *American Providence. (April 2005)*

While We're At It

❧ There's that old gibe about a nuclear bomb dropped on New York and eliciting the *Washington Post* headline, "Nuclear Attack on New York: Women and Minorities Hardest Hit." In an instance of life aspiring to parody, the *Post* headline about a mad sniper who drove around the D.C. area killing people at apparent random reads, "Arbitrary Victims, Identical Fate: County's Growing Diversity Reflected in Those Gunned Down." There's a bright side to everything. *(December 2002)*

❧ I am frequently asked whether there is much Catholic criticism of "Evangelicals and Catholics Together" (ECT). The answer is in the negative. Not that all Catholics are terribly enthusiastic about it, but most think it is no big deal that Catholics are in productive dialogue with evangelical Protestants. After all, the Catholic Church is in dialogue with almost everybody. It comes with being catholic. But there are exceptions. Catholic Apologetics International (CAI), for instance, devotes forty-three pages to criticizing an address I recently gave at Wheaton College in Illinois and concludes: "Father Neuhaus has shown himself to be an enemy of Christ, with a soothing voice and a flowery tongue that masks the Serpent's hiss. He wears the clothing of a sheep, but like a ravenous wolf he seeks to dissolve the Holy Church, and like Esau, to sell Her precious pearls of truth for a bowl of false and unholy ecumenical porridge." So you can see that some Catholics are not entirely approving of my work with ECT. I was not aware of CAI's somewhat pointed reservations until they were brought to my attention by that notable blogger Mark Shea, who is concerned about what he calls the Lidless Eye Crowd on the rightmost fringes of Catholicism. In my Wheaton address I, as usual, drew on the documents of Vatican II and statements of this pontificate such as *Dominus Iesus* (Jesus the Lord) and *Ut Unum Sint* (That They May Be One), but that, in the view of CAI, is just the problem. In another long essay from CAI, we are told that "it appears that Vatican II, in intention but not in fact, did redefine the perennial teaching of the Church." "That is to say that 'the Spirit of Vatican II,' as it is interpreted and applied by the more progressive innovators . . . appears to be exactly in line with what the Council itself intended to present." The Church teaches that Protestants are damned; Vatican II says they have means of grace and may be saved. The Church says that Jews are collectively guilty of the death of Christ; Vatican II says not. The Church says that religious freedom is a pernicious heresy; Vatican II affirms religious freedom. On each point, the CAI document cites earlier councils, popes, and saints in order to establish the "perennial teaching" of the Church. The unavoidable implication is that Vatican II was a false council and the pontificates of Paul VI and John Paul II are devoid of magisterial authority. Like his soulmates on the far left, the CAI author has no use for Newman's understanding of the development of doctrine, an understanding explicitly endorsed by the Magisterium since Vatican II. Every so-called development is, in fact, a radical change, a contradiction, and an effort to reform the irreformable. That Vatican II and subsequent pontificates are heretical is a thought not to be entertained lightly by a Catholic. Our author writes, "Please God, may I be wrong about this. If ever there was a time that I wished to be corrected and proved wrong, this is it." As it happens, in the essays on my work and on Vatican II, there is not the slightest indication that the author wishes to be corrected, never mind to be proved wrong. He entered into full communion with the Catholic Church only recently, believing he had found the rock (as in monolith) of inflexible and sedentary truths. It seems he was not prepared for the Church of ongoing pentecostal stirrings of the Spirit leading into the fullness of the truth that will not be exhaustively understood until "we know even as we are known." He seems to be saying, to paraphrase St. Augustine, "So late I knew you. So soon must I say good-bye." Where he might go from here, God only knows. Having put the burden of proof on those who believe that the Catholic Church has not fallen into heresy, we hope he will stop presenting himself as a Catholic apologist. In any event, the answer to the question whether there are Catholic critics of ECT is yes, but they are not very. If they are very Catholic, they are not very critical; and if they are very critical, they are not very Catholic. *(January 2003)*

❧ Columnist Mark Lowry of the *Fort Worth Star-Telegram* reviews what is billed as the Christmas show at Radio City Music Hall and complains, "A recreation of the biblical Christmas story, complete with live animals, wise men, and shepherds, drags on for a good twenty minutes. . . . To lure spectators of all faiths (and non-faiths) with the promise of an entertaining holiday revue, and then to ambush them with Christian theology, is dated and borderline offensive, especially at a time when understanding of other cultures and beliefs is more important than ever." Christmas at a Christmas show. Actually celebrating Christian culture and beliefs. What won't they impose upon us next. *(February 2003)*

❧ Aleksandr Solzhenitsyn's *Dvesti let Vmeste (1795-1995) (Two Hundred Years Together)* has yet to appear in English, but Daniel J. Mahoney has a splendid review essay on the first volume in *Society.* The "together" in the title refers to Russians and Jews, and Mahoney convincingly rebuts the slander that Solzhenitsyn's Russian patriotism entails a form of anti-Semitism. At the same time, Solzhenitsyn does not evade questions that some will not touch for fear of being charged with anti-Semitism. Mahoney writes: "Any adequate treatment of the Russian 'Jewish question' must sooner or later confront the difficult question of Jewish involvement in the various revolutionary movements of the late nineteenth and early twentieth centuries. Solzhenitsyn rightly insists that this question cannot remain 'taboo' for the serious historian of Russia and the modern world. But it is necessary for the historian to read carefully, displaying scrupulous respect for the facts and doing nothing to inflame already overheated passions. Solzhenitsyn condemns those extremist elements on the right who have irresponsibly blamed the Jews for the Bolshevik plague — even as he cannot ignore the fact that a disproportionate number of Jews participated in various leftist revolutionary movements. Solzhenitsyn confronts this delicate issue equitably and forthrightly. . . . [H]e praises the Jewish people for their positive contributions to capitalist economic development and democratic politics. He praises the commitment of many responsible Jewish leaders to the path of political moderation. But he also laments the 'unreasonable' choice of some de-Judaized Jews for totalitarian and revolutionary politics. This choice for revolution was unreasonable but understandable: the revolutionary intelligentsia welcomed educated Jews to their ranks and offered an easy path to assimilation for those Jews who had broken with the traditional Jewish community. The old regime, in contrast, vacillated between enlightened efforts at accommodation between Russians and Jews and imposing humiliating restrictions that could only feed revolutionary discontent. The revolutionaries not only welcomed Jews to their ranks but provided a messianic secular religion — a universalist political mission — to those who rejected the seemingly provincial and antiquated traditions of their fathers." As he has written before, notably in *August 1914,* Solzhenitsyn laments the assassination of Pyotr Stolypin, the Russian prime minister from 1906 to 1911, who he believes was the one man who could have conserved what was good in the old regime by making necessary adaptations, not least in granting full rights to Jews. Mahoney concludes, "This very Russian book does not draw any grandiose theoretical conclusions about 'the Jewish question.' But it reminds its readers of those universal traits of soul that are essential in every time and place: moderation, repentance, courage, balanced judgment, and statesmanlike dedication to the public good." If only such traits were more universal. *(May 2003)*

❧ This is unusual television fare. Promoting an upcoming segment on *Dateline,* Jane Pauley said, "Still ahead, the latest round of bloodshed and violence at abortion clinics." At last they are going to show what really happens at abortuaries: cutting bodies of babies in pieces, plucking out the bloody limbs one by one, puncturing the heads of infants and sucking out the brains. At last, one thought, at least one network has the nerve to tell the truth about abortion. Then Ms. Pauley completed her message: "The anti-abortion movement has been creeping to the edge of bloody fanaticism for a decade." *(May 2003)*

❧ Elaine Pagels of Princeton has another book out celebrating early Christian gnosticism. *Beyond Belief* is about the apocryphal Gospel of Thomas, written in the second century and much amended later, which Pagels prefers to the canonical Gospels, and especially to the Gospel of John. "One of its central messages," Pagels says in an interview with *Pub-*

lishers Weekly, "is that there is divine light within each person. Reacting to Thomas' teaching, the author of the Gospel of John has Jesus always declaring that Jesus is the only light of the world. . . . Thomas is not a specifically Christian book, if by Christianity one means believing that Jesus is the only Son of God. Thomas is not about Jesus, but about the recognition of the light within us all. In this way, Thomas has a close affinity with Jewish mysticism." Well, at least a close affinity with about 80 percent of everything in the "Spirituality" section of Borders or Barnes & Noble. The Gospel of Thomas as celebrated by Pagels is marvelously attuned to what Harold Bloom calls in a book by that title, *The American Religion,* namely, gnosticism pitched to a popular and apparently inexhaustible appetite for self-flattery. *(August/September 2003)*

❦ October 5 was the beginning of Respect Life Week, and also the beginning of National Coming Out Week. At Boston College — a school "in the Jesuit tradition" — the promotion of gayness trumped the protection of unborn babies. On the student calendar, only National Coming Out Week is mentioned. October 5 was "Solidarity Sunday," and "All masses on campus will have a GLBT theme." Some students asked that pro-life petitions be included in the prayers of the faithful that Sunday and were told that they were free to propose such petitions from the congregation but the official focus was on affirming gays. The week's announced activities included a talk on gay issues in athletics, an evening titled "Guess Who's Gay," and a talk by author and professional Bush-hater (his self-description) Michael Moore. So much for Respect Life Week at Boston College, a school "in the Jesuit tradition." *(December 2003)*

❦ I spend a good deal of time on campuses and confess to succumbing occasionally to a measure of jadedness about the state of higher education. Prestige schools that demand $40,000 in annual tuition often seem like the backwaters of American culture, an elaborately and expensively institutionalized form of extended day care for students not yet ready for the job market. Of course a determined student, a good library, and one or two intelligent mentors can make for a solid education almost anywhere. The frenzied race to get into "the best" schools has a lot more to do with networking than with education. Among the great weaknesses of the people who run our massive higher education system is that they are afflicted by the one thing that education is presumably intended to counter: ignorance. To cite but one instance at hand, and one that is at the heart of this journal's concern, a recent national survey asked administrators and students about the First Amendment. Only 21 percent of administrators and 30 percent of students knew that the First Amendment guarantees religious freedom. Only six percent of administrators and two percent of students knew that religious freedom is the first freedom mentioned in the First Amendment. Only 41 percent of administrators and 32 percent of students believe that religious people should be permitted to advocate their views by whatever legal means available. On the other hand, 74 percent of students and 87 percent of administrators think it "essential" that people be able to express their beliefs *unless* — and then come a host of qualifications, all amounting to the condition that their beliefs not "offend others." Commenting on the survey, Alan Charles Kors, a University of Pennsylvania historian, said, "If an antiwar group put up a poster of Iraqi children they claimed were maimed by George Bush, nobody would blink. But let a pro-life group put up a poster of an aborted fetus and suddenly it becomes, 'Well, they crossed the line.'" Students surveyed said they remember having heard something about the Bill of Rights back in high school. But then they moved on to higher things. *(February 2004)*

❦ Michael Lindsay writes that he is amused when he drives along Forty-Sixth Street in Minneapolis and sees the sign pointing to Faith Free Lutheran Church. I checked out the church's website and it seems they're firmly committed to the "solas" of Scripture and grace. So that's two out of three. Lutherans are not perfectionists, after all. *(March 2004)*

❦ It appears that the customary spine-removal ceremony in Episcopal consecrations is not part of the African Rite. After the Episcopal Church USA (ECUSA) affirmed an openly gay priest, the Rev. Gene Robinson, as bishop of New Hampshire, the Anglicans of Uganda formally announced that its communion with ECUSA had been broken. Herewith a letter from Archbishop Livingstone Mpalanyi Nkoyoyo on behalf of the Anglican Church of Uganda to ECUSA's Presiding Bishop, Frank Griswold: "Considering those things, we were shocked to receive a letter from you informing us of your decision to send a delegation to the enthronement of our new Archbishop in January, and your intention for the delegation to bring aid and assistance for the people who live in desperate conditions in the camps in Gulu that you have ignored for years. Recent comments by your staff suggesting that your proposed visit demonstrates that normal relations with the Church of Uganda continue have made your message clear: If we fall silent about what you have done — promoting unbiblical sexual immorality — and we overturn or ignore the decision to declare a severing of relationship with ECUSA, poor displaced persons will receive aid. Here is our response: The gospel of Jesus Christ is not for sale, even among the poorest of us who have no money. Eternal life, obedience to Jesus Christ, and conforming to his Word are more important. The Word of God is clear that you have chosen a course of separation that leads to spiritual destruction. Because we love you, we cannot let that go unanswered. If your hearts remain hardened to what the Bible clearly teaches, and your ears remain deaf to the cries of other Christians, genuine love demands that we do not pretend that everything is normal. As a result any delegation you send cannot be welcomed, received, or seated. Neither can we share fellowship nor even receive desperately needed resources. If, however, you repent and return to the Lord, it would be an occasion of great joy." Repent. Imagine that. *(March 2004)*

❧ Philip Hamburger's *Separation of Church and State,* published two years ago, has received a great deal of deserved attention and, for the most part, high praise (see FT, December 2000). Douglas Laycock, another distinguished scholar of the First Amendment religion clause, offers a sharp dissent in the *University of Chicago Law Review* (Fall 2003). In "The Many Meanings of Separation," Laycock contends that Hamburger's book — while providing massive and useful documentation of the ways in which separationism has been driven by anti-religious and, more specifically, anti-Catholic passions — deceptively limits "separation" to one meaning, namely, the "strict separationism" of, for instance, the 1948 *McCollum* decision with which the Hamburger book ends. Almost a half century later, Laycock argues, it is evident that the Supreme Court's construal of the religion clause is much more nuanced than Hamburger suggests. Laycock concludes: "If to some people separation means protection of religious activity from government, and to other people it means suppression or subordination of religious activity by government, then the phrase has no agreed core of meaning that will enable anyone to communicate. The phrase is deeply entrenched in American society and people will not quit using it. But the apparent lesson of Hamburger's book is that the phrase has no sufficiently agreed meaning to be of any use, and until we develop vocabulary that communicates distinct theories of separation, we should give up the phrase altogether. Thanks to Hamburger's careful history of actual usage, we now know that from the phrase alone, without an analysis of context, we have no idea what people mean by it." I'm not quite sure what to make of all this. I agree with Hamburger that, in the past and at present, the dominant use of "separation of church and state" in public discourse has aimed at limiting, muting, or excluding religious influence in our public life. I agree with Laycock that the most virulent forms of antireligious separationism, described in such detail by Hamburger, have not definitively triumphed. I also agree with Laycock that the "separation of church and state" also supports the freedom of religion from government interference. He is right to say that the phrase is deeply entrenched and will continue to be used until an alternative terminology gains currency. All of which leaves us with the observation that the phrase "the separation of church and state" is used in ways both hostile and friendly to religious freedom and, so long as it is with us, we must not tire of contending for its friendly use. *(April 2004)*

❦ When David B. Hart is on a roll, there is no stopping him. In the March issue of *The New Criterion* he offers an extended and scintillating overview of contemporary religion, culture, and civilization in America. (On the last he doesn't have much to say because he doesn't think there is much of it.) Most of the analysis will be familiar to our readers from what he and others have written in these pages. As you might expect, I'm in substantial agreement with the assessment he provides, although I think he exaggerates the importance of the "charismatic" in the present and future vitality of Catholicism and evangelical Protestantism. I have frequently cautioned against the propensity of some conservatives, especially Evangelicals, to claim that ours is a post-Christian society. That is, I contend, an easy out from engaging the tasks that are ours in an incorrigibly, confusedly, and conflictedly Christian America. Hart sets out another consideration to which we should attend: "For, if we succumb to post-Christian modernity, and the limits of its vision, what then? Most of us will surrender to a passive decay of will and aspiration, perhaps, find fewer reasons to resist as government insinuates itself into the little liberties of the family, continue to seek out hitherto unsuspected insensitivities to denounce and prejudices to extirpate, allow morality to give way to sentimentality; the impetuous among us will attempt to enjoy Balzac, or take up herb gardening, or discover 'issues'; a few dilettantish amoralists will ascertain that everything is permitted and dabble in bestiality or cannibalism; the rest of us will mostly watch television; crime rates will rise more steeply and birthrates fall more precipitously; being the 'last men,' we shall think ourselves at the end of history; an occasional sense of the pointlessness of it all will induce in us a certain morose feeling of impotence (but what can one do?); and, in short, we shall become Europeans (but without the vestiges of the old civilization ranged about us to soothe our despondency)." Hart acknowledges that he is not original in observing that "the vestigial Christianity of the old world presents one with the pathetic spectacle of shape without energy, while the quite robust Christianity of the new world often presents one with the disturbing spectacle of energy without shape." It is reasonable to believe that a more churchly and culture-forming shape of Christianity may be in process through efforts such as Evangelicals and Catholics Together and new Christian initiatives in philosophy, literature, and the arts. There are, to be sure, formidable obstacles but, if we resist the temptation to resign ourselves to ours being a post-Christian society, such initiatives could bear impressive fruit in the short term of the next hundred years or so. And in the long term, who knows what might happen? *(May 2004)*

❦ The *New York Times* reports that John Kerry became "combative" with reporters when asked about critics who say he does not follow Catholic teaching on questions such as abortion and same-sex unions. "Who are they?" he demanded. "Name them. Are they the same legislators who vote for the death penalty, which is in contravention of Catholic teaching?" He went on to explain: "I'm not a church spokesman. I'm a legislator running for president. My oath is to uphold the Constitution of the United States in my public life. My oath privately between me and God was defined in the Catholic Church by Pius XXIII and Pope Paul VI in the Vatican II, which allows for freedom of conscience for Catholics with respect to these choices, and that is exactly where I am." We had better tread lightly here. We're dealing with the inner sanctum of the conscience. This is a man who apparently has taken a private oath under the tutelage of a pope of whom most of us have never heard. Rumor has it that members of the very secretive Society of Pius XXIII are taught to be so careful about not imposing their religion that, just to be safe, they do not impose it upon themselves. It has also been said that "Pius XXIII" is a pseudonym used by Father Robert Drinan, a Jesuit who has contrived a moral rationale widely employed by Catholic politicians inconvenienced by Catholic teaching. I have no idea whether such rumors are true, but I have a strong hunch that during the course of this campaign we may be learning a great deal about Catholicism that nobody knew before. *(June/July 2004)*

❧ By the end of the nineteenth century, after much wrangling, Harvard had dropped *Veritas pro Christo et ecclesia* from its motto, settling for the one word, *Veritas*. This March, Columbia University redesigned its symbol, a crown with three crosses, by removing the crosses. Columbia was established 250 years ago as an Anglican college and chartered by King George II. Predictably, some conservatives lamented the change. Others, however, took comfort in the fact that the university, while no longer Christian, is still monarchist. *(June/July 2004)*

❧ Now I'm in for it. Please, hold off on the protests and let me explain. A long and generally fair story in the *New York Times* on Evangelicals and Catholics Together (ECT) says that I "confided" in the reporter, Laurie Goodstein, that there are aspects of Evangelical culture that Catholics are uneasy about, such as "the overly confident claims to being born again, the forced happiness and joy, the awful music." No, I'm not going to complain that I was quoted out of context, although of course I was. The context was an interview of well over an hour, and publishing it all would have taken up a large part of that Sunday's paper. Ms. Goodstein asked about tensions between Evangelical and Catholic religious cultures, and I offered an extended list of such tensions, including the items quoted above. The "overly confident claims" sound to many Catholics like the sin of presumption, while Evangelicals intend what they call "blessed assurance" or, if they are Calvinists, "the perseverance of the saints." The seemingly forced expressions of happiness and joy (I should have added "seemingly") reflect an Evangelical accent on the subjective and experiential, as distinct from the Catholic accent on the objective and sacramental. As for awful music, Catholics know that Evangelicals have no monopoly on that, but I had just been to an Evangelical rally in which the worship (or was it entertainment?) was an emaciated-looking young man with an electric guitar working himself into a frenzy with ten minutes of a loud and escalating screech, "Jeeeesus, I love YOU!!!" There is awful, and then there is really awful. But, mind you, all this was in the context of describing to Ms. Goodstein the stereotypes that Evangelicals and Catholics commonly have of one another. Don't get me wrong. I love Evangelicals. Some of my best friends are Evangelicals. Evangelicals are swell. (Chuck Colson, can you help me out here?) *(August/September 2004)*

"What can we do to show that the Eucharist is a communal activity? Greeting people at the door is a start. It alerts us to the fact that we are going to do something with others. . . . I have found some Catholics who think this whole 'welcoming' business is destroying our traditional sense of reverence and replacing it with some folksy, feel-good experience. This is a false conclusion. If you wish to invite a guest into your home, you must have space. To invite others into our hearts and our worship, we must make room for them. The enemy of reverence is not hospitality but arrogance." Despite my being intimidated by the flat assertion, "This is a false conclusion," I dare to wonder if the author, a professor of theology writing in *America,* might tolerate a modest dissent. Note the language: *we* are going to do something; *our* traditional sense of reverence; *your* home; *our* worship. Is there not something to be said for reverence for what *God* is doing in *His* house through the liturgy of the *Church,* the saints in heaven and pilgrims on earth? There are many conversion stories in which the narrator describes quietly entering a Catholic church, maybe even sneaking in, and being struck by the statues and candles, and, most of all, by the people kneeling in rapt devotion as the priest at the altar lifts the consecrated host and declares, "Behold, the Lamb of God who takes away the sins of the world." There may be one, but I have never read a conversion story in which a person was drawn to the Catholic Church by the kind of chumminess that one might encounter at a birthday party or around the water cooler at the office. "This is a false conclusion," rumbles our liturgist. I'm sorry, sir, but since I've had the temerity to go so far, I'll go a step further and, at the risk of your wrath, suggest that it is really not so important "to show that the Eucharist is a communal activity." That's not the point. The point is what God has done, and is doing in the Mass, reconciling the world to Himself through the sacrifice of Christ. The eucharistic community is created precisely by our turning away from ourselves and toward Christ. The wonderful friendliness of our wonderful selves is really quite beside the point. And to think otherwise is, well, arrogance. *(October 2004)*

❧ I don't know what kind of revolution Robert Reich, labor secretary in the Clinton administration, has in mind, but he does Robespierre proud. Writing in the July issue of the *American Prospect,* he contends that Christian fundamentalists pose a greater danger to America than people flying jetliners into skyscrapers. He writes, "Terrorism is a tactic, not a belief. The true battle will be between modern civilization and anti-modernist; between those who believe in the primacy of the individual and those who believe that human beings owe their allegiance and identity to a higher authority . . . between those who believe in science, reason, and logic, and those who believe that truth is revealed through Scripture and religious dogma. Terrorism will disrupt and destroy lives. But terrorism itself is not the greatest danger we face." By Reich's definition of "fundamentalist" and "religious zealot," one would have to include, to name but a few Presidents, Washington, John Adams, Lincoln, Wilson, Carter, Reagan, and, of course, George W. Bush. More impressively, the great majority of the American people are, by his measure, enemies of the democracy he envisions. Reich's are not offhand remarks after the third scotch but were written for publication in a magazine of liberal respectability and influence. The thing worth remarking is that most of those who inhabit his ideological fanum (from which "fanatic") likely consider his sentiments unexceptionable. Mr. Reich has written a book called *Reason: Why Liberals Will Win the Battle for America.* Recall the recipe for unicorn stew: first, get a unicorn. Robert Reich's recipe for liberal victory in America is similar: first, get rid of the Americans. *(October 2004)*

❦ "According to Webster's," some opponents of same-sex marriage like to say, "marriage is 'the state of, or relation between, a man and a woman who have become husband and wife.'" Not any more. The eleventh edition of Merriam-Webster's Collegiate Dictionary, as well as the American Heritage Dictionary and the Oxford English Dictionary, all now include a union between two persons of the same sex under the definition of marriage. And, in a few years, there will likely be an allowance for "two or more." Arthur Bicknell of Merriam-Webster says they don't take sides on controverted questions. "Our primary job as lexicographers is to create a painstakingly accurate and comprehensive record of the English language." In other words, their job is description, not prescription, and there is an argument to be made for that. The more important point is that defenders of marriage need to appeal to a higher authority than Webster's, such as natural law, clear reason, the common good, and — dare one say it? — the Word of God. *(December 2004)*

❧ If you don't like the Constitution, you can always rewrite it. Or resort to the creative use of ellipses. The American Civil Liberties Union has an impressive website on free speech. The opening paragraph introducing the website is this: "It is probably no accident that freedom of speech is the first freedom mentioned in the First Amendment: 'Congress shall make no law . . . abridging the freedom of speech, or of the press, or of the people peaceably to assemble, and to petition the Government for a redress of grievances.' The Constitution's framers believed that freedom of inquiry and liberty of expression were the hallmarks of a democratic society." The first freedom mentioned in the First Amendment is, of course, the free exercise of religion. It appears that among the liberties championed by the ACLU is that of taking liberties with the text of the Constitution. *(January 2005)*

❧ I expect many Americans only vaguely remember the Beslan massacre in Russia of last September. More than three hundred men, women, and children were slaughtered by Muslim fanatics. The men were killed first, and the older children were forced to throw the corpses of their parents out the window. Most of the children killed were shot in the back as they tried to run away. In an interview at a conference dealing with terrorism, Renato Cardinal Martino, head of the Pontifical Council for Justice and Peace, said, "We are facing a Fourth World War." For a moment it sounded as though he had been reading *Commentary*. But only for a moment. He continued, "We have to identify the causes. What provokes terrorism? Why? Until we have the answer, and until we try to address these causes, terrorism cannot be defeated." Later in the interview he said, "If a madman attacks me, obviously I have the right to defend myself. Society has the right to defend itself in the way it has always done when dealing with madmen. I've never said that there must be no use of force, and I've never called for the abolition of the use of arms." Whatever its other problems, the Cardinal's statement is a welcome clarification of his earlier and widely remarked assertion that there is today no such thing as a just war. *(February 2005)*

❦ Recall the grisly case in Missouri in which Lisa Montgomery killed by strangulation a woman who was eight months pregnant. The Associated Press reported: "Authorities said Montgomery, 36, confessed to strangling Bobbie Joe Stinnett of Skidmore, Mo., on Thursday, cutting out the fetus and taking the baby back to Kansas." What happened to the fetus? And where did Montgomery get a baby? Encapsulated in one sentence are the absurdities of thought and language that bedevil liberal talk about abortion. *(March 2005)*

❦ A reader found this on the Internet, so it must be true. A man in Charlotte, North Carolina, bought a box of very expensive cigars which he insured against fire. Having smoked them, he filed a claim, saying they had been lost "in a series of small fires." The insurance company balked, the case went to court, and the judge ruled in the man's favor, noting that the company did not specify what is an "unacceptable fire." The company was required to pay the fellow $15,000, but then had him arrested on twenty-four counts of arson. He was convicted and sentenced to twenty-four months in jail and a fine of $24,000. If true, it is a sobering tale, confirming me in the wisdom of smoking cigars that are inexpensive and uninsured. *(May 2005)*

III

Remembering Martin Luther King Jr.

I know it is a fact, but it is nonetheless hard to picture: Had he lived, Martin Luther King Jr. would now be seventy-three years old. Everybody of a certain age has memories, if only of television images; many were there when he spoke, others marched with him in Selma or Montgomery, and some of us were, albeit intermittently, drawn into his personal orbit. The last I count as one of the many graces of my life, and it no doubt explains why I read, almost compulsively, just about everything published about the man and the time. Now we have Marshall Frady's *Martin Luther King, Jr.*, the latest volume in the "Penguin Lives" series. It is a valuable addition to the many accounts we have of the man and the movement he led.

I am in the minority with my admiration for Ralph Abernathy's 1989 autobiographical account of the movement, *And the Walls Came Tumbling Down*. Abernathy was beyond doubt closer to King than anyone else. After the assassination, he took King's place as head of the Southern Christian Leadership Conference (SCLC), although he knew as well as anyone that he was no Martin Luther King. His book was harshly criticized for its candor about King's sexual vagaries, but other published accounts had been more explicit on that score. What I think got to many reviewers is that Abernathy refused to toe the line on the leftist ideology of the movement and even, in the early eighties, took a conservative turn, offering some favorable words on, of all people, Ronald Reagan.

His gravest violation of conventional tellings is that he declined to see black Americans as a victim class oppressed by white racism, or to depict the movement as a response of revolutionary rage. As he told the story, King was a privileged son of the black bourgeoisie of Atlanta and he, Abernathy, was the heir of a tradition of black dignity in a rural Alabama he describes in almost idyllic terms. Abernathy was daringly "incorrect," and he paid a steep price for it. "Though slavery as an institution was wicked and foreign to the will of our Lord," he wrote, "it was not uniformly cruel and abusive. Some slaves, in the midst of their degradation, were treated with a measure of Christian charity, just as some prisoners of war have always been treated better than others. In the worst of circumstances, the human heart is still a mysterious variable."

His grandparents were slaves, but did not understand themselves to be victims. "In Marengo County during the first half of the twentieth century, the name 'Abernathy' meant integrity, responsibility, generosity, and religious commitment — and it came to mean that largely through the life and testimony of the *black* Abernathys. . . . So I feel no shame in going by a last name to which my father and mother brought such character and dignity. It was *their* name. They didn't just borrow it from a long-dead white man. They paid for it with their exemplary lives and therefore owned it outright when they passed it along to me."

Abernathy says that as a boy he was aware of racial segregation, but to him and other blacks in Alabama it was no big deal if the white folks wanted to have their own drinking fountains and a separate entrance at the post office. What did rankle is that white folk wouldn't call his father "Mister." The demand for white courtesy, and respect for the dignity that black folk knew they possessed — that was the issue in what came to be called the civil rights movement. That was the issue when Rosa Parks refused to give up her seat, a refusal that sparked the Montgomery bus boycott to which Abernathy recruited Martin Luther King, Jr., thus launching them both on a tumultuous course that they could neither anticipate nor control.

A Legacy Not Well Served

That is in largest part the story of *And the Walls Came Tumbling Down:* how a modest campaign for basic human decency somehow exploded into an out-of-control movement that, picking up a curious mix of causes and characters along the way, was perceived as a revolutionary challenge to the fundamental institutions and beliefs of the country and the world. Oddly enough, Marshall Frady's *Martin Luther King, Jr.* tells much of the story in the same way, although Frady tends to be condescending, at best, toward Ralph David Abernathy. Abernathy is described as "a stocky, slow badger of a man with a drowsy-eyed, drooping face but a droll and rollicking earthiness, who in their special comradeship over the years was to serve as something like King's Falstaff." At another point: "There was already, of course, the dutiful Abernathy, [King's] baggy, dolorous-faced, waggish Sancho Panza [who was] totally steadfast." It was easy to underestimate Abernathy, as I too learned. He did play the clown at times, but at times of crisis there was no one whose intuitive judgment King trusted more.

On the other hand, Frady has a high estimate of Jesse Jackson. In 1996 he published *Jesse: The Life and Pilgrimage of Jesse Jackson,* and in the present book he writes: "Jesse Jackson, after founding his own movement organization in Chicago, would eventually convert what was perhaps the largest victory of King's apostleship — the claiming of the vote for all blacks — into two surprisingly impressive guerrilla presidential campaigns in 1984 and 1988: as it turned out, this aide who came latest to King, and was perhaps most mistrusted by him, would come closest to developing into his heir as the single most eloquent symbol of pride and hope for masses of black Americans." All the worse for masses of black Americans, in the judgment of many. Frady attempts to excuse even Jackson's smearing of his shirt with King's blood on April 4, 1968, and then going on television to present himself as the anointed heir.

King mistrusted Jackson with good reason, and the following decades have vindicated that mistrust as Jackson has time and again acted as an opportunist, an ambulance chaser, and a publicity hound, who has skillfully exploited the memory of the movement by turning it into a lucrative extortion racket for shaking down corporate America. With a few honorable exceptions, such as Andrew Young, King's legacy has not been well served by those closest to him. While excusing Jackson, Frady is appropriately critical of Coretta and the children for their continuing efforts to tightly control and financially milk the relics of the martyr.

Days of Delirium

Frady captures well the exhilaration of the time. "The civil rights movement became the nation's latest attempt to perform in the South an exorcising of its original sin, and it turned out our most epic moral drama since the Civil War itself." All of us at the time had a dream of possibilities hitherto unimagined. For this young inner-city pastor in black Brooklyn, as for so many others, a new world was aborning. John XXIII was Pope, John F. Kennedy was President, and Dr. King had sighted the promised land of "the beloved community." As Wordsworth said of an earlier moment of tragically disappointed hope, "Bliss was it in that dawn to be alive, / But to be young was very heaven!" Frady puts it nicely: "They were days delirious with belief." I do not want to exaggerate my own delirium. After all, I was a Lutheran, attuned to "two-kingdom" skepticism about social change and steeped in Reinhold Niebuhr's understanding of the ironies of history. But, as much as a Niebuhrian Lutheran could be, I too was caught up in the epic moral drama.

The story line of the drama was challenged early on by young blacks high on the delirium of their own radicalism who derided King as "de Lawd" and had little patience with his devotion to nonviolence. SNCC, the Student Nonviolent Coordinating Committee, at first worked closely with King, but soon fell into the hands of violence-prone nonstudents incapable of coordinating anything, but masterful in generating rage. The cry of "Black Power" was heard in the land, and later would come the murderous Black Panthers. Stokely Carmichael, whom Frady describes as "the long lean black Robespierre," hijacked SNCC, declaring, "I'm not gonna beg the white man for anything I deserve. I'm gonna *take it!*" Frady writes: "Romanticism about the movement in the liberal salons of the North had begun shifting to its incendiaries like Carmichael, with their terminal cynicism about the efficacy of the ethic of nonviolence, their Malcolm [Malcolm X] mentality of a final, bitter acceptance of the human condition as one of hopeless racial antagonism. What seemed to be happening everywhere around King, in fact, was something like the tidal ebbing of faith in Matthew Arnold's *Dover Beach:* a withdrawal to naked shingles of anger." In his devastating depiction of the liberal salons of the North, Tom Wolfe would write of the "radical chic" that has not yet disappeared entirely, and may never disappear, from what are deemed to be the commanding heights of the culture.

In an early (1970) book, *King: A Critical Biography,* David Lewis argued that King was much more of a radical than was generally believed. Lewis writes, and Frady quotes him approvingly, that in "the nation's canonization of Martin King . . . we have sought to remember him by forgetting him." Frady says that King's message "inexorably evolved into an evangelism against what he saw as the moral coma of the country's whole corporate, technological order: its loud and vicious void of materialism . . . and the measureless vandalism this new kind of high-tech barbarism was visiting not only on the life of America, but elsewhere in the world, most luridly at that time in Vietnam. In effect, he came to pit himself against his entire age." I am not persuaded that King ever came to a systematic endorsement of the kind of ideological radicalism that Lewis and Frady attribute to him.

Not So Radical

King was an exuberant rhetorician, and rhetoric has a way of getting out of hand. Frady gives due attention to King's dependence on Stanley Levison, a wealthy New York lawyer and wheeler-dealer, who dropped his membership in the Communist Party lest it become an embarrassment to King. The Old Left with its ties to communism was an integral part of much of what was viewed as mainstream liberalism in the 1960s. Even the more established liberal organizations that maintained an "exclusionary clause" against Communists did not take seriously the claim that communism posed a domestic threat. The great threat of the time was thought to be anticommunism, as evident in the rambunctiously reckless attacks of Senator Joe McCarthy and the catchall term of opprobrium, "McCarthyism." King's refusal to break with Levison, despite pressures from the FBI and others, indicates not that he was a Communist puppet or had embraced Marxist ideology but simply that he was a good liberal, although less scrupulous about — probably because less knowledgeable about — the Old Left with which more establishment liberals were so unhappily familiar.

King, writes Frady, "was to arrive in the end at a kind of Christian socialism of conscience, once professing to a friend, 'If we are to achieve real equality, the United States will have to adopt a modified form of socialism.'" But of course. Almost everybody in the left-liberal orbit of the time professed to be a socialist of one kind or another. King is quoted as saying at a private retreat of movement leaders that "something is wrong with the economic system of our nation . . . something is wrong with capitalism." The liberals at the time who did not claim to be socialist had no inhibitions in declaring themselves strongly opposed to capitalism. They were typically for a "third way" between socialism and capitalism. In those days, in those circles, actually affirming capitalism was simply beyond the pale. Frady quotes King telling David Halberstam, "You have got to have a reconstruction of the entire society, a revolution of values." Of course. What liberal preacher or politician has not said the same, and said it many times? Depending on what unhappy aspect of society is being deplored, conservatives frequently say the same.

In my movement days, I would, when feeling mischievous, observe that I was not and never had been a socialist. This would predictably meet with startled incredulity, and the discussion would inevitably turn to what is meant by socialism. I would usually end up by saying something like this: "If by socialism, you mean reforms in the political economy that help the poor to be more fully included in the opportunities and responsibilities of society, then I admit to being a socialist." This almost always met with great relief, my faux pas was forgiven, and I was restored to ideological communion. If the above formula is accepted as the definition of socialism, I'm very much a socialist today.

I do not for a moment deny that there were hard-core socialists, ideological Marxists, and, probably, even active collaborators with communism in the leadership of the movement. There is every reason to believe Dr. King knew that and he should have been more concerned about it than he apparently was. He thought he could use them, and he was probably at times used by them. But I am confident that he and his closest associates, such as Abernathy and Young, were not among them. His most radical program for change was the Poor People's Campaign launched in 1968. It was supposed to bring many thousands of people to encamp on the Washington Mall until the government agreed to expend an annual $30 billion in expunging poverty, committed itself to full employment, a guaranteed annual income, and the building of 300,000 low-income housing units each year. After his assassination in April, a bedraggled and dispirited SCLC tried to go ahead with the plan, ending up a few weeks later with a handful of supporters holding out in mud-besotted tents before federal rangers moved in to clear them out and clean up the mess. It was an inglorious ending to a misbegotten plan.

King's occasional rhetoric of "revolutionary" change and the proposals of the Poor People's Campaign do not, I think, support the claims of Lewis, Frady, and others that he was an ideological socialist, never mind a revolutionary in the Marxist vein. That was a time when radical talk seemed to be the mainstream. A few years later, George McGovern's presidential campaign would embrace most of the proposals of the Poor People's Campaign. McGovern was wrong, and he may have been dumb, but he was not a revolutionary bent upon overthrowing the constitutional or economic order. He was what was then de rigueur among most liberals — a "radicalized" liberal. So also with Martin Luther King.

By his own admission, Dr. King was by 1968 frustrated, tired, and confused. I recall conversations at the time when some were urging him to launch a presidential "peace campaign," or to join with Senator Eugene McCarthy in the challenge to Lyndon Johnson. He spoke about his uneasiness with the ambiguities of electoral politics in all its forms, and the need to recapture the uncomplicated moral drama of Birmingham and earlier campaigns in the South. In New York, a few months before his death, we had lunch, together with Young and Al Lowenstein, an activist who would later be murdered by one of his protégés, and King turned philosophical about the limits of political change. It was a leisurely and convivial lunch. The restaurant had been alerted that "the famous Dr. King" was coming, and the waiter assumed that the white man in the clerical collar must be he, and so throughout the lunch addressed me as "Dr. King." It both astonished and amused that one of the most famous people in the world was not recognized, and King enjoyed it immensely, taking the opportunity to smoke cigarettes throughout lunch, a regular habit that he usually indulged only in private. Among many other things, we talked about the abiding wisdom of Reinhold Niebuhr and the need to recognize the distinction between the morally imperative and the historically possible, agreeing also on the moral imperative to press the historically possible. It was the last time I saw him.

Disenchantment

I am surprised that the editors of the Penguin Lives chose Marshall Frady to do the book on Dr. King, or maybe it is they who are surprised by the book he wrote. Had this been the received picture of King in the years following his death, it is likely that his birthday would not be a national holiday. "The fact is," writes Frady, "King was always to fail more often than he would succeed." He rightly notes that the Montgomery bus boycott launched in 1956 did not prevail but was rescued by a federal court order. Six years later, "Birmingham had become the first clear, authentic victory, actually won in popular confrontation and struggle, for King's movement of nonviolent mass protest." After his emergence from obscurity in Montgomery, King had only twelve years to live, and it is fair to say that Birmingham was the only such victory. The effort to take the movement to the North, to Richard Daley the Elder's Chicago, was a disaster. King's courtly Southern ways did not resonate with the slum dwellers of the North. He was not angry enough. As he said, "You just can't communicate with the ghetto dweller and at the same time not frighten many whites to death." At that time, Malcolm X was exulting in frightening whites to death, and King looked moderate — i.e., weak — by comparison.

He led marches for housing desegregation through white neighborhoods of Chicago, meeting with outraged anger. At one point he said, "I have never seen so much hatred and hostility on the faces of so many people as I've seen here today." Frady writes, "He had in fact come up against the innermost reality of racism in America." The larger fact is that King had no plan for the racial integration of Chicago, nor did anyone else. Nor, except for a few mainly upper-income neighborhoods, has anybody come up with a successful plan for integrating housing to this very day. After Montgomery, King had said, "I'm worried to death that people will be expecting me to pull rabbits out of a hat for the rest of my life." A problem with Frady's account, it seems to me, is that he is among those who judge King by whether he succeeded in pulling rabbits out of a hat.

In his calculation of success and failure, Frady tends to be dismissive of the inherent worth of King's preaching, exhortation, inspiration. Every preacher who has been around a while finds consolation in the promise of Isaiah that "the word shall not return void." To preach well *is* success. I recall rallies when, in the course of his preaching, King would hold forth on the theological and moral foundations of the movement. The klieg lights and cameras shut down, only to be turned on again when he returned to specifically political or programmatic themes. "Watch the lights," he commented. "They're not interested in the most important parts." But as for the judgment that King finally achieved very little, Mr. Frady might recall his own statement that the chief consequence of King's legacy was securing the vote for all blacks. No little achievement, that.

Death in Mid-Passage

Frady tends to agree with those who say that King died at the right time and in the right way. "Some have since suggested that it was just at the point where King seemed passing irretrievably into decline that he came by the terrible exaltation of violent martyrdom — a kind of historical editing, before the disillusionment could become total, that spared him from what could well have become a progressive marginality and tiresomeness and bankruptcy of his image. . . . If King had lived, most likely he would, with his increasingly radical gospel, have departed steadily further from the temper and received liberal sophistication of his times, drifting to the outermost fringes of apparent relevancy."

I am inclined to the view that Dr. King was taken in mid-passage; he was not yet forty and nobody knows what he might have become and might have done. He might have departed further "from the temper and received liberal sophistication of his times," not because of the radicalism that Frady attributes to him but because of a deeper radicalism grounded in the Christian gospel. I have entertained the hope that King would have confronted the epoch-defining moral crisis posed by what then was called, long before *Roe v. Wade,* "liberalized abortion law." That is no more than a hope. I have no idea what he would have done with respect to this crisis of all crises in our time. But recall that Jesse Jackson, to his credit, was a powerful defender of the unborn for several years after 1968. About abortion he declared, "The war on poverty has been replaced by the war on the poor and the most defenseless." To his great shame, he promptly switched sides when he was bitten by national political ambitions. Had King lived and continued in his aversion to politics, it is reasonable to hope that he would have made the obvious connections between the civil rights struggle and abortion, both being the cause of expanding and defending the community of human dignity. That is, of course, no more than a hope, and we will never know.

Abernathy was severely castigated for writing about King's deep moral flaws, but he tended to treat them as somehow incidental to his character and work. In Frady's portrait, they are more central to understanding what he depicts as the tragedy of Martin Luther King. That King plagiarized a large part of his doctoral dissertation at Boston University is now well known. Frady describes this as "an inclination to casual textual appropriation that was to become an unhappy habit of King's." That the books that were published under his name were, for the most part, written by others is not so well known. There is no doubt, however, that he really is the author of the classic "Letter from Birmingham Jail." Yet plagiarism is not the chief sin.

"The Pelvic Issues"

Dr. King was, for all that was great about him, an adulterer, sexual libertine, lecher, and wanton womanizer. In this he set the moral tone for others. Of the movement leaders Frady writes, "They were . . . a raunchy troupe for the most part, some roistering outrageously at times among whatever likely young ladies were at hand — the movement generally, for that matter, was hardly 'a sour-faced, pietistic' adventure, one veteran has since attested; 'everybody was out getting laid.'" King was a celebrity always surrounded by likely young ladies. On his last night on earth — the night of the unforgettable declaration, "I have seen the promised land" — King returned to the motel and "flung himself into a final, all-night release into carnal carousal" with no less than three women in succession. For years the FBI and, through the FBI, political opponents had tapes of King's nocturnal debauches and attempted to use them for purposes very much like blackmail. Coretta knew, and put on a brave public face of not knowing. The major reporters from newspapers and television networks knew but, Frady writes, "none of this material found its way into their reportage, a restraint virtually inconceivable in these times, meaning, of course, that King would very likely never have survived now as the figure he was then."

I did disagree once. When, shortly after his death, the first book appeared detailing this shadowed side of King's life, *The King God Didn't Save* by John A. Williams, I reviewed it very critically in the *New York Review of Books.* The evidence, I wrote, was hearsay, third- and fourth-hand, circumstantial, unsubstantiated, and highly improbable. I could not write that review today. The book was shoddy and sensationalistic, but thirty years later most of its substantive claims appear to be supported by more reliable witnesses. I had no personal knowledge of Dr. King's sexual wanderings, and I suppose it is possible that I did not see what others saw because I did not want to see it. To be forced to acknowledge that the stories are probably true — no, almost certainly true — still makes me sick. For the fact is that I admired and loved King, and still do. Then and now, I think it possible and necessary to make a crucial, albeit not unambiguous, distinction between the very broken earthen vessel and the treasure of truth that vessel contained and so powerfully communicated.

This must also be said: from very early on, the rhetoric and habits of the movement evinced a recklessly casual attitude toward sexual morality. It became a cliché in activist circles that there were many more Bible passages condemning inequality of wealth and other injustices than there were condemning sexual misconduct. Conventional religion was routinely assailed for being inordinately preoccupied with "morality from the belly button down." Among liberals to this day these are derided as "the pelvic issues." The movement at its best, by which I mean the civil rights movement through the mid-sixties, contained moral ingredients that would later become the libertine "counterculture" of drugs and sexual license. That was the turn, joined most decisively by the agitation for the abortion license, that resulted in my breaking ranks with the left. That turn among left-liberal activists, extending through the 1970s, also has a strong bearing on today's scandals about miscreant sexual conduct by clergy, Protestant and Catholic, who were formed by, and conformed to, the aberrations of the time.

What Jesus Promised

Martin Luther King Jr. was a Christian. Despite all. As we are all, in the final analysis, Christians despite all. Many of his biographers, and the public school texts, tend to downplay that. Much is made of his having been enlightened by reading Gandhi, and he is frequently depicted as a forerunner of New Ageish spirituality. But King was emphatic in asserting, "This business of passive resistance and nonviolence is the gospel of Jesus. I went to Gandhi through Jesus." Frady and others have recounted his telling of the time in Montgomery when he was first receiving death threats and wanted out. Frady tells it this way:

> He was overwhelmed with woe over his own unworthiness, his life of bourgeois privilege even during this ordeal into which he had led the city's black community, and finally about the superficiality of his "inherited" call into the ministry, although he "had never felt an experience with God in the way that you must . . . if you're going to walk the lonely paths of this life." As he later recalled that late night hour of desolation, "I couldn't take it any longer" and "tried to think of a way to move out of the picture without appearing a coward." Dropping his head into his hands, he suddenly realized he was praying aloud in the midnight hush of the kitchen: "Lord, I'm down here trying to do what's right. . . . But Lord, I'm faltering, I'm losing my courage. And I can't let the people see me like this. . . . But I've come to the point where I can't face it alone." And at that moment, as King would tell it, he seemed to hear "an inner voice . . . the voice of Jesus," answering him: "Martin Luther, stand up for righteousness, stand up for justice, stand up for truth. And lo, I will be with you, even until the end of the world." That voice of Jesus, King recounted, "promised never to leave me, no, never to leave me alone."

A few days after the assassination, I took part in a huge memorial service in Harlem. The service was reported on the evening news. The reporter, microphone in hand, stood in front of St. Charles Borromeo Catholic Church and said, as I recall his words, "And so today there was a memorial service for the slain civil rights leader, Dr. Martin Luther King. It was a religious service, and appropriately so, for, after all, he was the son of a minister." That rather totally missed the point, as the point has been missed so often in the years since then.

Marshall Frady depicts a man desperately riven and driven. "In King's lapses into that 'lower self' he so often decried, one sensed an extraordinarily harrowed man — caught in the almost insupportable strain of having to sustain the high spirituality of his mass moral struggle, while living increasingly in a daily expectation of death — intermittently resorting to releases into sweetly obliterating riots of the flesh. He seemed thus to move through some endlessly recycling alternation between the transcendently spiritual and the convulsively carnal." At a later point he writes: "In the widening beleaguerment of his latter years, it would sometimes seem as if he were, as in the Keats ode, 'half in love with easeful death,' almost wishful for its surcease from all travail, proposing once that he just might withdraw into a fast 'unto death.'"

I have no doubt there were times when that was the case. He was, after all, for twelve years and almost daily on the receiving end of death threats, thought he had come close to being killed several times, and was finally gunned down. Of course he thought about death more than most people have occasion to think about death. But it was in those latter years, especially the last two years, that I came to know him personally. Not on a day by day basis, to be sure, but enough to form a firm judgment of the man. I was impressed not by any morbid preoccupation with failure and mortality but by what appeared to be his inner peace, an almost triumphant tranquillity. Surrounded as world-class celebrities are by groupies and sycophants, he seemed not to be taken in by it all. I most clearly remember thinking, "Here is a man who has his ego under control. He knows who he is, and who he is not." I admired, and I envied, that. And that, despite all, is the way I remember him to this day.

Marshall Frady and others are right: if everything was

known then that is known now, Dr. King would early have been brought to public ruin, and there would almost certainly be no national holiday in his honor. But God writes straight with crooked lines, and he used his most unworthy servant Martin to create in our public life a luminous moment of moral truth about what Gunnar Myrdal rightly called "the America dilemma," racial justice. It seems a long time ago now, but there is no decline in the frequency of my thanking God for his witness and for having been touched, however briefly, by his friendship, praying that he may rest in peace, and that his cause may yet be vindicated. *(October 2002)*

While We're At It

❦ As you might imagine, thousands of books come through this shop, and relatively few can be considered for serious treatment, or any treatment at all. *Birdwatching in Vermont,* for example, didn't stand a chance, and when the postman spotted *Breaking Open the Head: A Psychedelic Journey into the Heart of Shamanism* and wanted to borrow it, nobody objected. We come up with little games in making necessarily quick judgments about books. There is, for instance, the best "focus-group title." That's when in every part, and taken as a whole, the title reflects keen market testing. The winner this season is Martin E. P. Seligman's *Authentic Happiness: Using the New Positive Psychology to Realize Your Potential for Lasting Fulfillment.* Bingo. "Happiness" is, of course, the original happy word. The qualifying "authentic" signifies that the author is aware of phony happinesses on offer. "Using" appeals to the pragmatic assumption of what ideas are for. "New" resonates with a neophiliac culture. "Positive," of course. Who wants anything negative? "Psychology" may have only a niche appeal, but accompanied by such an armory of qualifiers, it is hoped that any skepticism will be overwhelmed. "Realize" and "Potential" may seem redundant, except that the latter is needed for the inclusion of the crucial "Your," assuring the reader that Seligman is not going to impose anything. He only wants to help you be the wonderful person you are. "Lasting" is an implied guarantee that you will never have to buy another book like this again. As for "Fulfillment," see above on "Happiness." Seligman and Free Press have come up with the generic title for the entire genre of self-help books, meaning books that pander to the delusion that the simply marvelous "real me" is just waiting to be released from the me of life so far. And now I expect I will hear from a reader or two who will say their lives were turned around by the book. To which I can only say, Congratulations. But you might want to give the "Lasting" a bit more time. *(October 2002)*

❦ "Cutting Icons Down to Clay Feet." The heading of the review signals that Ben Brantley, theater critic of the *New York Times,* has found another "transgressive" work to celebrate. This one is by Jean Genet, the French writer, pedophile, sadomasochist, and homosexual prostitute who was jailed not for buggery but for burglary. Lionized bad boy of the literary elite, Genet had a long list of degradations to his credit, including having sex with the Stalinist philosopher Jean-Paul Sartre. The play, written in the 1950s, was titled *Saintette,* which Alan Cumming — on whom Brantley also did a fawning profile — adapted as *Elle.* It is about a pope (not this one, Brantley assures us) who knows that "she" is faking it but feels compelled to go through the motions of the Catholic thing. Daring, *non?* The message is simple-minded and repetitive, Brantley admits, but the presentation is "richly theatrical entertainment" and goes beyond "homosexual campiness" to reach new heights of "the impeccably vulgar." While Mr. Brantley finds decadence and blasphemy entertaining, when well done, he is by no means indifferent to the question of "redeeming social merit," to use the legal phrase for tolerable obscenity. "What *Elle* makes of the themes of sacrificial celebrity and the world's hunger for human gods," he writes, "seems painfully pertinent just now." That is undoubtedly meant to mean something. Perhaps that Jean Genet's and his pleasure in mocking the pope is not unmixed with pain. It is a sad duty, but somebody has to do it. Giggle, giggle. *(November 2002)*

❧ In the absence of an argument, change the subject. Peter Singer of Princeton, writing in *Free Inquiry,* the secular humanist publication, responds to my commentary on our debate at Colgate University ("A Curious Encounter with a Philosopher from Nowhere," FT, Public Square, February 2002). After offering his idiosyncratic — and, if I may say so, lamentably ill-informed and literalistic — view that the Scriptures have nothing to say about abortion or the creating and destroying of embryos for research purposes, and may, in fact, approve of suicide, he changes the subject to Matthew 19 and Jesus' counsel to the rich young man to sell all he has and give the money to the poor. Professor Singer exults, Gotcha! It has come to his attention that most Christians do not sell all they have and give the proceeds to the poor! He also notes that FT carries an advertisement for a Catholic investing service, in clear violation of the words of Jesus to "take no thought for the morrow." Gotcha again! Prof. Singer writes, "Father Neuhaus denies that the Christian ethic tells us to share extensively with the poor." That, of course, is nonsense. Singer writes, "I have advocated, without any appeal to religion, that those of us who are sufficiently comfortably off to be able to spend much of our income on frivolities like restaurants, the theater, fashionable clothes, and vacations abroad should give a substantial proportion of our income to organizations working to assist the world's poorest people." On that we are in complete agreement, and I am glad to be assured that Prof. Singer, who is very comfortably off indeed, does that. I also agree that such generosity need not be religiously motivated but can be in response to a sense of natural justice. What I do deny is that Prof. Singer's laudable concern for world hunger is relevant to his support for creating and destroying human life in the laboratory, for the unlimited abortion license, and for a policy permitting the killing of children who are already born but, because of some defect, are no longer wanted. The debate is not about whether Peter Singer is in some respects a nice person, nor is it about whether all Christians live in a manner consistent with the Christian ethic (however he misconstrues that ethic). He is and they don't. The debate is about this "philosopher from nowhere" and his advocacy of the morally monstrous. Were I in Prof. Singer's position, I, too, might want to change the subject. Much to be preferred, of course, is that he would change his mind. *(November 2002)*

❦ It is hardly a surprise that Peter Singer, the philosopher from nowhere, is a proponent of world government. He employs a very familiar trope: "The twentieth century's conquest of space made it possible for a human being to look at our planet from a point not on it, and so to see it, literally, as one world. Now the twenty-first century faces the task of developing a suitable form of government for that single world." He recognizes that the idea of world government, which in its modern form goes back at least to Immanuel Kant, has its skeptics. "There is little political support for such ideas at present. Apart from the threat that the idea poses to the self-interest of the citizens of the rich nations, many would say it puts too much at risk, for gains that are too uncertain. It is widely believed that a world government would be, at best, an unchecked bureaucratic behemoth that makes the bureaucracy of the European Union look like a lean and efficient operation. At worst, it would become a global tyranny, unchecked and unchallengable. Those thoughts have to be taken seriously. They present a challenge that should not be beyond the best minds in the fields of political science and public administration, once those people adjust to the new reality of the global community and turn their attention to issues of government beyond national boundaries." The bureaucrats of the European Union will likely be insulted, and rightly so, by the suggestion that they don't have "the best minds in the fields of political science and public administration." Remember Bill Buckley's line about the Harvard faculty and the Boston telephone directory. *(December 2002)*

❦ They're going to die anyway, so why not derive some good from their deaths? We even talk about "redeeming" the tragedy of so many deaths. Many years ago, the Methodist ethicist Paul Ramsey discussed how seductive this way of thinking and talking is. Then the subject was using aborted fetuses for research purposes; now the debate is about using embryos in research related to stem cells, cloning, and such. Writing in the *Weekly Standard,* Lutheran ethicist Gilbert Meilaender provides grist for moral reflection: "The issue of embryo research is not precisely the same as fetal research, of course, but the insight into our ready recourse to the quasi-religious language of finding some redeeming good in what we do is illuminating. We need to think again about the spare-embryo argument. Initially appealing as it may be, offering it seems a chance to move forward with research while still drawing a significant moral line, it begins to lose its force the longer we ponder it and the harder we press on it. The very form of the argument — 'he'll die anyway; we might as well get some good from his dying' — seduces us into supposing that all moral evils must be forms of 'harm.' 'No harm, no foul' may work well for officiating basketball, but it does not work well for sorting through our moral obligations. Reducing all moral evils to harm, we blind ourselves to issues of dignity and justice — as if, for example, we would not wrong a permanently unconscious person by selling tickets for others to observe him. We need to slow down, think again, and draw back, lest we train ourselves to think in ways that diminish us as a people. Perhaps this means — though it's hard to say for sure — that the pace of medical progress must be slower than it could be. If so, that only means that here, as in so many other areas of research, we accept and honor necessary moral limits. For, as Paul Ramsey also put it, 'the moral history of mankind is more important than its medical history.'" *(December 2002)*

❧ *Militant Islam Reaches America* by Daniel Pipes (Norton) makes some important points, Judith Miller allows in the *New York Times Book Review.* But his description of the threat posed by militant Islam, or Islamism, has a sometimes "intemperate tone" and, more important, lacks balance. "His prescriptions for what he calls the world's most dangerous movement," Ms. Miller writes, "barely mention the need to defend America's secularism or the extent to which secular laws, values, and traditions are under attack not only by militant Muslims but also by the Bush administration and its allies on the Christian right." But of course. Islamists fly passenger planes into skyscrapers, execute homosexuals and political dissenters, forbid women to show their faces in public, and threaten the world with weapons of mass destruction. But how about the religious fanatics at the Family Research Council who encourage family stability, urge the protection of unborn children, and support parental choice in education? She got you there, Dan Pipes. *(December 2002)*

❧ Long ago, when I was a student at Concordia College (now Concordia University) in Austin, Texas, I was greatly impressed by a sermon that kept returning to the theme, "God has no grandchildren. He only has children." The preacher's point was that faith cannot be inherited; that each of us become children of God by our own act of faith. I do not reject that insight when I observe that, in saying Mass today, there are few parts of the rite that so consistently touch my heart as the phrase before the Sign of Peace, "Look not on our sins, but on the faith of your Church." The

Church does believe with me, and for me. We do have grandparents and brothers and sisters and cousins and a host of the faithful both here and in glory who sustain us in faith. This truth was brought to mind in reading an address on "The Question of Authority" by Cardinal Cormac Murphy-O'Connor of Westminster, England. He cites the commentary by Henri de Lubac on the statement by the third century Origen, "For myself, I desire to be truly ecclesiastic." I have written a good bit on what it means to be an "ecclesial Christian," and some say they are puzzled by the phrase. I mean what de Lubac writes in *The Splendor of the Church:* "Anyone who is possessed by a similar desire will not find it enough to be loyal or obedient to perform exactly everything demanded by his profession of the Catholic faith. Such a man will have fallen in love with the beauty of the house of God; the Church will have stolen his heart." Which is to say that Christ has stolen his heart. Murphy-O'Connor notes that today the word "authority" is so problematic because it is habitually associated with power. But ecclesial authority is grounded in love, the love of God in Christ. He writes: "The Church has nothing to offer but Jesus Christ. The reality that the Church offers to our world is Christ, his gift of forgiveness and his gift of love. These are given in his word, in his sacraments, in his presence, through the power of the Holy Spirit. Like Peter in the Acts of Apostles, we say, 'I have neither silver nor gold but I give you what I have: in the name of Jesus Christ, the Nazarene, walk,' and Peter then took him by the hand and helped him to stand up (Acts 3:6-7). If Christ's is the authority of the Church, Peter is the model of its exercise. He is also a sign of the paradox which is our experience of human weakness and God-given strength. Peter was given the power of the keys, but it was not because he was strong or because he was faithful. He was, for some considerable time, neither. He betrayed Jesus out of his own mouth. His shame and his moral collapse at that moment was utterly disabling. Surely Peter is the least authoritative and trustworthy of founders? One might think so; but it is here that something of the mystery of God's graciousness and freedom is revealed and, as with the cross, we discover a truth which is a source of incomprehension (perhaps even scandal) to many. The answer is that we can trust Peter precisely because he has fallen, because he is weak, because he is forgiven, and because he is raised up to service. We trust him because in him we see God's power working in our human weakness. Peter knew from his own experience the depth of the gift he offered; he knew that it was neither his gift nor his authority but that of the One he denied and yet loved. Like each one of us, he experienced not only his own need of forgiveness; he experienced first hand from where that forgiveness comes. He was both empowered and commissioned to go out and to offer that same forgiveness to the whole of mankind. He was indeed the rock on which the Church was founded. She, like Peter, speaks not out of any kind of false strength, but out of her experience of weakness. And she speaks God's truth that she lives and experiences every day. This is the authentic voice of the Church, a voice enriched with the gifts our Lord has given her and emboldened and quickened with the authority with which he has invested her: 'Go therefore and teach all nations, baptizing them in the name of the Father and of the Son and of the Holy Spirit, and know that I am with you always, even to the end of time.'" *(February 2003)*

❦ Things are getting awfully complicated. The Sunday bulletin of Prince of Peace Lutheran Church in Springfield, Virginia, notes that at communion people have the choice of individual cup or chalice, real wine or nonalcoholic wine. Then there is this: "On the pulpit side a male communion assistant will serve the common cup; a female communion assistant will serve the individual cups. On the baptism side, the procedure will be reversed." In my Lutheran boyhood we were told that form and philosophical explanations such as "transubstantiation" didn't matter. "The only thing that matters," it was said, "is that you are receiving the Body and

Blood of Christ." Now so many things seem to matter. *(May 2003)*

❧ The mischievous *Forum Letter* is up to it again. It reports that at a Rocky Mountain Synod meeting in Colorado Springs, Bishop Mark Hanson, head of the ELCA Lutherans, spoke on a sexuality study in which that communion is embroiled. Certainly, he said, "we're not going to base our position with regard to homosexuality on seven passages from Scripture." One pastor leaned over to a brother and said, "Isn't that more than we have on the institution of the Lord's Supper?" *(August/September 2003)*

❧ An Episcopalian friend expressed her puzzlement that the Episcopal Church can so cavalierly jettison doctrines while taking such a firm stand on questions of funding and authority. Paul Marshall of Freedom House came up with a possible answer in a statement by Karl Marx in his preface to the first volume of *Das Kapital:* "The English Established Church will more readily pardon an attack on 38 of its 39 articles than on 1/39th of its income." But we know that Marx got everything wrong. Well, almost everything. *(December 2003)*

❧ Hilaire Belloc writing from the Sahara as he pondered the ruins of Timgad: "We sit by and watch the Barbarian, we tolerate him; in the long stretches of peace we are not afraid. We are tickled by his irreverence, his comic inversion of our old certitudes and our fixed creeds refreshes us; we laugh. But as we laugh we are watched by large and awful faces from beyond: and on these faces there is no smile." The theater world is abuzz with the effort to mainstream Tony Kushner's *Angels in America: A Gay Fantasia on National Themes.* The show was wildly acclaimed on the Great Gay Way that Broadway has become. It is titteringly asked whether dumb, plodding, pious, bourgeois, so very ordinary America is ready for this scintillating inversion of its old certitudes and fixed creeds, in the half-hope that the answer is in the negative, thus providing further proof of the genius and, yes, the courage of Mr. Kushner and, by extension, of the herd of independent minds who join in his contempt for our repressive society that would, don't you know, jail him if it could. Mr. Kushner has also written a little book, *Save Your Democratic Soul!: Rants, Screeds, and Other Public Utterances.* Civil discourse is not his shtick. His agent says that in his many campus appearances Mr. Kushner "prefers to speak to progressive audiences open to change." But of course. Because old certitudes are no longer certain and fixed creeds no longer so fixed, people who cannot help but know better nervously applaud the assault on what they used to call their convictions, thus appeasing the great god Progress who might otherwise be displeased. Their nervous approval is offered in the hope of avoiding the terrible judgment of the priesthood of comic inversion that they are too witless to join in the fun of trashing what, to their embarrassment, they know they believe. They are keenly aware that their every response is ruthlessly scrutinized by the queer eye for the straight guy. Their laughter is forced, however, for, try as they might, they cannot quite rid themselves of the suspicion that they are being watched also by those large and awful and unsmiling faces from beyond. *(February 2004)*

❧ Progress is a jealous god. Upon being the first Episcopal bishop to ordain a lesbian, the late Paul Moore declared that, whenever he was faced with a difficult moral decision, he chose change, the way of the future. Albert R. Hunt begins his *Wall Street Journal* column with, "I am a convert to accepting gay marriages." He says he was uncomfortable with the idea at first. "But times are changing. When I asked my seventeen-year-old son if he supported gay marriage, he shrugged and replied, 'Sure. What's the big deal?'" After having done his homework on the subject, Hunt goes on to echo Andrew Sullivan's usual talking points, but the clinching argument is that "younger Americans are not encumbered with many of the hang-ups and prejudices of their elders; the tide is with change." And if you are not convinced by that, there is the fact that gay marriage has about it "a sense of ultimate inevitability." Well, there you are. Hunt acknowledges that the great majority of Americans are against gay marriage and a majority appears to favor a constitutional amendment to preclude it, but that only means he is among the elect of those who are ahead of their time. "The times are changing." "The tide is with change." Some things never change. *(March 2004)*

❧ "Water, An Essential Element of Life." That is the lead item in *Origins,* a Catholic documentary service. "Water, an Essential Element of Life" is a major and perhaps eagerly awaited statement by the Pontifical Council on Justice and Peace. Last year was the UN International Year of Water. The statement declares, "Sufficient and safe drinking water is a precondition for the realization of other human rights. There is a growing movement to formally adopt a human right to water." Without drinking water, people cannot live and therefore cannot exercise their rights. Obversely, those who have drinking water can violate the rights of others. "When water is scarce, competition for limited supplies has led nations to see water as a matter of national or regional security," the pontifical council has concluded. "Access and deprivation underlie most water decisions. Hence, linkages between water policy and ethics increasingly emerge." Moreover, "the poor suffer far more from the scarcity of water than do the wealthy." The principal difficulty involving water today, the pontifical council discovered, "is not one of absolute scarcity but of distribution." It seems that some places have too much water and other places have too little. There is an unconfirmed report that under discussion at the UN is an International Year of Air. If that ambitious step is taken, informed observers say, the Pontifical Council on Justice and Peace will be ready with a major statement, "Air, An Essential Element of Life." *(March 2004)*

❦ Apparently it's becoming the thing with rich kids who have lots of Jewish friends. They go to Bar Mitzvahs and Bat Mitzvahs and find the parties really cool. For example, Laura Jean of Dallas, whose parents are Methodist, had a really big bash, which the *Wall Street Journal* says "looked like a Bat Mitzvah, without the religion." Said Laura Jean, "I wanted to be Jewish so I could have a Bat Mitzvah. Having the party fulfilled that." More precisely, having the party fulfilled wanting to be Jewish in order to have a party. Don't blame the kids, but what are the parents, if they are thinking, thinking? *(April 2004)*

❦ "Jews, Muslims, Christians — we are all children of Abraham and people of the Book." Not so, says the French historian Alain Besançon, writing in *Commentary*. "What Kind of Religion is Islam?" is a hard-hitting critique of what Besançon views as a false ecumenism eager to find commonalities with Islam that do not exist. Not incidentally, this misguided effort disadvantages Judaism since it is claimed, for instance, that Islam honors Jesus and Mary while Judaism does not. But the Jesus/Issa honored in the Koran as a messenger of Allah is not the Jesus whom Christians worship, writes Besançon. He is supposedly born of Mariam, the sister of Aaron, and is neither a redeemer nor a mediator between God and man. And, of course, he does not die on the cross, since a double is substituted for him. Moreover, Allah is not the God of Abraham who reveals himself through historical events, but a distant and impersonal power that makes everything happen immediately; not through the nature and history of his own creation but according to his omnipotent whim. Thus the determinism and fatalism at the heart of Islamic religion. "These then," writes Besançon, "are some of the elements that conduce to misunderstanding when Christians and Jews approach Islam. Such outsiders may well be struck by the religious zeal of the Muslim toward a God whom they recognize as being also their God. But this God is in fact separate and distinct, and so is the relation between

Him and the believing Muslim. Christians are accustomed to distinguish the worship of false gods — that is, idolatry — from the worship of the true God. To treat Islam suitably, it becomes necessary to forge a new concept altogether, and one that is difficult to grasp — namely, an idolatry of the God of Israel. To put it another way, Islam may be thought of as the natural religion of the revealed God." The concept is indeed difficult to grasp and not, I think, entirely convincing. Yet Besançon's critique is a necessary caution against the kind of interreligious dialogue that slides too easily into wishful thinking. "The Qur'an," he writes, "is neither a preparation for biblical religion nor a retroactive endorsement of it. In approaching Muslims, self-respecting Christians and others would do better to rely on what remains within Islam of natural religion — and of religious virtue — and to take into account the common humanity that Muslims share with all people everywhere." Christians seeking dialogue with Muslims have to begin somewhere, and Besançon's bare minimum is one starting point. Despite the fundamental differences that he underscores, however, other Christians and Muslims may, with eyes wide open to the difficulties, try to tease out greater religious commonalities. This is one of the great tasks of this century, and the alternative to pursuing it may be open-ended and unlimited warfare by Islam against the infidels, meaning chiefly Christians and Jews. *(October 2004)*

❦ Despite our unflagging efforts, aided by outside proofreaders, typos still crop up from time to time. With new technologies of electronic transmission we cannot even blame the fabled "printer's devils." So it is with considerable relief that we received the following item forwarded by a reader who found it on the Internet: "I cdnuolt blveiee taht I cluod aulaclty uesdnatnrd waht I was rdanieg. The phaonmneal pweor of the hmuan mnid. Aoccdrnig to rscheearch at Cmabrigde Uinervtisy, it deson't mttaer in waht oredr the ltteers in a wrod are, the olny iprmoatnt tihng is taht the frist and lsat ltteer be in the rghit pclae. The rset can be a taotl mses and you can sitll raed it wouthit a porbelm. Tihs is bcuseae the huamn mnid deos not raed ervey lteter by istlef, but the wrod as a wlohe. Amzanig." Amazing indeed. *(November 2004)*

❦ "None of this is by accident. For a couple of decades now, there has been a systematic attempt to dilute the sacred message of Christmas while elevating the prominence of Hanukkah and Kwanzaa (the latter a recent secular invention)." Conspiracy theory, anyone? The quote is from a Catholic League press release reporting on their careful counting of the seasonal cards produced by the major greeting card companies. There were 443 Christmas cards, with only nine featuring the religious significance of Christmas. That's two percent. Of the thirty-three Hanukkah cards, twenty-six, or 79 percent, feature a Star of David or Menorah. The Kwanzaa cards are all areligiously ethnic. In the Christmas cards department, there is also a "Risqué" line and a "Rude" line on offer. These feature, inter alia, S&M gear and a near-naked female angel asking, "Ever make an angel in the snow?" You get the idea. There are no "Rude" or "Risqué" Hanukkah or Kwanzaa cards. It is not plausible that this circumstance reflects simply a business decision on the part of the card companies. In a country where nearly 90 percent of the people claim to be Christian and, curiously enough, even more say that Jesus was born of a virgin, the predominance of "Christmas" cards mocking or blaspheming the meaning of the day — or simply ignoring it — cannot be explained by market dynamics. I don't know if conspiracy is the right word. Conspiracy implies a measure of collusion. Maybe the major greeting card companies, for some unknown reason, employ an inordinate number of people who are Christophobes, people who have hatred or contempt for Christ and Christianity. I am open to more convincing explanations. *(December 2004)*

❧ As is well known, the constitution of the European Union very pointedly makes no reference to Christianity in its preamble alluding to European identity. This fall the leaders of member nations gathered in Rome to formally sign the constitution. The signing took place on the Capitolino, a beautiful square designed by Michelangelo. The leaders were photographed sitting beneath a huge statue of the fifth-century Pope Innocent I. In the same room is a fine bust of the emperor Constantine. One expects that some of the politicians had a hard time remembering that Christianity played no part in the formation of Europe. *(January 2005)*

❧ Who should decide about when and where to go to war? After discussing the criteria of just war, the *Catechism of the Catholic Church* says, "The evaluation of these conditions for moral legitimacy belongs to the prudential judgment of those who have responsibility for the common good" (§2309). That's not good enough, writes Father Drew Christiansen in *America,* a Jesuit magazine. "In light of the war in Iraq, it appears that the *Catechism* needs updating. The revision should take into account recent church teaching and the example of the pope, bishops, and faithful in opposing war. It should acknowledge the fallibility and the failures of political leaders. Above all, it should affirm the right and responsibility of the public to set a limit in public opinion to the warmaking of elected political elites." A great idea. Like, you know, maybe we could have elections in which candidates debate their differences about the war and other, like, really important things, and then maybe the winner, like, gets to be president. Hey, it might be worth giving it a try. *(February 2005)*

❧ Of the books one goes back to again and again, Augustine's *City of God* is near the top of the list. I have it in mind to do a florilegium of quotes from that great work one of these months. Last summer I once again read it through up at the family cottage in Quebec and was struck as I had not been before by how much of a Roman Augustine was. The conventional notion is that Augustine was writing the book as the Empire was collapsing around his head and he was proposing the heavenly city as the alternative to the ruin of all temporal orders. It is not quite that simple. "The Roman Empire," he wrote, "has been shaken rather than transformed, and that happened to it at other periods, before the preaching of Christ's name; and it recovered. There is no need to despair of its recovery at this present time. Who knows what is God's will in this matter?" While all temporal orders are marked by the lust for power and earthly glory, not all are equal. Augustine quotes approvingly a passage from the pagan historian Sallust that might put some readers in mind of another temporal order that some are now (mistakenly) calling an empire: "As soon as their power advanced, thanks to their laws, their moral standards, and the increase of their territory, and they were observed to be very flourishing and very powerful, then, as generally happens in human history, prosperity gave rise to envy. Neighboring kings and people therefore made trial of them in war: only a few of their friends came to their help: the rest, paralyzed with fear, kept well out of danger. But the Romans, alert both in peace and war, acted with energy, made their preparations, gave mutual encouragement, advanced to meet the enemy, and with their arms defended their liberty, their country, their parents. Then, when they had by their courage dispersed those perils, they brought help to their friends, and won friendship rather by rendering services than by receiving them." Especially in the first half of *City of God,* the reader may be puzzled about why Augustine goes into such extraordinary detail in engaging and rebutting the myriad superstitions and wrongheaded philosophies of the pagan world. But then, when one recognizes how much of a Roman Augustine was, the puzzlement vanishes. These were his people, his peers, his fellow intellectuals; they were leading others astray and, in doing so, imperiling also the worldly good of their common life in the Empire. Augustine certainly had no delusions that any temporal order, including the Roman Empire, could provide the lasting peace of right order. Only the City of God could do that. But the City of God, on its journey through time from Abraham to the consummation of the kingdom of Christ, is not indifferent to questions of approximate justice in the city of man. Augustine's is a perspective to be recommended to Christians of our time, and of all times until Our Lord returns in glory. I make no claim that the discovery of Augustine the Roman is original with me, but, in this rereading of *City of God*, it became more strikingly evident to me. *(March 2005)*

❦ Come this time of year and the indomitable Cardinal Newman Society sends out its list of Catholic colleges sponsoring a performance of *The Vagina Monologues*. The performance entails, as I understand it, women getting their kicks by talking as dirty as possible about their sexual fantasies. This year's list included Nazareth College and St. John Fisher College in Rochester, New York. Upon investigation, however, it was determined that the Diocese of Rochester no longer recognizes the two schools as Catholic. So they join Marist College in Poughkeepsie, New York, as schools decertified by the Church. According to the 1990 Vatican document *Ex Corde Ecclesiae* ("From the Heart of the Church"), such schools are not to advertise themselves as Catholic, but of course that is not binding in U.S. law. The standard equivocation employed by dubiously Catholic or definitely not Catholic schools is "in the Catholic tradition" or, sometimes, "in the Jesuit tradition." Proceeds from last year's performance of *Monologues* at St. John Fisher went to Planned Parenthood. Fisher, the bishop of Rochester, England, was one of the most renowned scholars of the land, a friend of Erasmus, who alone among the English bishops refused to acquiesce in King Henry's adultery and pretension to being the Supreme Head of the Church in England. After imprisonment in the Tower, he was beheaded on June 22, 1535, and shares a day on the Church's calendar with another martyr,

St. Thomas More. One wonders what, if anything, is taught about St. John Fisher at the college that bears his name. While hypocrisy may be the tribute that vice pays to virtue, one would like to think that somebody there might succumb to a twinge of decency and suggest a name change. And then there is Nazareth. I suppose it might be argued that the name is a purely geographic reference, although, admittedly, a rather odd one for upstate New York. Brighter students probably know that the school was named for somebody really famous who came from Nazareth, or visited Nazareth and, like, really liked it, or whatever. *(May 2005)*

IV

Dostoevsky and the Fiery Word

When I was young and under the compulsion to affect a deeper experience of life than I had, I was fond of quoting Whittier's sage-sounding observation that the saddest words of tongue or pen are simply these, "It might have been." They can be words of profound regret and even bitterness about the roads not taken, but they can also be spoken without sadness in grateful recognition of one's creatureliness. Being a creature of time and limited possibilities, no matter how much I've done, what I've done is so pitiably small, but I choose to believe it was mine to do. Decisions were made; and I've never gotten over my first discovery that the word *decision* is derived from *decidere,* which means to cut off. In deciding for this and then for that, from which followed the other thing, I cut off what might have been. But it is only in moments of ungrateful rebellion against my creatureliness that I resent the fact that what might have been was not. Most of the time I think about what might have been not in resentment but in wonder.

I know for sure that I will never do the monumental thing done by Joseph Frank. I have published, quite literally, millions of words on subjects so various that many, if not most, of them escape recall. I am regularly asked by graduate students in search of something or someone to write about what I meant by one thing or another that I wrote ten or twenty or even thirty years ago. I wrote that, did I? What I wrote is usually not an embarrassment, although there is a touch of awkwardness in not remembering.

The same might have been the case with Joseph Frank. After all, he was a professor of comparative literature and understood himself to be a literary critic. He could very well have ended up giving papers at the Modern Language Association on transgressive gendering or other topics of felt academic urgency. But then — to our good fortune and, I trust, to his gratification — he got interested in Dostoevsky. He started out to write a modest book on the novels, but then, as he rather understates the matter, "my initial intention would grow in size and scope." Decades later, we have the fifth, final, and very big volume of a biography that will be a standard reference for as long as there are people interested in Dostoevsky, which I like to think will be until Our Lord returns in glory. It is titled *Dostoevsky: The Mantle of the Prophet, 1871-1881* (Princeton University Press, 794 pp., $35). Frank is now professor emeritus and I cannot help but wonder, not without a smidgen of what I trust is unsinful envy, what must be the satisfaction of a writer's life commandeered by one grand project.

Frank invested his life in exploring everything pertinent to understanding the life and work of Fyodor Mikhailovich Dostoevsky: the language, the social and political changes, the literary rivalries, the loves, the illnesses, the frustrations. It seems there is almost nothing left unexplored. The fifth volume picks up at the point of Dostoevsky's return to Russia from four thoroughly disquieting years in the West and includes the writing of *A Raw Youth, The Diary of a Writer,* and, by far the most important, *The Brothers Karamazov.* The last is, I dare say, the greatest novel ever written, and the only novel I have read and reread year after year, always with increased pleasure and admiration. Frank writes:

> No previous work gives the reader such an impression of controlled and measured grandeur, a grandeur that spontaneously evokes comparison with the greatest creations of

Western literature. *The Divine Comedy, Paradise Lost, King Lear, Faust* — these are the titles that naturally come to mind as one tries to measure the stature of *The Brothers Karamazov.* For these too grapple with the never-ending and never-to-be-ended argument aroused by the "accursed questions" of mankind's destiny.

A Definite Argument

I would not quibble with a word of that. And yet, in the very same passage Joseph Frank makes a claim that is repeated in various forms throughout his biography. With that claim I have not only a quibble but a very definite argument. In fact, I have the temerity to suggest that Frank is simply wrong when he writes that *Karamazov* is about "the great theme that had preoccupied [Dostoevsky] since *Notes from Underground:* the conflict between reason and Christian faith." I am keenly aware that Joseph Frank probably knows as much about Dostoevsky as any person alive. For all his undoubted knowledge, however, I am persuaded that he misunderstands texts that are crucial to his claim that Dostoevsky's lifelong obsession was with the presumed conflict between reason and what Frank persistently calls "irrational faith." Since that claim is key to, in some ways *the* key to, his construal of Dostoevsky's life and work, this is no little disagreement. But I will come back to that. First it is necessary and fitting to note, indeed to relish, other aspects of Frank's achievement.

Underscoring the subtitle "The Mantle of the Prophet," the fifth volume employs as its epigraph Pushkin's "The Prophet." Pushkin had died in 1837, and there is no doubt that Dostoevsky believed that he, Elisha-like, had inherited his mantle. On several notable occasions, he gave public recitations of the poem that were marked with such fervor of devotion that the audience sensed that one even greater than Pushkin was here. The poem speaks of a "six-winged seraph" who cuts open the author's breast and presses into the wound "a glowing livid coal."

There in the desert I lay dead,
And God called out to me and said:
"Rise, prophet, rise, and hear, and see,
And let my works be seen and heard
By all who turn aside from me,
And burn them with my fiery word."

Dostoevsky evinced the conviction of having been divinely commissioned in a manner that was diffident, almost shy, and utterly devoid of braggadocio. He was anxious about falling short of the task bestowed. An admirer describes her meeting with Dostoevsky: "Most sharply of all remains in my memory the following trait, quite outstanding in Dostoevsky, his fear of ceasing to understand the young generation, of breaking with it. . . . There was not at all any fear of ceasing to be a beloved writer or of decreasing the number of his followers and readers: no, he obviously regarded a *disagreement* with the young generation as a human *downfall,* as a moral death. He boldly and honorably defends his intimate convictions; and at the same time somehow fears not fulfilling the mission entrusted to him, and inadvertently losing his way."

Frank supplies a number of instances in which Dostoevsky seems almost to be pandering to the youth, so worried is he about not losing touch with the shifting currents of thought and yearnings for change. His is not, however, the embarrassing sixties-ish posturing of so many of the hoary-headed among today's intellectuals. Dostoevsky's wisdom embraced the creatureliness of his aging and mortality. His anxiety was not for himself but for the mission, for the prophecy that will be carried to fulfillment by the successor generation and their children. Frank is especially strong in depicting the churnings of avant-garde opinion, of political and social movements, from sundry socialisms of atheistic and engineering varieties to populist efforts by intellectuals to reconnect with the "simple faith" of the Russian peasantry. For long stretches, *Dostoevsky* is as much social and political history as it is an examination of the man's thought and writing. To which Frank would no doubt say, with justice, that the two are inseparable.

Dostoevsky understood himself to be the prophet of a new world in which historical possibility intersected with resurrection hope. I confess that I had always found the ending of *Karamazov* something of a let-down. There Alyosha Karamazov, the youngest of the three brothers, is surrounded by the boys remembering their poor and shabbily treated friend. Alyosha addresses them:

> "Ah, children, ah, dear friends, do not be afraid of life! How good life is when you do something good and right!" . . .
>
> "Karamazov, we love you!" a voice, which seemed to be Kartashov's, exclaimed irrepressibly. . . .
>
> "Hurrah for Karamazov!" Kolya proclaimed.
>
> "And memory eternal for the dead boy!" Alyosha added again.
>
> "Karamazov," cried Kolya, "can it really be true, as religion says, that we shall all rise from the dead, and come to life, and see one another again, and everyone, and Ilyushechka?"
>
> "Certainly we shall rise, certainly we shall see and gladly, joyfully tell one another all that has been," Alyosha replied, half laughing, half in ecstasy.

And then they went off, hand in hand, to the meager funeral meal. As I say, the ending always seemed to me to be marred by an excess of sentimentality, leaving me with the hope that it might have been redeemed by the second volume of *Karamazov*, focusing on Alyosha, that Dostoevsky did not live to write. But Frank helped me to understand the fitness of the ending, charged as it is with the conviction that the love exemplified by Alyosha is a world-transforming force. At the same time, Frank's treatment of Dostoevsky as prophet of a world-transforming word lacks a certain weightiness, and I think the reason is that he does not, for whatever reason, take seriously Alyosha's, and Dostoevsky's, eschatological hope. Perhaps it is because that hope is part of the faith that Frank calls, with puzzlement often indistinguishable from dismissiveness, "irrational."

"From Them I Accepted Christ"

The socialists who took a populist turn in trying to utilize Christianity without Christ viewed Dostoevsky's reverence for the faith of the Russian people as naive, romantic, and, yes, irrational. Dostoevsky responds that he is well aware of "the transgressions" of the Christ-loving people, but, referring to the years in Siberia, he also knows much more. "I lived with them for some years, shared meals with them, slept alongside them, and was myself 'numbered among the transgressors'; I worked with them at real, backbreaking labor and at a time when others were playing at liberalism and snickering about the people. So don't tell me that I don't know the people! I know them; it was from them I accepted Christ into my soul again, Christ whom I had known while still a child in my parents' home and whom I was about to lose when I, in my turn, transformed myself into a 'European liberal.'" One can hardly exaggerate the disdain that attends Dostoevsky's use of the words "European liberal."

Dostoevsky's animus toward European liberalism and Roman Catholicism — which to his mind were of a piece — is another thing that can hardly be exaggerated (see Rodney Delasanta's "Dostoevsky Also Nods," FT, January 2002). There are, Dostoevsky said, three ideas contending for mastery over the world. One is "the Catholic idea" embodied in France and at the heart of French socialism. "For French socialism is nothing other than the *compulsory* unity of humanity, an idea that derived from ancient Rome and that was subsequently preserved in Catholicism." Rome is infinitely devious and resourceful. It is by no means the antithesis of socialism. "Having lost the kings as its allies," said Dostoevsky, "it will surely rush to the demos." Indeed, socialism is simply the secularized version of Catholicism with its claim to universal domination, and the Church is eager to re-sacralize it. Dostoevsky was on to something. There were and are Catholics who think that way. Today's readers will recall the late and unlamented efforts of "liberation theology" to establish under Marxist auspices what would be, in effect, a new Christendom.

The second great force is "the Protestant idea" that, Dostoevsky said, goes back far before Luther but gained new strength with the unification of Germany in 1870. As Frank describes his thought, "Like the Slavophiles, Dostoevsky views Protestantism as fundamentally a *protest* against Latin Catholic civilization, hence containing nothing positive of its own and ultimately leading to atheism and nihilism." And the third great force is, of course, "the Slavic idea" incarnated in Orthodoxy and the Russian faithful. Despite the eighteenth-century efforts of Peter the Great to introduce westernizing corruptions, Dostoevsky believed in the fundamental religious and social integrity of Holy Russia. Russia is, for Dostoevsky, the Redeemer Nation, and his fantastical claims for the moral, spiritual, and even intellectual superiority of the Russian people know no bounds. Frank deals with all this in detail, and is particularly deft in his treatment of what we today can only describe as Dostoevsky's anti-Semitism. "Yiddism," he believed, was a culture within a culture, a people within a people, and therefore a culture and people undermining the integrity and destiny of Orthodox Russia.

Critics, one notes in passing, have been exceedingly harsh in their treatment of Dostoevsky's nationalism. It is said with derision that, in view of the overthrow of the Tsar, the Bolshevik revolution of 1917, and the subsequent history of the Soviet Union, Dostoevsky was a lamentably poor prophet. To which the response is that his prophetic office did not consist in predictive powers but in bearing witness to a truth and possibility that, tragically, were shattered by the facticity of history. As Richard Pipes and other historians have underscored, there was nothing inevitable about the Bolshevik takeover. One can readily conjure other and credible scenarios in which Tsardom and Orthodoxy might have cooperated in the realization of something approximating Dostoevsky's hopes.

Even with respect to predictive powers, the magnificent Legend of the Grand Inquisitor, related by Ivan Karamazov, was eerily prescient in its understanding of the dynamics that would become twentieth-century totalitarianism. Frank observes in a footnote that "Dostoevsky's nightmare vision of the surrender of inner freedom for untroubled security was also a predecessor of the literary genre of dystopia, represented by such works as Eugene Zamiatin's *We,* Aldous Huxley's *Brave New World,* and George Orwell's *1984.* The motif of deception — the Grand Inquisitor's pretense to speak in the name of the true Christ — is closer to the Communist model."

Dostoevsky is harshly criticized also for his support of the Russian effort to recapture Constantinople as the capital of Orthodoxy. That effort is commonly derided as an exercise in unbridled jingoism, but it is by no means evident today that France and, more particularly, England ("perfidious Albion") were on the side of the angels in opposing Russia's effort. The "what if" arguments of history are interminable, but a believable case can be made that today's "clash of civilizations" and the attendant war against terrorism might be less threatening, or have been avoided altogether, had Christian Russia succeeded in turning back, at least in part, the Muslim conquest. One might even push the question a bit further and speculate that, on the basis of what he foresaw then, Dostoevsky would not have been surprised by what many view as today's unfolding conquest-by-immigration as Islam relentlessly presses upon a spiritually and demographically dying Europe. Dostoevsky's eye was ever attentive to the larger patterns of history.

A key to understanding Dostoevsky is "fantastic realism," a phrase he himself used to describe his work. Frank explains it nicely:

> He is always striving to apply to the present the mode of apprehension that he sees as a psychological datum in relation to the past. He looks for the essence of the passing and contemporary by projecting it into the future and *imagining* its completion (which makes it "fantastic"), but then, with an unflinching moral-social and psychological realism, dramatizing all the consequences of this future, as if it had already occurred or was coming into being.

This fantastic realism is closely tied to Dostoevsky's appreciation of original sin, although he is not comfortable with that terminology snatched from the Augustinian vocabulary of the West. The ever so progressive spreaders of the "European" disease deny the reality of human guilt and freedom, contending that fault and destiny lie with social and economic arrangements. Dostoevsky rejects this in no uncertain terms:

> It is clear and intelligible to the point of obviousness that evil lies deeper in human beings than our socialist-physicians suppose; that no social structure will eliminate evil; that the human soul will remain as it has always been; that abnormality and sin arise from that soul itself; and, finally, that the laws of the human soul are still so little

known, so obscure to science, so undefined, and so mysterious, that there are not and cannot be either physicians or *final* judges.

The Question Is Freedom

There it is, and it will not go away: the question of the soul. It brings us back to the aforementioned disagreement with Joseph Frank, a disagreement which, I regret to say, is inescapable and basic. I regret to say it because it seems almost a sin against gratitude for the enormous gift that is his *Dostoevsky*. But it must be said: the driving motif around which Dostoevsky's life and work cohere is not the conflict between "reason and irrational faith." It is, rather, the conflict between freedom and the enemies of freedom, however variously disguised. It is between the affirmation and the denial of the reality of the human soul.

The simple Russian people knew they had souls. Dostoevsky fiercely defended popular Christian piety, even when it appeared to be superstitious and fantastical. In response to a critic he writes, "They need sacred objects by their side, visible, as reflections of Godliness. One must believe, aspire to the invisible God, but revere Him on earth with simple customs that are related to Him. You can tell me that such belief is blind and naive, and I will reply that faith should be that way. We can't all be theologians." And, we might add, a good thing too. The people are not theologians, but, as we shall see, Dostoevsky, although an artist and not a theologian in any academic sense, is given to careful theological reflection. Joseph Frank is inclined to disparage this at almost every turn. He describes Dostoevsky's Weltanschauung as one of "apocalyptic intuitions of impending cosmic chaos, religious irrationalism, and mystical nationalism" — and they are all of a piece. At several points, Frank even compares Dostoevsky with Kierkegaard in what he calls his intuition of the "total irrationality and subjectivity" of faith.

Yet he also quotes, without attempting to explain, Dostoevsky's emphatic rejection of the claim that faith is irrational. The real irrationality, Dostoevsky insists, is represented by forms of Enlightenment, and often atheistic, rationalism that he sometimes terms "Euclidian." "Infinite wisdom," says Dostoevsky, "crushes the mind of man, but he seeks it. Existence must be unquestionably and in every instance superior to the mind of man. The doctrine that the mind of man is the final limit of the universe is as stupid as stupid can be, and even stupider, infinitely stupider, than a game of checkers between two shopkeepers." That may be described as an affirmation of the supra-rational, but it is not, as Frank claims, "irrational." It is, rather, a conclusion to which Dostoevsky is compelled by reason.

A critic writes to Dostoevsky in what Frank describes as a "tone of lofty professorial self-assurance" — about the infantile and irrational nature of religious faith. To which Dostoevsky responds, "You could regard me from a scientific point of view, but not so arrogantly when it concerns philosophy, although philosophy is not my specialty. . . . It is not like a child that I believe in Christ and profess faith in him, but rather my *hosanna* has come through the great *crucible of doubt,* as the devil says in that same novel of mine" *(Karamazov).* As for science, Dostoevsky is all for it, but what is called science is unscientific and irrational, or just plain "stupid," when it refuses to take seriously faith and that to which faith points. "The tremendous fact of the appearance on earth of Jesus, and all that came after that, in my opinion demand scientific elaboration. But at the same time, science cannot reject the meaning that religion does have for humanity, if only as a historical fact that is staggering in its continuity and tenacity. The conviction that humanity has about *coming in contact with another world* is also very significant and cannot be resolved [by dismissing it as 'infantile']."

Again, his point is that Euclidian rationalism is not rational enough, and dogmatically atheistic science is unscientific. It is not with Kierkegaard but with Pascal that Dostoevsky should be compared. The heart has its reasons, and as with Pascal and, earlier, with Augustine — although there is no evidence that Dostoevsky was conscious of borrowing from either on this score — there is the awareness of love as a way of knowing. In *Karamazov,* the chattering Mme. Khokhlakova has picked up bits of fashionable atheism and responds to the saintly Father Zosima's statement of faith, "But how is one to prove it?" It is surely Dostoevsky who speaks through Zosima when he says that no "proof" is possible but one knows "by the experience of active love. If you attain to perfect self-forgetfulness in the love of your neighbor, then you will believe without doubts and no doubt can possibly enter your soul."

Irrational Rationalism

Frank says that the rationalist Ivan Karamazov "refuses to make the leap of faith" that would allow him to believe in Christ and his world-transforming power. But it is not a Kierkegaardian leap of faith that is at issue. In the very same passage he quotes Ivan saying that "even if at the moment of eternal harmony, something so precious will come to pass that it will suffice for all hearts, for the comforting of all resentments, for the atonement of all the crimes of humanity . . . even then, though all that may come to pass, I won't accept it." Then Frank himself comments, "Ivan now finds himself in the same position as those unbelievers mentioned earlier who would not accept miracles even if they were accomplished before their very eyes." Precisely. But Frank fails to recognize the import of what he has just said. The problem with Ivan is not that he "refuses to make the leap of faith" but that he is blinded to reality by his irrational rationalism.

Frank is similarly confusing the reader, I believe, when he speaks of Dostoevsky's "visionary beliefs" that the promise of Christ and the possibility of world-transforming love will be realized. Of his Christian faith Dostoevsky writes, "If I believe that the truth is here, in those very things in which I put my faith, then what does it matter to me if the whole world rejects my faith, mocks me, and travels a different road?" To which Frank comments, "Here speaks the voice of his 'ridiculous man,' whose dream of the ideal cannot be shaken by the skepticism and incredulity of those who laugh at his preachments. The value of such an ideal, he says, cannot 'be measured in terms of immediate benefit, but is directed toward the future, toward eternal ends and absolute joy.' This is the vision that Dostoevsky upholds as the Russian answer to Western 'enlightenment.'"

That is not a peculiarly Russian answer, however, but simply the Christian answer, which, of course, Dostoevsky believed the Russian soul was uniquely capable of making. Jesus told his disciples that they would be rejected, mocked, and persecuted. Dostoevsky's words are those of all faithful disciples who, as Jesus said, "continue in the truth." They are the words of the martyrs, martyrdom being the frequent fate of prophets. For Dostoevsky, faith is required by the reason that it complements and completes. I hesitate to go so far as James Scanlan in his recent book, *Dostoevsky the Thinker*, in almost making of Dostoevsky a systematic theologian, but there is no denying that Joseph Frank is simply tone-deaf to the philosophical and religious coherence of Dostoevsky's thought. It is a remarkable and in some ways an admirable thing that Frank could discipline himself to devote decades of his life to, and write thousands of pages on, a figure who most critically defined himself by reference to a Christian faith for which Frank has little sympathy and, it would appear, even less curiosity.

Frank writes, "For Dostoevsky, it was a moral-psychological *necessity* of the human personality to experience itself as free." It is necessary to say also that his hard fought conviction, on the far side of his battle with doubts to the contrary, is that the human soul *is* free, and is that by virtue of Christ. The inescapably Christian logic that permeates his work, and especially

Karamazov, is discovered in the two sayings of Jesus: "I am the way, the truth, and the life" and "You will know the truth and the truth will make you free." Man is free to choose good and evil. That, too, is part of the dignity of being human. Thus Dostoevsky writes that, if criminals are not punished, "you only plant cynicism in their hearts, you leave them with a seductive question and with contempt for you yourself." Frank criticizes that as a "sanctimonious plea" for punishment in order to uphold "age-old inherited pieties of the Russian people." I think not. What Dostoevsky insists upon upholding is the moral agency of the human person.

Frank applies his master template of "reason versus irrational faith" in his interpretation of Father Zosima's critique of rationalistic socialism. He says Zosima is criticizing those who "rely on reason alone," but he is in fact criticizing the irrationality of their view of reason. "They have," says Zosima, "more fantastic dreams than we. They aim at justice but, denying Christ, they will end flooding the earth with blood." Indeed, "were it not for Christ's covenant, they would slaughter one another down to the last two men on earth," and then the last two would kill one another in their fantastic effort to establish the rule of reason apart from the truth of Christ. In our awareness of the consequences of communism's "scientific" doctrine of history in terms of "dialectical materialism" and other rationalist fancies, Dostoevsky, speaking through Fr. Zosima, seems startlingly prescient.

Frank writes that *Karamazov* is about "the moral-psychological struggle of each of the main characters to heed the voice of his or her own conscience, a struggle that will always remain humanly valid and artistically persuasive whether or not one accepts the theological premises without which, as Dostoevsky believed, moral conscience would simply cease to exist." Frank is right about conscience as a witness to human freedom in Dostoevsky's thought, but I expect Dostoevsky would be exceedingly impatient with Frank's essentially aesthetic treatment of conscience apart from the truth to which conscience testifies. Similarly, in the haunting account of Ivan's dialogue with the devil — whether in his fevered imagination or at some other level of reality — the devil taunts Ivan with the fact that his Euclidian rationality cannot account for his determination to help his brother Dimitry. "You are going to perform an act of heroic virtue and you don't believe in virtue; that's what tortures you and makes you angry, that's why you are so vindictive." And that's why, Dostoevsky would have us understand, Ivan's version of reason is so irrational.

The Majestic Legend

And then there is the majesty of the Legend of the Grand Inquisitor. I have sometimes said, only half jokingly, that, if there is one piece of literature that might be added to the biblical canon, it is the Legend. Of course it reflects Dostoevsky's animus toward Catholicism, but it depicts the temptation to which religion, and all forms of Christian religion, not just Catholicism, are susceptible. Many books have been written on the Legend, and many more no doubt will be. Suffice it to say that the Legend is emphatically not about "the conflict between reason and faith." It is about the inextricable relationship between freedom and truth. The Grand Inquisitor, with a perversely heroic virtue for which he is prepared to be damned, spends the night explaining to the silent Jesus why he was wrong about truth and freedom. Mankind cannot bear the truth, and is eager to surrender freedom in exchange for the security of lies. The Church has corrected Jesus' disastrous mistake, the Inquisitor explains, and Jesus has no right to return at this late date to threaten the Church's necessary and, yes, noble work. Jesus — the way, the truth, and the life — says nothing in response. "The old man longed for him to say something, however bitter and terrible. But he suddenly approached the old man in silence and softly kissed him on his bloodless, aged lips." The Inquisitor shudders and, reversing his earlier sentence of death, opens the cell door. "'Go,' he says, 'and come no more — come not at all, never, never.' And he let him out into the dark squares of the town."

There is so much that is missed in Dostoevsky, and in *Karamazov* especially, when one imposes upon his writing the interpretative template of "the conflict between reason and faith." Christian faith is the necessary template. Consider the question of theodicy posed to Alyosha by Ivan in an argument painfully concentrated on the undeserved suffering of children. It is the ever vexing question of the Holy Innocents. Alyosha has no neat catechism answer for his brother, and Dostoevsky acknowledges in a letter about *Karamazov* that Ivan's argument is nearly "irrefutable." But then there is the suffering, and then the death, of innocent Ilyusha. Is he or Alyosha the "Christ-figure" here, or are they both that? What has happened with Ilyusha participates in the mystery of redemptive suffering. I quoted earlier Alyosha's words on resurrection. Immediately prior to that, he addresses the boys:

> Let us make a compact here at Ilyusha's stone that we will never forget him, or each other. And whatever happens to us later in life, let us always remember how we buried the poor boy at whom we once threw stones. Let us always remember how good it was when we were together, united by a good and kind feeling which, for the time we were loving that poor boy, made us perhaps better than we are. . . . If a man carries many such memories with him into life, he is safe to the end of his days, and if one has only one good memory left in one's heart, even that may be the means of saving us. Perhaps we may even grow wicked later on, but however bad we may become, yet when we recall how we buried Ilyusha, how we loved him in his last days, and how we have been talking like friends all together, at this stone, the cruelest and most mocking of us will not dare to laugh inwardly at having been kind and good at this moment.

In the ending of *Karamazov,* at Ilyusha's stone, they who are free to choose otherwise know freedom in having chosen love. The knowledge of that possibility "may be the means of saving us." It is, Dostoevsky proposed, also a possibility for the transformation of society. Only months before his death he wrote about how the European rationalist rejects that possibility, claiming that "if the Christians take over, they will immediately begin to massacre the non-Christians." Dostoevsky responds, "On the contrary, complete freedom of faith and freedom of conscience is the soul of true Christianity. *Believe freely* — that is our formula. The Lord did not step down from the cross to inculcate belief *by force* of external miracle, but precisely wished for freedom of conscience. That is the soul of our people and of Christianity."

To which Joseph Frank remarks, "Nothing better than such a passage illustrates the baffling mixture in Dostoevsky of an advocacy of the most reactionary social structures in the name of the most liberal principles." The use of "reactionary" and "liberal" in this context reflects secular liberalism's habit of mind, precisely the habit of mind that Dostoevsky identifies as "European." I suggest that Frank finds the passage "baffling" because he fails to see that Dostoevsky is proposing a way to more firmly ground freedom, including political freedom. Freedom must be grounded in the truth, which is ultimately the truth of love, of redemptive suffering, revealed in Christ. One may fault Dostoevsky's idea of social transformation as implausible or naive or impracticable on any number of scores, but it is hardly reactionary. It is visionary. Or, as Dostoevsky would undoubtedly say, it is prophetic.

Return to the scene where Ivan is challenging Alyosha's faith most relentlessly, demanding an answer to his story of the general who unleashes his dogs on the peasant boy, and to the catalogue of other cruelties against the innocents that he has related. Alyosha is taken aback, allowing that it would be intolerable to accept happiness on the foundation of the unexpiated blood of even one innocent child. Ivan demands to know whether there is "in the whole world a being who would have the right to forgive and could forgive" such injustice. Then Alyosha remembers, and bursts out, "But there is a Being and He can forgive everything, all *and for all,* because He gave His innocent blood for all and everything. You have forgotten Him, and on Him is built the edifice, and it is to Him they cry aloud, 'Thou art just, O Lord, for Thy ways are revealed!'"

It is not true that Joseph Frank's *Dostoevsky* has forgotten Him, but the crucified and risen Christ is safely contained in the category of the irrational. By having Dostoevsky's story told in conventionally liberal terms of the conflict between reason and faith, the reader is spared the demand for decision about the truth that, Dostoevsky insists, will make us free. For the student of Dostoevsky, it is not necessary to share his faith in order to try to understand his faith. An account of Dostoevsky that does not invite a decision about what was most decisive for Dostoevsky — without which he says he could not understand himself, and without which he cannot be understood — is sadly flawed.

And God called out to me and said:
"Rise, prophet, rise, and hear, and see,
And let my works be seen and heard
By all who turn aside from me,
And burn them with my fiery word."

I come away from Joseph Frank's biography thinking, "It might have been." The sadness is in knowing that many readers, rightly admiring Frank's monumental labors, and having much enjoyed an interesting story nicely told, will close the fifth and final volume with a sense of quiet satisfaction. Unburned. Not even singed. *(March 2003)*

While We're At It

❧ I suppose I must plead guilty. Jody Bottum, that incorrigibly pedantic nitpicker at the *Weekly Standard,* charges me with carelessness in attributing to James Joyce the statement that the Catholic Church is "Here Comes Everybody." He notes that in *Finnegans Wake* Joyce does play on the initials of H. C. Earwicker — HCE — employing the phrase, "Here Comes Everybody," but nowhere can Mr. Bottum find the phrase applied to the Church. I can't either. Mr. Bottum complains that my apparent mistake is now being replicated "everywhere on the Internet," which is probably something of an exaggeration. Barring a kind reader's supplying a vindicating reference, I assume that somewhere along the line, probably years ago, I found the formulation attributed to Joyce and took the attribution at face value. So, pending further clarification, please do not use it. I am trying to be grateful to my friend Jody Bottum for depriving me of a great line. *(October 2002)*

❧ Here comes everybody (as James Joyce, it seems, did not describe the Catholic Church), and Pius X Church in Tulsa, Oklahoma, does mean everybody. I snitch from Martin Marty's *Context* the ad that Pius X ran, urging people to "come home" to the Church. The ad includes a special welcome to "single, twice-divorced, under thirty, gay, filthy rich, black and proud, poor as dirt, can't sing, *no habla Ingles,* married with pets, older than God, more Catholic than the pope, workaholic, bad speller, screaming babies, three-times divorced, passive-aggressive, obsessive-compulsive, tourists, seekers, doubters, bleeding hearts . . . oh, and you." The call to holiness, said Vatican Council II, is universal, and everybody has to begin somewhere. *(November 2002)*

❧ Here comes not quite everybody wanting to help me keep my "Here Comes Everybody" title for the Catholic Church in play, despite Jody Bottum's cavils. It is pointed out that the Catholic columnist Tim Unsworth titled his memoir *Here Comes Everybody,* attributing it to James Joyce. And Anthony Burgess' introduction to Joyce is titled "Here Comes Everybody," with apparent reference to the Church. Thanks for the efforts, but now if somebody could come up with evidence that Joyce actually said the Church is "Here Comes Everybody." *(December 2002)*

❦ Now we're getting somewhere. Long-suffering readers know that I was fond of citing James Joyce to the effect that the Catholic Church is "Here Comes Everybody." Until the pedantic Jody Bottum, our poetry editor, spoiled the fun by claiming that nowhere in the Joyce corpus is "H.C.E." applied to the Catholic Church. Several erudite readers, invoking Joycean fragments, have in recent months suggested ways of rehabilitating my wonted usage, for which I am grateful. Now arrives a helpful reflection from Craig Payne of Indian Hills College in Ottumwa, Iowa. Is it possible that what was not seen by the Ivy League has been revealed to Indian Hills? Mr. Payne suggests that the text of *Finnegans Wake* supports the application of H.C.E. to the Catholic (and particularly the Irish Catholic) Church. His letter is submitted in evidence: "In the ongoing dream of Mr. Porter, Porter's dream persona, Humphrey Chimpden Earwicker (HCE), appears to have become identified at one point with Finn MacCool, the legendary or semi-legendary Irish hero of the third century a.d., leader of the Fianna warriors. MacCool is partly human and partly divine; in later stories, he is also described as being of gigantic stature. Anyway — during this sequence the following passages occur: 'The great fact emerges that after that historic date all holographs so far exhumed initialled by Haromphry bear the sigla H.C.E. and while he was only and long and always good Dook Umphrey for the hunger-lean spalpeens of Lucalizod and Chimbers to his cronies it was equally certainly a pleasant turn of the populace which gave him as sense of those normative letters the nickname Here

Comes Everybody. An imposing everybody he always indeed looked, constantly the same as and equal to himself and magnificently well worthy of any and all such universalisation. . . . [F]rom good start to happy finish the truly catholic assemblage gathered together in that king's treat house of satin alustrelike above floats and footlights . . . in a command performance by special request with the courteous permission for pious purposes the homedromed and enliventh performance of the problem passion play of the millentury, running strong since creation, A Royal Divorce . . .' A few lines later comes a reference to 'the christlikeness of the big cleanminded giant H. C. Earwicker throughout his excellency long vicefreegal existence . . .' 'Here Comes Everybody,' then, is the other partly human and partly divine Irish giant, the universal and 'truly catholic' assemblage, gathered 'for pious purposes' to watch yet another performance of a passion play, a play which has run ever since creation, when the 'Royal Divorce' took place. And one more point: this passage is presented at precisely the point where the 'christlikeness of the big cleanminded giant' HCE is called into serious question, by accusations of sexual misconduct involving himself and a youngster (a girl, in this case). I'm pretty sure this will clear up nothing, as is the case with most Joyceana. However, it was worth a try." It was, I think, more than a worth a try. It may not be the find of the millentury, but my hunch is that Mr. Payne has hit pay dirt with respect to the ecclesiological significance of H.C.E. *(February 2002)*

❧ You know the old — very old — one about the fellow taking the Rorschach test who is told by the psychiatrist that he has a dirty mind, and he responds, "You're the one showing the dirty pictures." Well, it seems the Centers for Disease Control (CDC) was sponsoring a workshop on "Great Sex" as part of a Stop AIDS Project. CDC promised the event would provide "some fun interactive intimacy games to help you keep sex safe and hot!" People sending e-mails to protest the program discovered that their messages were never received. CDC computers were blocking the messages because they contained "obscene" materials that violated government decency standards. The obscene materials in question were the materials used by CDC to publicize the workshop. Your government at work. Against itself. *(November 2002)*

❦ Also on the thirtieth anniversary of *Roe v. Wade,* Medical Students for Choice, an organization at Johns Hopkins, threw a party. The invitation read: "Come learn about what's being done to train new providers and ensure that a woman's right to choose is both safe and accessible! Come and eat birthday cake!" Birthday cake in honor of *Roe v. Wade?* Perhaps this is an instance of overdetermined postmodernist irony, but I doubt it. Here the rule applies: do not seek for further explanations when stupidity will do. *(April 2003)*

❦ "Jesus Plus Nothing: Undercover among America's Secret Theocrats." That's the title of a big heavy-breathing story in Lewis Lapham's *Harper's.* The author, a Jeffrey Sharlet, sneaked himself into a Christian fellowship in Washington, D.C., that aims at evangelizing influentials both foreign and domestic. The group's leader, Doug Coe, is also involved in organizing the annual National Prayer Breakfast, at which Presidents since Eisenhower have made an appearance. Mr. Sharlet, pretending sympathy, lived and worked with members of the group for several weeks at their house near Washington. His long article swings between cheap sneers at the group's evangelical piety and warnings against their sinister "theocratic" belief that Jesus is Lord of the whole world. Jesus is everything, they say, hence the "Jesus plus nothing" of the article's title. We are informed that one young man in the group has a laugh "that made him sound like a donkey," and another has "a chin like a plow, and he sang in a choir." *Harper's* has got real class. I have indicated before my reservations about the theologically dubious religious boosterism of events such as the National Prayer Breakfast, and there are no doubt valid criticisms to be made of Mr. Coe's enterprise. This article, however, is no more than a juvenile rant. The responsibility for the publication of this distasteful exercise rests with Mr. Lapham, who once again leaves no doubt that he wants his readers to despise conservative Christians, maybe all who are more than nominally Christian. And he wants his readers to be afraid. Those Christians don't believe in democracy. How could they? They believe that Jesus is Lord. And they really don't like liberals. Be very afraid. *(May 2003)*

❦ "I respect and admire the French, who have been a far greater nation than we shall ever be, that is, if greatness means anything loftier than money and bombs." That is Thomas Fleming, editor of a paleoconservative magazine called *Chronicles,* cheering France's anti-American turn this past March. It serves as the epigraph to David Frum's long article in *National Review* of March 19, "Unpatriotic Conservatives." In response to inquiries: Yes, Frum gets right the story of the emergence of paleo sectarianism when, in May of 1989, the Rockford Institute of Illinois, publisher of *Chronicles,* forcibly ejected us from the offices of the Center for Religion and Society here in New York. We had established the Center in 1984 and I became increasingly uneasy with what was understandably viewed as the racist and anti-Semitic tones of *Chronicles* under the direction of Fleming, its then new editor. I was preparing to break the connection with Rockford and go independent when one rainy Friday morning Rockford executives showed up, fired the entire staff, put us out on the street, and changed the office locks. We could have done without the melodrama, but every May 5 we have a gala staff luncheon to celebrate the occasion. As for the Rockford Institute and *Chronicles,* it is perfectly understandable if you never heard of them until now. It is just as well. (Some day I may get around to writing up my notes on the possibility of morally licit Schadenfreude.) *(June/July 2003)*

❧ Some church bulletin bloopers are legendary. Here are a few that a reader has gleaned from a local newspaper. "The sermon this morning: 'Jesus Walks On the Water.' The sermon tonight: 'Searching for Jesus.'" "For those of you who have children and don't know it, we have a nursery downstairs." "Remember in prayer the many who are sick of our community. Smile at someone who is hard to love. Say 'Hell' to someone who doesn't care much about you." "Don't let worry kill you. Let the church help." "Ladies, don't forget the rummage sale. It's a chance to get rid of those things not worth keeping around the house. Don't forget your husbands." "The Low Self-Esteem Support Group will meet Thursday at 7:00 p.m. Please use the back door." "Weight Watchers will meet at 7:00 p.m. at the First Presbyterian Church. Please use large double door at the side entrance." "Please place your donation in the envelope along with the deceased person you want remembered." Finally, this one, which I've seen before, is not only legendary but, I suspect, apocryphal: "The associate minister unveiled the church's new tithing campaign slogan last Sunday: 'I Upped My Pledge — Up Yours.'" *(February 2004)*

❧ "All citizens have the right and responsibility to contribute to the common good through the payment of taxes," declares a new statement by the Catholic bishops of Iowa. The bishops go on to say that "taxes should be based on one's ability to pay." (That used to be called progressive taxation.) Further, the bishops say, "From those to whom much has been given, much should be expected." I may be wrong about this, but I think Our Lord was speaking about what God expected, not what the government expected. The bishops do not dismiss corporal works of mercy, voluntarism, and giving to church-related programs that help the needy. "Works of charity will always be a personal responsibility for Christians. But private charities cannot substitute for what the public sector can do through the just collection and distribution of tax monies." No matter how much public good faith-based efforts may do, the government, we are given to understand, has a monopoly on "the public sector." The bishops' statement brings back warm memories of seminary days when we were taught that charity must give way to justice, that voluntary initiatives were but stopgap measures until we created a just society in which government would attend to all human needs. So much has happened since then: the mediating institutions revolution, the communitarian movement, the discovery of "social capital," the end of the socialist dream, Reaganomics, supply-side economics, the Clinton welfare reforms, faith-based initiatives, the teachings of John Paul II on the free society, and on and on. Along with fond memories, the bishops' statement stirs a measure of envy. In a world of rapid and often troubling change, what bliss it must be to teach social doctrine in Iowa. *(March 2004)*

❦ Brian Anderson of *City Journal* and his wife, Amy, send their five-year-old to kindergarten at a Catholic school in Westchester County, New York. At a parents' meeting, the pastor, Father "Bill," announced a new curriculum in which he would be teaching peace studies. He went on to explain that we must not let September 11, 2001, be hijacked by the warmongers, that we must address the root causes of terrorism, and that there are fanatics on our side as well. With these and other half-truisms did he discomfort the parents. Anderson writes: "Ultimately, Father Bill's 'peace studies,' like other political causes espoused by church leaders since the 1960s, undermines the Church's already battered moral authority. My son's experience illustrates the point. After a service presided over by Father Bill, he told me: 'You must never war, Daddy — that's what Father says.' I had to correct him: Sometimes there are bad men in the world, and we need force to stop them. On reflection, he had no problem with that. One of his favorite television shows is 'Justice League,' chronicling the (often violent) adventures of Superman, Batman, and other heroes as they oppose monstrous villains. However, now he's likely to treat all of what Father Bill says with greater skepticism. The pastor's radicalism hasn't outweighed the other advantages of choosing a Catholic education for our boy. But it sure has made that choice less satisfying." The most important line there is about the skepticism implanted in the boy. When clergy teach opinion as doctrine, they invite the suspicion that doctrine is no more than opinion. *(March 2004)*

❦ I don't want to make too much of it, but Peter Singer of Princeton University, whom I have regularly referred to as "the philosopher from nowhere," has a long essay in the *New York Review of Books* on the thirtieth anniversary of the animal rights movement. The essay immediately preceding his is a reflection on a novel by Aleksandar Hemon, *Nowhere Man.* There is possibly an editor there with a sense of humor. Singer's ethical utilitarianism is a form of rationalism that rigorously prescinds from tradition, habit, instinct, or anything that smacks of authority, especially religious authority. This leads him to a position of equal consideration for all sentient beings. The core question, he writes, is this: "Should all and only human beings be protected by rights, when some nonhuman animals are superior in their intellectual capacities, and have richer emotional lives, than some human beings?" Singer answers that question in the negative and declares that those who disagree are guilty of "speciesism." His contention is "that a difference of species is not an ethically defensible ground for giving less consideration to the interests of a sentient being than we give to similar interests of a member of our own species." Question: If a house containing a healthy chimp and a severely retarded child is on fire, which would Peter Singer try to rescue? Maybe neither, since a utilitarian argument might be made that neither is worth risking the more valuable life of Peter Singer. I would like to think, however, that his human decency would trump his ethical theory and he would try to rescue the child. But maybe not. *(March 2004)*

❦ Good news, according to the advertising magazine *Brandweek*. Focus-group studies show that products advertised on "edgy" television programs do not suffer significant damage to their image. "Edgy" is the new word for vulgar. Advertisers used to worry that the sleaze would rub off on their products. But now, *Brandweek* declares, "marketers can get a bang for their buck buying into edgy programs." What matters morality, never mind good taste, when the alternative is a bang for the buck? *(April 2004)*

❦ I hear from readers who wonder why there are fewer comments in this space on the distortions, falsehoods, and general inanition of the *New York Times*. Frankly, it is because the *Times* is increasingly tedious and I spend less and less time with it. It has long been a liberal paper, of course, but in recent years it has become increasingly strident and unprofessional in its leftwing advocacy. Picking out this item or that for criticism seems unsportsmanlike, like shooting fish in a barrel. One increasingly looks at the *Times* in the way one looks at the *Village Voice* or the *Nation*, just to see what the left is up to. But old habits die hard, and I do look at the *Times* almost every morning. And from time to time, one comes across something worthy of comment. For instance, a while back there was a long editorial titled "Frank Talk About Abortion." It is now generally recognized that the pro-abortion advocates are on the defensive, and this had the appearance of an editorial reassessment of the question. It was unusual in that it took up the entire space for editorials. The editors begin with some grave chin-pulling about the "unfortunate consequences" of recent turns in the abortion debate. "Among the most disheartening is the widespread impression that the pro-choice movement does not regard abortion as a serious matter, and that women seeking to terminate a pregnancy require a condescending reminder from Congress to understand that the fetus they are carrying is a potential life." Hope is sparked by an editorial subtitle, "Finding Common Ground." Aha, one thinks, at last the pro-abortion forces, who have up to now been unwilling to give an inch, are open to an accommodation. "The wisest line," the editors write, "is the one laid down by the Supreme Court thirty years ago in *Roe v. Wade:* Government should have the right to step in only when the fetus has developed fully enough to be able to exist on its own." So, the *Times* is ready to support the legal protection of the unborn after the point of viability? Well, not quite. The editorial is occasioned by, and strongly opposed to, the partial birth abortion ban. In other words, the government does not have the right to step in even to protect a healthy baby who is being killed in the very process of leaving the birth canal. The editors' only other specific proposal in the service of "finding common ground" is that government should promote "effective sex education and easier access to contraception, including over-the-counter availability of the so-called morning-after pill." Did I, in a triumph of hope over experience, approach this editorial with the thought that maybe the *Times* would have something to say that did not insult the intelligence of its readers? Yes, I honestly did. Call me naïve, or call me charitable, I really am exceedingly reluctant to give up on the possibility of intelligent public discourse and respectful engagement with opposing arguments. And so, despite all, there may still be occasional references to the *Times* in this space. *(May 2004)*

❦ Here's an invitation to a lecture at the Harvard Club. "Empty Chairs and Empty Altars: How Will the Church Be Without All the Priests and Nuns?" The lecture is sponsored by the Jesuit School of Theology at Berkeley and *America* magazine. I don't think I'll go. The usual phrase is full pews and empty altars, which contrasts the burgeoning Catholic population with the diminishing number of priests. In any event, the question in the lecture title would seem to have an obvious answer. If there are no people and no priests, there will be no Church. Or is it only the nuns who sit on chairs? Whatever. One is struck by the number of people who seem to relish the shrinking of priestly ranks. The other day I received a long letter sent to parishioners by the pastor of a large metropolitan church — also Jesuit, I'm sorry to say. It explained in excruciating detail why, given present patterns, the parish, which now has three priests, would in a decade or two likely have to share one priest with several other parishes. There was no suggestion of a possible change in present patterns, such as, to cite one obvious possibility, the encouragement of more priestly vocations. One might describe the tone of the letter as fatalistic. Except for a few upbeat references to the multiplication of lay ministries and proposals for other professionals taking over traditionally priestly tasks. It is anticipated that the one priest some years hence will play a role of teaching, sacramental presence, and general oversight. In other words, the priest would be in a position traditionally held by a bishop. Which leads one to suspect that maybe all the talk about the inevitable decline in the number of priests is not fatalistic at all. Rather, and however perversely, it reflects something hoped for. To paraphrase Huey Long, Every Priest a Bishop. *(June/July 2004)*

❦ It's been a while since I've had occasion to remark on Peter Singer of Princeton University, the aging bad boy of moral philosophy. But now Gerald Nora, a second-year medical student, sends me the dust jacket of the 1996 edition of Singer's *Rethinking Life and Death.* Mr. Nora is right in suspecting that the blurbs "praising" the book might have been chosen by Professor Singer's enemies. For instance, there is this from the *Washington Post:* "Far from pointing a way out of today's moral dilemmas, Singer's book is a road map for driving down the darkest of moral blind alleys. . . . Read it to remind yourself of the enormities of which putatively civilized beings are capable." Precisely. If you want a roadmap for driving down blind alleys, this is it. Then there is this from the publisher: "A profound and provocative work in the tradition of Aldous Huxley's *Brave New World.*" Precisely again. Even more precisely, it is in the tradition of thinking that Huxley so powerfully warned us against. *(June/July 2004)*

❧ I have from time to time been critical of Alan Wolfe, Boston College's man on religion and public life and contributing editor at the *New Republic*. So I'm not surprised when, in a recent article, he refers to "the small and sectarian journal First Things." One might, very delicately, observe that the *New Republic* is almost as small and is a great deal more sectarian, if sectarian means narrowly preoccupied with partisan politics. Although I expect that by "sectarian" he means religious. Wolfe is reviewing books on atheism in America and, as a self-described nonbeliever, wishes that some of the authors were less fervently religious in their atheism. He is more sympathetic to *Doubt: A History* by Jennifer Hecht because "Hecht is the rare doubter who can simultaneously disagree with people of faith while granting them respect and taking their ideas seriously." That is obviously how Mr. Wolfe would like to think of himself. And in his books, such as *One Nation, After All* and *The Transformation of American Religion*, it is how he claims most Americans think. Religion and nonreligion, he writes, "raise first questions about the world that deserve heated exchange." But such questions must be kept safely distanced from our public life, and he indulges himself by whacking the Bush administration for violating that liberal dogma. "Whatever our differences over faith," Wolfe writes, "Americans belong to a common political community in which, assuming that we will continue to live together, we must find ways of talking to each other not just past each other." I am resigned to living together with Alan Wolfe but confess that it would be a great deal easier if he followed the example he says is set by Ms. Hecht in granting others respect and taking their ideas seriously — notably the ideas of those who disagree with Mr. Wolfe's belief that liberalism trumps truth and that, therefore, "first questions" must be banished from public life. Contra Mr. Wolfe, first questions — as in "We hold these truths to be self-evident" — are the foundation and not the enemy of the continuing American experiment. He says we must find ways of talking to each other and not just past each other. I am talking to you, Alan. *(August/September 2004)*

❧ There's an outfit called the Rainbow Sash Movement whose purpose is to encourage lesbians and gays to don a rainbow sash and present themselves for Communion at Catholic cathedrals on Pentecost Sunday. The idea, of course, is to protest the allegedly oppressive homophobia of the Catholic Church. In some places, Chicago for instance, priests are instructed to politely deny the sacrament, and they wave the protesters by, sometimes adding a blessing and a prayer for the reordering of sadly disordered lives. The point is, according to the Archbishop of Chicago, that those who would exploit the Eucharist by turning it into a political protest are manifestly not rightly disposed to receive the Body of Christ. In Chicago, Rainbow Sash succeeded in getting a few news stories about their being turned away at the altar. Other places, Los Angeles for instance, took a different tack. The cardinal archbishop there is on record as being opposed to politicizing the Eucharist by imposing sanctions on notoriously pro-abortion politicians. Los Angeles is also known to be, as it is delicately said, a gay-friendly place. The archdiocese not only announced that it would not turn away protesters but sent a message to the Rainbow Sash Movement saying that they would be warmly welcomed at the altar of the new Cathedral of Our Lady of the Angels. Nobody with sashes showed up. What's the point of going to Mass if you're going to be denied a confrontation? I would not be surprised if some gay activists in L.A. are upset about the archdiocese depriving them of their right to be rejected. And just imagine the hurt feelings of an ever-so-welcoming archdiocese scorned. In the theater of gay agitprop, players should stick to their designated roles. In Chicago, the archdiocese had the satisfaction of being Catholic, and gay activists the satisfaction of being oppressed. It was a win-win proposition. In Los Angeles, it seems that everybody lost. *(October 2004)*

❧ Yes, yes, we know, although we thank you for bringing it our attention. The spine of the October issue read "Octobeer 2004." As in Oktoberfest? The covers were all printed before the mistake was caught and to correct it would have cost thousands of dollars and a delay in getting the issue into the mail, so we let it be. Speculation that the misprint reflected the German extraction of persons associated with FT is entirely unfounded. There was, however, among copy editors desperate to make light of their egregious oversight, some discussion of making "Octobeer" an annual tradition. Be assured that the idea has been nipped in the Bud. *(December 2004)*

V

Getting Along at the Altar

In the course of a "self-interview" in his book *Signposts in a Strange Land*, Walker Percy discussed his becoming a Catholic Christian. What attracted him, he said, was "Christianity's rather insolent claim to be true, with the implication that the other religions are more or less false." In our time when "truth" is commonly put in ironic quotes, there is something bracingly contrarian in such a statement. Contrarianism can easily morph into crankiness, however, as witness Christians obsessively disputing and dividing over their supposedly singular grasp of the fine points of truth. The line between faithful insolence and egregious arrogance is not always clear. But the truth is that truth obliges, and sometimes truth divides. That is among the truths underscored in John Paul II's fourteenth encyclical, *Ecclesia de Eucharistia* (The Church of the Eucharist), issued on Thursday of Holy Week last.

"Can't we all just get along?" The plaintive question of Rodney King during the 1991 Los Angeles race riots elicited a warm response from millions of Americans. Throughout the fractious history of Christian differences, many have asked the same question, and nowhere is it asked so insistently as at the point of intercommunion in the Eucharist. Many Christian communities, weary of the differences that divide, have answered that there is no reason at all why we can't all just get along at the altar. I was impressed a while ago by a sign in a college chapel at Oxford that said all Christians were invited to share in Holy Communion — as well as those of other religions and no religion who wish to participate in, if I remember the wording correctly, this "symbolic act of the unity of humankind." One recalls the response of Flannery O'Connor to Mary McCarthy at that New York dinner party: "If it's just a symbol, to hell with it." O'Connor reports the incident in a letter to a friend. Usually unmentioned is what she immediately adds: "That was all the defense I was capable of, but I realize now that this is all I will ever be able to say about it, outside of a story, except that it is the center of existence for me; all the rest of life is expendable." That is pretty much what John Paul is saying in *Ecclesia de Eucharistia.*

Ecclesia de Eucharistia is about many things other than intercommunion. It is, in part, a movingly personal statement of the Pope's experience of the Eucharist as "the source and summit" (Vatican II) of the Christian life and of his own life as a priest. It is, as is to be expected in an encyclical, a reprise of Catholic teaching on the Eucharist, drawing richly on scriptural, patristic, and conciliar sources. I was struck by the way it highlights the chief themes of the Eucharist as set forth in the 1930 classic by the Lutheran theologian and archbishop of Uppsala, Yngve Brilioth, *Eucharistic Faith and Practice, Evangelical and Catholic,* and then further developed by Father Louis Bouyer and others in writings that informed the great movement for liturgical renewal prior to the Second Vatican Council: the Eucharist is commemoration, thanksgiving, communion, sacrifice, and the mystery of Christ's abiding presence on the pilgrim way to eschatological fulfillment. Each of these themes is lifted up, and some are freshly explored and expanded in *Ecclesia de Eucharistia.* The encyclical is at its heart ecclesiological. That is to say, it is about the Church as the Church is formed by the Eucharist. The title is telling: not the Church *and* the Eucharist, but the Church of the Eucharist. This is the ecclesiological context for the asking of the question, Why can't we all just get along at the altar?

The subject has an autobiographical dimension. I was

reared and ordained a pastor in the Lutheran Church–Missouri Synod (LCMS). That body practiced and, at least officially, still practices "closed communion," or, as some prefer, "close communion." Only members of the LCMS or of bodies formally in "pulpit and altar fellowship" with the LCMS were admitted to Holy Communion. Formal fellowship, in turn, was based on "complete doctrinal agreement" with the LCMS. Since propinquity is a common source of tensions, most particular attention was paid to avoiding intercommunion with other Lutherans who professed a seductive approximation of doctrinal agreement. (The stricter Wisconsin Synod did not countenance even prayer at the dinner table with other Lutherans.) A good thing about the LCMS at its best is that it cared about doctrine. To paraphrase Walker Percy, it made the rather insolent claim to be true, with the implication that the other Lutheran-isms, never mind non-Lutheran communions, are more or less false.

Of course, the logic of closed communion had ecclesiological implications. When the logic was robustly believed and practiced in the LCMS, a clear distinction was made between the visible and the invisible Church. Only God knows who belongs to the invisible Church. It was allowed that, by a "felicitous inconsistency," even Roman Catholics might belong to the invisible Church and thus be saved. Things are more transparent when it comes to the visible Church. It was taught that the LCMS, along with bodies in complete doctrinal agreement with the LCMS, was "the true visible Church on earth." Needless to say, the proposition that God established the true visible Church on earth in St. Louis, Missouri, in 1847 struck other Christians as somewhat counterintuitive. To be fair, some in the LCMS held a more nuanced version of the teaching, and the magisterial authority of Francis Pieper's *Christian Dogmatics* is not what it was during the first half of the last century. But the LCMS was right in seeing that the question of communion and intercommunion necessarily entails a doctrine of the Church.

That is the argument made also by *Ecclesia de Eucharistia.*

A great difference is that the LCMS defined the reality of the Church entirely by doctrine. *Sola doctrina,* so to speak. The true Church is constituted, in effect, by a school of theology and those who adhere to it. The Catholic understanding, by way of sharpest contrast, is that the Church is the People of God through time, identified and sustained by apostolic doctrine and ministry, by the holiness of saints and those called to be saints, and by the faithful doing of the sacramental things — above all the Eucharist — that Jesus commanded his disciples to do. The question of intercommunion as it is addressed by *Ecclesia de Eucharistia* is, then, the question of ecclesiology: whether the Catholic Church is what she claims to be.

She claims to be the Church of Jesus Christ most fully and rightly ordered through time. Or, to use the language of Vatican II, the Church of Jesus Christ uniquely "subsists" in the Catholic Church. She does not claim to be the Church exhaustively or without remainder. Other Christians are, by virtue of baptism and faith, in "real but imperfect communion" with the Catholic Church. As, conversely, Catholics are in real but imperfect communion with other Christians. The Council readily acknowledges that the signs of saving and sanctifying grace, including outstanding marks of holiness, are sometimes more evident among those outside than within the boundaries of the Catholic Church. Why, then, can't we all just get along at the altar?

No Place for Duplicity

Ecclesia de Eucharistia fills in the necessary background to the statement of the U.S. conference of bishops that is to be found in the Mass guides or bulletins of Catholic parishes:

> We welcome our fellow Christians to this celebration of the Eucharist as our brothers and sisters. We pray that our common baptism and the action of the Holy Spirit in this Eu-

charist will draw us closer to one another and begin to dispel the sad divisions which separate us. We pray these will lessen and finally disappear, in keeping with Christ's prayer for us "that they may all be one."

Because Catholics believe that the celebration of the Eucharist is a sign of the reality of the oneness of faith, life, and worship, members of those churches with whom we are not yet fully united are ordinarily not admitted to Holy Communion. Eucharistic sharing in exceptional circumstances by other Christians requires permission according to the directives of the diocesan bishop and the provisions of canon law. Members of the Orthodox Churches, the Assyrian Church of the East, and the Polish National Catholic Church are urged to respect the discipline of their own Churches. According to Roman Catholic discipline, the Code of Canon Law does not object to the reception of Communion by Christians of these Churches.

Ecclesia de Eucharistia underscores that this is not just an institutional rule that defies the high value our culture places on "inclusiveness." The Pope writes: "The Eucharist, as the supreme sacramental manifestation of communion in the Church, demands to be celebrated in a context where the outward bonds of communion are intact. . . . Christ is the truth, and he bears witness to the truth (cf. John 14:6; 18:37); *the sacrament of his body and blood does not permit duplicity*" (emphasis added). The encyclical says that the Church understands "an ecclesiology of communion [to be] the central and fundamental idea of the documents of the Second Vatican Council." Intercommunion without a shared ecclesiology of communion is the enemy of authentic unity. John Paul puts it this way:

> Precisely because the Church's unity, which the Eucharist brings about through the Lord's sacrifice and by communion in his body and blood, absolutely requires full communion in the bonds of the profession of faith, the sacra-

> ments, and ecclesiastical governance, it is not possible to celebrate together the same eucharistic liturgy until those bonds are fully reestablished. Any such concelebration would not be a valid means and might well prove instead to be an obstacle to the attainment of full communion by weakening the sense of how far we remain from this goal and by introducing or exacerbating ambiguities with regard to one or another truth of the faith. *The path toward full unity can only be undertaken in truth.* In this area, the prohibitions of church law leave no room for uncertainty. (Emphasis added)

The encyclical quotes a 1993 document of the Congregation for the Doctrine of the Faith, "On Some Aspects of the Church Understood as Communion": "Every Eucharist is celebrated in union not only with the proper bishop, but also with the pope, with the episcopal order, with all the clergy, and with the entire people. Every valid celebration of the Eucharist expresses this universal communion with Peter and with the whole Church, or objectively calls for it, as in the case of the Christian churches separated from Rome." The objective call for such universal communion is evident in the "churches" of the East, as distinct from the "ecclesial communities" resulting from divisions in the West. As I have written elsewhere, the only thing that is lacking for full communion between the Orthodox East and the Catholic West is full communion. That reconciliation between East and West — so that, as John Paul has often said, "the Church can again breathe with both lungs" — has not been achieved is undoubtedly the greatest single disappointment of this pontificate.

Apostolicity

In the Nicene Creed, Christians profess the Church to be "one, holy, catholic, and apostolic." *Ecclesia de Eucharistia* stresses in particular the importance of apostolicity. It is to the apostles that Jesus entrusted the Eucharist, and "it is in continuity with the practice of the apostles, in obedience to the Lord's command, that the Church has celebrated the Eucharist down the centuries." Apostolic practice is joined to apostolic faith. "With the help of the Spirit dwelling in her, the Church keeps and hands on the teaching, the 'good deposit,' the salutary words she has heard from the apostles." "Here too," says John Paul, "the Eucharist is apostolic, for it is celebrated in conformity with the faith of the apostles. At various times in the 2,000 year history of the people of the new covenant, the Church's Magisterium has more precisely defined her teaching on the Eucharist . . . precisely in order to safeguard the apostolic faith with regard to this sublime mystery. This faith remains unchanged, and it is essential for the Church that it remain unchanged."

Then there is the question of apostolic ministry. The encyclical cites the *Catechism of the Catholic Church*'s assertion that the Church "continues to be taught, sanctified, and guided by the apostles until Christ's return through their successors in pastoral office: the college of bishops, assisted by priests, in union with the successor to Peter, the Church's supreme pastor." John Paul adds, "Succession to the apostles in the pastoral mission necessarily entails the sacrament of holy orders, that is, the uninterrupted sequence from the very beginning of valid episcopal ordinations. This succession is essential for the Church to exist in a proper and full sense." Needless to say, not all Christians agree with this understanding of apostolic fidelity. But despite the divisions at the altar that it necessarily entails, the Catholic Church is bound by it. The conviction is that a unity purchased at the price of evasion or duplicity cannot be a unity pleasing to God.

The above-mentioned distinction between the visible and invisible Church also comes into play. The Pope writes:

> The celebration of the Eucharist cannot be the starting point for communion; it presupposes that communion al-

ready exists, a communion which it seeks to consolidate and bring to perfection. The sacrament is an expression of this bond of communion both in its invisible dimension, which in Christ and through the working of the Holy Spirit unites us to the Father and among ourselves, and in its visible dimension, which entails communion in the teaching of the apostles, in the sacraments, and in the Church's hierarchical order. The profound relationship between the invisible and the visible elements of ecclesial communion is constitutive of the Church as the sacrament of salvation. Only in this context can there be a legitimate celebration of the Eucharist and true participation in it. Consequently, it is an intrinsic requirement of the Eucharist that it should be celebrated in communion and specifically maintain the various bonds of that communion intact.

The Uncompromisable Goal

The Church's commitment to full Christian unity is, as this pope has repeatedly said, irrevocable. Catholics must be in dialogue with Christians who do not share the Catholic understanding of apostolic fidelity, they should develop cooperative relationships in work and witness, and they can engage in common prayer and worship. But they cannot receive communion at other altars lest they "condone an ambiguity about the nature of the Eucharist and consequently fail in their duty to bear clear witness to the truth." Such intercommunion is sometimes seen as a mark of ecumenical progress, but, in fact, the practice "would result in slowing the progress being made toward full visible unity." On the other hand, common services of prayer, worship, and Bible study may "prepare for the goal of full communion, including eucharistic communion, but they cannot replace it." The uncompromisable goal of ecumenism, in the Catholic understanding, is full communion.

But what about the statement that non-Catholics are "ordinarily" not admitted to Holy Communion? The answer is that exceptions to the rule are indeed extraordinary and made for compelling pastoral reasons. John Paul writes, "In this case, the intention is to meet a grave spiritual need for the eternal salvation of an individual believer, not to bring about an intercommunion which remains impossible until the visible bonds of ecclesial communion are fully reestablished." He then repeats what he wrote in the encyclical *Ut Unum Sint* (That They May Be One): "It is a source of joy to note that Catholic ministers are able in certain particular cases to administer the sacraments of the Eucharist, Penance, and Anointing of the Sick to Christians who are not in full communion with the Catholic Church but who greatly desire to receive these sacraments, freely request them, and manifest the faith which the Catholic Church professes with regard to these sacraments." Catholics, on the other hand, "may not receive communion in those communities which lack a valid sacrament of orders." Those churches in communion with Peter and the Orthodox are held to have a valid sacrament of orders.

"The ecclesial communion of the eucharistic assembly," the encyclical states, "is a communion with its own bishop and with the Roman pontiff." St. Ignatius of Antioch is cited: "That Eucharist which is celebrated under the bishop, or under one to whom the bishop has given this charge, may be considered certain." And Vatican II: "The Roman pontiff, as the successor of Peter, is the perpetual and visible source and foundation of the unity of the bishops and of the multitude of the faithful." From the beginning, the Church understood that fellowship at the eucharistic table defined the boundaries of those who are and those who are not in full communion with one another and with Christ. St. Paul writes, "Let a man examine himself, and so eat of the bread and drink of the cup" (1 Corinthians 11:28). John Paul quotes a homily of St. John Chrysostom: "I too raise my voice, I beseech, beg, and implore that no one draw near to this sacred table with a sullied and corrupt conscience. Such an act, in fact, can never be called 'communion,' not even were we to touch the Lord's body a thousand times over, but 'condemnation,' 'torment,' and 'increase of punishment.'" St. Augustine is called to witness: "Christ the Lord hallowed at his table the mystery of our peace and unity. Whoever receives the mystery of unity without preserving the bonds of peace receives not a mystery for his benefit but evidence against himself."

For many Christians, and for not a few Catholics, this teaching on intercommunion is both incomprehensible and offensive. In ecumenical circles, our division at the altar is commonly described as tragic, and it is that. In those communities, however, where the Eucharist is not understood or practiced as "the source and summit" of Christian existence, the use of the word "tragic" is somewhat hyperbolic. When non-Catholics speak of the tragedy of our not being united in eucharistic celebration, the tragedy they often have in mind is the "narrow" and "rigid" position of the Catholic Church. In the Catholic understanding, however, we really cannot do what others, and we, earnestly want to do, and that really is tragic because our "real but imperfect communion" is objectively ordered to, yearns and groans for, its perfection in eucharistic communion. But the Eucharist and other sacraments do not belong to the Church, to do with them as we wish. The Eucharist belongs to Christ, is Christ, and of that mystery we are the ministers and stewards. "The sacrament of his body and blood does not permit duplicity."

The End of Ecumenism

Consider, too, that, were we now to act on our desire for a common celebration of the Eucharist, that would be the end of ecumenism, of the quest for the unity that Christ intends for his disciples. Eucharistic communion is the consummate expression of our unity in Christ. Were we to pretend that it had already been achieved, we would all be free to return to our several and separate religious communities and associations and go about business as usual. It would be not only the end of ecumenism but the end of faithfulness to the truth, as God has given us to know the truth. Is this bread and wine symbolic of Christ's spiritual presence, or is this the body and blood of the crucified and risen Lord in the fullness of his humanity and divinity? Never mind. Does Christ intend an apostolically ordered community through time with a teaching authority under the guidance of the Holy Spirit, or is belief determined by private judgment or majority vote? Never mind. For that matter, is Jesus true God and true man? Never mind. What matters is that we all call ourselves Christians, and Christians "do this in memory of him," regardless of our conflicted understandings of what, in fact, we are doing, and of what, in fact, if anything, Christ is doing in our doing of it. This way of thinking is the way of duplicity in which we succeed in deceiving only ourselves. It would signal the end of the quest for unity in truth. A sure way not to reach a destination is to pretend that you have arrived before you get there.

An evangelical reader writes about an earlier comment on the Catholic Church's commitment to unity being irrevocable. "That's exactly what worries me," he says. "The Catholic Church will never give up until all of us return to Rome." In a recent lecture in England, Walter Cardinal Kasper, head of the Pontifical Council for Christian Unity, said, "We do not advocate an ecumenism of return. Ecumenism is not a way back; it is a way ahead into the future. Ecumenism is an expression of a pilgrim Church, of the people of God, which in its journey is guided, inspired, and supported by the Spirit, which guides us in the whole truth" (John 16:13). Of course there is always a necessary return to the sources *(ressourcement)*, especially the Scriptures and the fullness of the apostolic tradition. But it is precisely the sources that mandate and inform the spirituality and hard work of ecumenism, which is directed toward the future. That future may be a long way off. Christian unity, like world evangelization and much else to which we are called, must be seen against an eschatological horizon.

When the prayer of Jesus in John 17 is fulfilled, it will not be a matter of Baptists or Presbyterians becoming Roman Catholics. There will be but one Church, and it may well be that distinct traditions of theology and practice, now embodied in separated denominations, will continue, perhaps in the form that such traditions continue in ordered communities such as the Benedictines, Dominicans, and Franciscans today. But this is in the realm of speculation. In truth, nobody knows what the institutional form of visible unity among all Christians would look like. We can know that we will be united in the proclamation of the gospel, in sacramental life, in discernible continuity with apostolic ministry through time, and in communion with Peter. But even communion with Peter, perhaps the major stumbling block at present, will have different forms then. That was the bold proposal of John Paul II in the encyclical *Ut Unum Sint,* where he invites separated communities to join in exploring how the Petrine ministry might better serve as an instrument of unity. But this we know for certain: the cause of unity cannot be served by duplicity at the altar. If the Eucharist is the "source and summit" of the Church's life, it must be maintained as the place and moment of uncompromised honesty, or else all hope for unity in truth is abandoned. There is no remedy for the painful absence of full communion other than full communion in the fullness of the truth that Christ intends for his Church.

Ecclesia de Eucharistia is about much more than ecumenism. But because the Church is of the Eucharist, and all Christians are, however imperfectly and confusedly, engaged in the life of the one Church, it is very importantly about ecumenism. The encyclical urges us to recognize that overcoming our differences begins with recognizing that our differences make a difference. In our longing for the eucharistic destination of the unity that is ours, the way forward is the way of prayer, honest dialogue, patience, and disciplined restraint. *(October 2003)*

Remembering and Forgetting

When the much-celebrated architect Philip Johnson died this year at age ninety-eight the obituaries made little or no mention of his politics. In the days following, some commentators took note of this glaring omission. To be more precise, the omission was glaring only to those who remembered his politics. The worlds pertinent to supporting his celebrity status had long since decided to forget. Johnson was an enthusiastic backer of Hitler. In the 1930s he tried to organize a pro-Hitler fascist party in this country. He published a rave review of *Mein Kampf,* and he was part of the cheering crowds at the 1938 and 1939 Nuremberg rallies. He followed German troops invading Poland and watched the burning of Warsaw. "It was a stirring spectacle," he wrote. Being rich and famous, some might infer, means never having to say you're sorry. When on rare occasions his sordid past was mentioned, Johnson observed that he was also criticized for some of his artistic flirtations and would say with an impish smile that he had always been a "whore." I am told his admirers found this charming. He was a whore, but he was their whore.

Others have been treated very differently. In 1986, Kurt Waldheim, former UN general secretary, was treated as a nonperson when it was discovered he had served in the Nazi SS. Charles Lindbergh, at one time perhaps the most admired man in America, was destroyed by his "America First" effort to keep the country out of World War II. After the war, Martin Heidegger was permanently denied an academic post for his collaboration with the Nazis. Ezra Pound was locked up for years in St. Elizabeths mental hospital in Washington for his wartime broadcasts on behalf of Mussolini. And of course the witless young Prince Harry was excoriated in headlines around the world a while back when he thought it clever to show up at a party dressed as a soldier of the Afrika Korps, complete with swastika. There is also the case of Herbert von Karajan who never apologized for his Nazi past yet continued, until his death in 1989, to be the honored conductor of orchestras in all the great halls of the world. And Leni Riefenstahl, the gifted filmmaker and Hitler propagandist, was honored at the 2004 Academy Awards for her lifetime achievements.

How does one explain the dramatically different treatment of people guilty of similar offenses? Columnist Ann Applebaum, who is also author of a remarkable book on Soviet oppression, *Gulag* (see FT, November 2003), writes: "In the end, I suspect the explanation is simple: People whose gifts lie in esoteric fields get a pass that others don't. Or, to put it differently, if you use crude language and wear a swastika, you're a pariah. But if you make up a complex, witty persona, use irony and jokes to brush off hard questions, and construct an elaborate philosophy to obfuscate your past, then you're an elder statesman, a trendsetter, a provocateur and — most tantalizingly — an enigma." That is no doubt a large part of it, although Pound was punished, as was Heidegger, albeit more mildly, and their gifts were undoubtedly "in esoteric fields." But their punishment was in the immediate aftermath of "the last good war," when the line between good and evil seemed less ambiguous.

The erratic course of forgetting and remembering, of absolving and punishing, can also be explained by reference to another tyranny and those who supported it. In our culture-commanding institutions today, including the leadership of the once influential old-line churches, there are thousands upon thousands who enthusiastically backed Stalin, Mao, Ho Chi Minh, Castro, and others whose victims number in the many millions. After the fall of Saigon in April, 1975, hundreds of thousands of "boat people" fled to their death at sea, while hundreds of thousands of others were driven into reeducation camps, in many cases never to be heard from again. I had been a leader in the "peace movement" — the quotes are now necessary and maybe were then — and helped organize a protest against the brutality of the Hanoi regime. We asked 104 movement leaders to sign the protest and the split was almost exactly even. Those refusing to sign subscribed to the doctrine of "no criticism to the left." No matter what they did, leftist regimes represented the historical dynamic of progress; they were the wave of the future and therefore above any criticism that might slow their course. It was a pity about the victims, but most of them probably deserved it, and, anyway, "you can't make an omelet without breaking eggs."

There are things not to be forgotten. At the height of Mao's cultural revolution in which as many as thirty million died, the National Council of Churches published a booklet hailing China as an admirably "Christian" society. In 1981, *60 Minutes* did an hour-long program on the National Council of Churches' support for Marxist causes, and I spoke with Morley Safer about religious leaders who had become "apologists for oppression." That was the end of some important friendships, or at least I thought they were friends. I was then a much younger man, learning slowly and painfully what many had learned before. Allegiance to the left, however variously defined, was a religion, and dissent was punished by excommunication. There was for a long time no romance so blinding as that with the Soviet Union. Malcolm Muggeridge wrote witheringly about Lenin's "useful idiots" — Western progressives on pilgrimage to the Soviet Union, from which they returned with glowing accounts of "the future that works." There was also Whittaker Chambers' *Witness,* Robert Conquest's *The Great Terror,* Alexander Solzhenitsyn's *Gulag Archipelago* — all of them dismissed as right-wing propaganda. To be sure, there were those who had a change of mind, and even instances of something like public penance. In a famously lucid moment, the late Susan Sontag shocked a Town Hall audience by saying that the readers of *Reader's Digest* had a better understanding of Communism than did readers of the *New York Review of Books.* Much earlier, William F. Buckley had launched *National Review* with the help of apostates from "the god that failed." Yet up to the present the hard left, not so reduced in numbers and influence as some claim, is enraptured; not usually by Communism but by a Marxian analysis of oppression and imperialism joined to a more or less consistent anti-Americanism.

Yes, Philip Johnson should have apologized for his repugnant politics, and because he didn't he should have paid the price of being denied the fame and wealth so uncritically bestowed. But it is almost too easy to excoriate, hunt down, and punish the remaining collaborators with Hitler. That was a long time ago, and they are very old now. Not so with the unrepentant apologists for oppression from the Old Left, the New Left, the Maoists, the cheerleaders for the Sandinistas, and those who make slight effort to disguise their hope for America's defeat in the war on terror. In many instances they hold positions of influence on the commanding heights of culture. There may not be much that can be done about our circumstance. Nobody should want to revisit the experience of the House committee on un-American activities. And it is impossible to imagine something like South Africa's Truth and Reconciliation Commission that was set up after the end of apartheid, since with the great divide in our society and its politics there is no end in sight. We have to try to get along with one another as best we can, keeping our disagreements within the bounds of civility. But, as was not done in the case of Philip Johnson, we should remember. *(May 2005)*

The Conservatism of Andrew Sullivan

"As a simple empirical matter, we are all sodomites now, but only homosexuals bear the burden of the legal and social stigma." Thus says Andrew Sullivan in a long article in the *New Republic* occasioned by the Texas law against sodomy now before the Supreme Court. As he has done many times before, Mr. Sullivan presents himself as a Catholic who is trying to help the Church update its antiquated views on human sexuality. And again he misrepresents, and then triumphantly rebuts, a crazy-quilt of arguments which he attributes to Aquinas and other worthies, including contemporary natural law theorists. Finally, for Mr. Sullivan, what is "natural" is what people actually do, and what people actually do sexually should not be censured so long as it is "private, adult, and consensual." Most people do not adhere to the Church's teaching that the sexual act is rightly ordered within the unitive and procreative bond of marriage. People do all kinds of disordered and downright kinky things and therefore are, says Mr. Sullivan, de facto sodomites. Here, as Mr. Sullivan is given to saying, is the money quote:

> It is hard to see why . . . sexual pleasure, fantasy, and escape are somehow inimical to human flourishing — and there's plenty of evidence that their permanent or too-rigid suppression does actual psychological and spiritual harm. Relationships that include sexual adventure and passion and experimentation are not relationships of 'disintegrated' people but relationships in which trust is the prerequisite for relief, release, and renewal. The meaning of these sexual experiences is as varied as the people in them. And there are many contexts in which to understand these sexual experiences other than as purely procreative. You can think of sex — within marriage and in other relationships — as a form of bonding; as a way to deepen and expand the meaning of intimacy; as a type of language even, where human beings can communicate subtly, beautifully, passionately, without words. And, in a world where our consumer needs are exquisitely matched by markets, in which bourgeois comfort can almost anesthetize a sense of human risk and adventure, sex remains one of the few realms left where we can explore our deepest longings, where we can travel to destinations whose meaning and dimensions we

cannot fully know. It liberates and exhilarates in ways few other experiences still can. Yes, taking this to extremes can be destructive. And yes, if this experience trumps or overwhelms other concerns — the vows of marriage, the trust of a faithful relationship, the duty we bear to children — then it can be a social harm. But the idea that expressing this human freedom is somehow intrinsically and always immoral, that it somehow destroys the soul, is an idea whose validity is simply denied in countless lives and loves.

A Matter of Taste

Mr. Sullivan, who is a conservative on some matters, is, in principle if not in disposition, a sexual libertine. This is disguised from some by his sleight of hand in contending that "gay marriage" would bring homosexual excesses under the domesticating influence of a conventional institution. But he leaves no doubt that such unions are but one of innumerable choices homosexuals might make in the pursuit of "sexual adventure and passion and experimentation." He allows that "taking this to extremes can be destructive," but who is to say what is extreme, especially if such adventure is private, adult, and consensual? Answering that question was exactly the project of Michel Foucault with his "limit experiences" in the bathhouses of San Francisco before he died of AIDS. The above statement by Sullivan could as well have been made by Norman O. Brown in his defense of the unbridled libido, which he marketed as "polymorphous perversity." Mr. Sullivan likely deems the positions of such as Foucault and Brown to be extreme, meaning that they are not to his taste, although he has written elsewhere about the erotic charms of anonymous sex with strangers.

A couple of months ago a major Catholic university held a symposium on "the reconstruction of Catholic sexual ethics," and invited me to debate Andrew Sullivan. I declined. Mr. Sullivan has no interest whatever in reconstructing a

Catholic sexual ethic, or any other kind of ethic that might propose constraints or moral orderings on the satisfaction of sexual desires, apart from a few narrowly defined causes of possible "social harm." The meaning — including moral meaning — of sexual relationships "is as varied as the people in them." That some things might be right or wrong "is an idea whose validity is simply denied in countless lives and loves" of people who have persuaded themselves that their ways of pursuing adventure, passion, and experimentation is right for them. Mr. Sullivan knows that living in defiance of Christian morality does not imperil the soul — nothing "destroys" the soul — because his soul and the souls of others who do likewise are in such great shape. Such is the perfect circularity of moral solipsism.

Mr. Sullivan is a self-declared sodomite. In his writing about his own proclivities and practices, he presents himself as a conservative sodomite. Manifestly uneasy about being a bad Catholic, he does not, like other bad Catholics, confess his sin, but writes endlessly about why the Church is wrong and he is right about what he and others do. Perhaps sensing that he is not getting much of anywhere with that argument, he resorts to declaring, "We are all sodomites now." The discerning reader will recognize that the *tu quoque* defense (You're one, too) is the last refuge of the defender of the indefensible. *(June/July 2003)*

While We're At It

❦ Some schools mean it when they say they are Catholic. For instance, Mark A. Sargent, dean of the law school at Villanova University in Philadelphia, writes, "Our Catholic identity is not casual, sentimental, or merely historical."

While the school has many non-Catholic faculty and students, he observes, Villanova remains a Catholic university. The occasion for clarifying all this was a fellowship program in which some students elected to work for pro-abortion organizations. The argument was made that, if the program cannot support abortion, it should just as clearly not support capital punishment. Dean Sargent's response is marked by what might be described as uncommon lucidity: "Occasionally, we will not do something because we are Catholic. We will not do something that conflicts with our Catholic identity. Such situations are rare, but sometimes we must take a stand. We do so when the conflict is so fundamental and unambiguous that we, in effect, have no choice. Association of Villanova with advocacy for abortion rights presents one such conflict. The fellowship program provides summer stipends for Villanova law students working without pay for public interest organizations. It is funded by an auction, in which Villanova students, faculty, staff, and alumni participate. The program is not an independent student activity. Our name is associated with every aspect of it and makes it go. Our tax-exempt status is used. The auction takes place in our building. The law school administers the funds, and our staff members help organize the program as part of their jobs. Students receiving the stipends are known as Villanova Public Interest Fellows. It is indisputably a Villanova Law School program. A Villanova program obviously cannot be associated with advocacy for abortion rights. Though many individual Catholics believe that there should be some legal right to abortion, the Church's teaching on the topic is fundamental and unambiguous. We have no choice but to ask program fellows working in our name to agree not to engage in such advocacy. They are, of course, free to take jobs outside the program doing whatever they want. But as program fellows they represent us, and they cannot represent us in advocacy for abortion rights. Some might accuse us of hypocrisy in not banning the program work with advocates of capital punishment and other causes that they believe have the same status as abortion in Catholic teaching. What they do not understand is that the status of these issues in Catholic teaching is very different from that of abortion. Take capital punishment, for example. The Pope has asked Catholics to conclude that capital punishment is insupportable. I agree with him completely. But his statements on the issue were not made with the authority that requires the faithful obedience of all Catholics and Catholic institutions, unlike the Church's position on abortion. Indeed, many orthodox supporters of the Pope have disagreed with him on this issue and argued that the Catholic tradition does not support abolition of capital punishment. The law school is thus not compelled to disassociate itself from advocacy for capital punishment as it is from advocacy for abortion rights. This is significant, because we are reluctant to constrain our students unless we absolutely must. With respect to abortion, we must. With respect to capital punishment, it is a matter of choice. We could choose to disassociate ourselves from it on Catholic grounds because we are convinced by the Pope's arguments. And during the next academic year we, as a community, will consider the difficult question of whether we should make that choice. To take time to think hard about what we should do regarding capital punishment is not hypocrisy, but prudence. The need to make a prudential decision about the ambiguous question of capital punishment does not make a principled decision about the unambiguous question of the Church's teaching on abortion hypocritical." One hopes that Dean Sargent's argument will be read, and emulated, by leaders of other schools for whom the name Catholic is not "casual, sentimental, or merely historical." *(June/July 2003)*

❦ I remember visiting Goree Island in Senegal. It was thirty years ago, and I braced myself against the emotional impact that it evoked. Goree Island is the place where captured Africans were collected and shipped off to slavery in the New World. Your local paper reported that President Bush was there in July, but it likely did not report much of what he said there, which is a pity. Was JFK the last President whose moments of eloquence were widely celebrated and declared to be historic? School children learned them as the words of Kennedy, not of Ted Sorenson or other gifted speechwriters. We're a long way from Lincoln's scribbling the Gettysburg Address on the back of an envelope. Although, more recently, we've learned about those legal pads of Ronald Reagan, and how he wrote out some of his best lines. But we've grown more sophisticated, perhaps more jaded, about presidential speeches. Of course, with Bush there is the factor of partisan prejudice in the media, and the belief that he is illegitimately President. Add to that the assumption that he is dumb and inarticulate. Such biases have blocked much attention being paid the remarkable presidential rhetoric — in the noblest meaning of that term — of the last nearly three years. So Mike Gerson drafted the speech; the fact is that the President of the United States approved it, delivered it, and, for all I know, rewrote it. His words at Goree Island deserve to be called historic. He said: "For 250 years the captives endured an assault on their culture and their dignity. The spirit of Africans in America did not break. Yet the spirit of their captors was corrupted. Small men took on the powers and airs of tyrants and masters. Years of unpunished brutality and bullying and rape produced a dullness and hardness of conscience. Christian men and women became blind to the clearest commands of their faith, and added hypocrisy to injustice. A republic founded on equality for all became a prison for millions. And yet in the words of the African proverb, 'No fist is big enough to hide the sky.' All the generations of oppression under the laws of man could not crush the hope of freedom and defeat the purposes of God. In America, enslaved Africans learned the story of the Exodus from Egypt and set their own hearts on a promised land of freedom. Enslaved Africans discovered a suffering Savior and found he was more like themselves than their masters. Enslaved Africans heard the ringing promises of the Declaration of Independence — and asked the self-evident question, 'Then why not me?'" Then Bush mentioned William Wilberforce and others who early on recognized the evil of slavery and agitated against it. "These men and women, black and white, burned with a zeal for freedom, and they left behind a different and better nation. Their moral vision caused Americans to examine our hearts, to correct our Constitution, and to teach our children the dignity and equality of every person of every race. By a plan known only to Providence, the stolen sons and daughters of Africa helped to awaken the conscience of America. The very people traded into slavery helped to set America free." He concluded with this: "The evils of slavery were accepted and unchanged for centuries. Yet, eventually, the human heart would not abide them. There is a voice of conscience and hope in every man and woman that will not be silenced — what Martin Luther King called 'a certain kind of fire that no water could put out.' That flame could not be extinguished at the Birmingham jail. . . . It was seen in the darkness here at Goree Island, where no chain could bind the soul. This untamed fire of justice continues to burn in the affairs of man, and it lights the way before us." Powerful stuff, that. School children could learn, and no doubt are learning, a great deal that is less worthy of their attention. *(October 2003)*

❦ The ELCA Lutheran church council has finally come out with its long awaited statement, *Message on Commercial Sexual Exploitation.* At the risk of spoiling the suspense, they're against it. But Richard O. Johnson, associate editor of *Forum Letter,* thinks they may be against it for the wrong reasons, or at least not for the most crucially right reasons. He writes: "We're not in favor of lust, either, but its traditional place among the seven deadly sins suggests that in the Christian view, lust is sinful in and of itself, and most of us are guilty. The penitent doesn't generally come to the confessor and say, 'I've sinned by looking at pornography, and thereby I've exploited women and children and magnified social injustice.' No, the penitent has the good sense to know there is sin here, much deeper than exploitation. It is the sin of lust, 'the desire of the flesh.' It stands on its own two feet, thank you, and doesn't really need a train of social and economic consequences to make it evil. Hidden in the middle of the message is a statement that we at the ELCA 'teach the difference between loving sexuality and sexual violence and exploitation.' One would hope we do. But if that is all there is at the heart of this church's teaching on human sexuality, we have missed the boat entirely. What if the church council's message had been something like this: 'We are to fear and love God so that in matters of sex our words and conduct are pure and honorable, and husband and wife love and respect each other' *(Small Catechism).* It would have left out a lot of psycho-social rhetoric, to be sure, and perhaps it would be too simple in a complex world. But it would have saved a lot of paper, it would have been read by a lot more people, and it would have had, one thinks, a lot more staying power." *(November 2002)*

❦ "I think atheists tend to be pretty individualistic people and when people tell them what to do they might go the other way," says Dave Anderson, director of the Washington State branch of American Atheists. That fierce individualism may keep down the numbers showing up for the "Godless Americans March on Washington," scheduled for November 2. The communitarian spirit seems to be storming a final redoubt. "We're here, and we want to share the country with everybody else," says Mr. Anderson. "There's a need for fellowship amongst atheists. God might not be part of it, but I think it's important to meet people who have similar beliefs." Even atheism is going wimpy. *(November 2002)*

❦ I won't go so far as to say that some of my best friends are, but some of my friends are ethicists, and I don't want to be too hard on them. But from time to time I've been compelled to note that hiring someone to watch the ethical store — whether the subject be bioethics or business ethics — is a dubious undertaking. By the very structure of the relationship to what they're supposed to be watching, ethicists end up being more lapdogs than watchdogs. Gordon Marino, a philosopher at St. Olaf, notes that the business ethics industry is doing very well at $2 billion per year, but business ethics is not doing so well, as witness Enron, WorldCom, and other scandals. What is basically wrong with the ethics industry, says Professor Marino, is the idea that we can subcontract the work of moral judgment. "First, there are simply no grounds for believing that a person can become an authority on matters moral in the same way that he might on market strategies; that is, by mastering the appropriate information and literature. You can memorize Kant and still be a moral dunce. As Aristotle taught us, moral percipience and judgment are not the product of reading moral treatises and applying them to case histories. Aristotle counsels that if you need moral guidance seek out a person who has succeeded in living a moral life rather than someone who has succeeded in memorizing moral arguments. More important than the lack of philosophical foundation, the idea of ethics experts invites us to believe that the ethical implications of what I am doing are not my business but rather the business of the ethics office down the hall. After all, if there are experts on ethics, then who am I, a nonexpert, to pass moral judgments? Be they ethics audits, codes, or 'ethics fitness seminars,' none of the numinous pseudo-products of the ethics industry will restore integrity to commerce. The issues that provoked the present crisis were not overly subtle. You don't need a weatherman to know which way the wind blows, and CEOs do not need a business ethicist to tell them right from wrong. What they need is the character to do the right thing, which is to say, the mettle to avoid the temptation to talk themselves out of their knowledge of right and wrong even if that knowledge lowers their profit margins." *(December 2002)*

❧ David Horowitz is pressing a proposal that has thrown many academics into a tizzy. He wants universities to adopt an Academic Bill of Rights that will assure, amidst a multitude of other diversities, "intellectual diversity." Everybody in the academy is fervently devoted to diversity, until you put "intellectual" in front of the word. The eminent and self-described sophist Stanley Fish does not like the Horowitz proposal one little bit. It is, he says, a "Trojan horse of a dark design" to infiltrate conservatives into positions of academic influence. On campuses, says Fish, the culture wars are being won by those who promote women's studies, Latino studies, African-American studies, postmodern studies, gay-lesbian-transgender studies, and the like. But their critics have won the war of public opinion, convincing Americans that "our colleges and universities are hotbeds (what is a 'hotbed' anyway?) of radicalism and pedagogical irresponsibility where dollars are wasted, nonsense is propagated, students are indoctrinated, religion is disrespected, and patriotism is scorned." Horowitz's Academic Bill of Rights, Fish declares, would inaugurate the oppressive rule of ideological "balance" when the only purpose of a university is "to seek the truth." It is hard to know what to make of Fish's protest. In other writings, he is scornfully dismissive of the idea that there is such a thing as "the truth." Maybe it is just that Fish likes the academy's domination by insouciant nihilisms and doesn't want to see that challenged. Of course Horowitz is a conservative and would like to see more people in the academy challenging the likes of Fish. His proposal is a very odd Trojan horse, however, since no secret is made of its intent. Stanley Fish, sophist that he is, is never happier than when people say it is hard to know what to make of what he says. As for the meaning of "hotbed," I trust that Professor Fish is not above resorting to a dictionary where it is defined as "a bed of soil heated by fermenting manure." *(May 2004)*

❧ At a recent campus lecture, a superannuated radical from olden days interrogated me sharply on how I, the radical hero of his youth, could now be so conservative. And I thought of a line from Joseph Epstein, that master — he prefers to think of himself as the only surviving practitioner — of the occasional essay: "Sooner or later, either a man grows up or he pulls his gray hair back into a pony tail." *(June/July 2004)*

❧ A good many conservatives think that the National Endowment for the Arts (NEA) is a good example of the kind of thing government has no business doing. It may not have changed minds but it blunted complaints when President Bush appointed Dana Gioia the chairman of the NEA. Gioia is a distinguished poet and has a way of winsomely engaging those who disagree with him, as many do. He was also our Erasmus Lecturer last year and we are looking forward to publishing his text, which, we are assured, is undergoing final, final revision. With Gioia in charge, the administration has even increased, modestly, the NEA's $139 million budget, which is about the budget line for paper clips in government agencies thought to matter in Washington. But of course the NEA matters greatly to many people in the arts. John Rockwell, a critic at the *New York Times,* is deeply ambivalent about the new management at the NEA. He doesn't exactly call for a return to the tumultuous times of Andres Serrano's "Piss Christ," Chris Ofili's "Blessed Virgin of the Elephant Dung," or the late Robert Mapplethorpe's "X Portfolio," which celebrated the nuances of anal intercourse, but Mr. Rockwell does seem to miss the good old days. Rockwell's reflection is titled, "Help for the Old and Safe, Neglect for the New and Challenging." He notes that Gioia is promoting traveling Shakespeare companies to do live theater in small cities, schools, and military bases, along with touring groups performing jazz and other American masterpieces. Rockwell writes, "This is all well and good. Really it is. But it does provoke some questions." When he has to assure the reader that he "really" thinks this is all well and good, the reader may suspect he doesn't really mean it, and it turns out he doesn't. Gioia says his program is a "win-win" approach to the arts, to which Rockwell protests: "But what happened to multicultural disdain for dead white European males? If touring Shakespeare is such a win-win deal, just how does transgressive, transsexual, multiracial, confrontational performance art 'win'?" How indeed. Thus, according to Rockwell, does Gioia neglect "the new and challenging." One might respond that *Macbeth* is a great deal more challenging than Mapplethorpe and, as for the latter being new, pornography goes way on back. Rockwell complains, "Rich people support major arts institutions disproportionately, and rich people are mostly conservative." It is true that a disproportionate amount of financial support for the arts comes from rich people. It probably has something to do with the fact that rich people, generally speaking, have more money than poor people. As for rich people being "mostly conservative," however, one has to wonder whose patronage made the likes of Serrano, Ofili, and Mapplethorpe rich. Adolescents of all ages who would prove they are artists by behaving badly and shocking the grownups also want to be rich. They understandably grouse that not enough money goes to support the "transgressive, transsexual, multiracial, confrontational performance art," but such bad behaviors would not abound without a lot of people paying for them. And some of what Mr. Rockwell and others deem "new and challenging" may, it is quite possible, some day be recognized as art worth preserving as part of the American heritage. Of the NEA approach Rockwell writes, "Certifying masterpieces and making them available to all is not inherently evil." That is a magnanimous concession. Evil perhaps, but not inherently evil. Then comes an even greater concession: "Edgy art was made long before public arts support became a reality in this country; not all rich patrons are conservative." So it seems the new and the challenging are safe after all. And all without taxpayers being forced to pay for being insulted by the antics of those who hold them in contempt. It may not be entirely a win-win approach, and it may not change the minds of those who think the NEA should be abolished, but the direction taken by Dana Gioia holds the promise of preserving and sharing a heritage of proven achievement, to which the work of those who outgrow their captivity to "the new and challenging" may one day be admitted. *(August/September 2004)*

❦ Holiday greetings or Christmas greetings? Every year about this time, the arguments begin anew. William Devlin, the founder of the Urban Family Council in Philadelphia, has come up with a notice that might be posted in public places in order to preempt the contentious and litigious: "Legal Disclaimer: 'Merry Christmas' (hereafter 'The Greeting') . . . this announcement is not intended to offend, alienate, foster hate, or be a precursor for any egregious acts (legal or illegal), thoughts, words, or deeds. 'The Greeting' is made only in the context in which it may be legally received, if in fact, it is received at all. It is not intended to be nor should it be, in any way, connected to any other type of greeting, real or imagined, past, present or future. No references to any persons, things, or substances, animate or inanimate, real, fictional, or otherwise should be assumed by the reader or receiver of the greeting (hereafter, 'the greetee'). The 'Greeting' is not being made to (nor will tenders be accepted from or on behalf of) nonbelievers in 'The Greeting' in any jurisdiction in which making and/or accepting the greeting would violate that jurisdiction's laws or feelings (also refer to local statutes and ordinances related to 'The Greeting'). In any jurisdiction in which perceived 'greeting' is not welcomed nor agreed upon by all 'greetees,' then the 'greetor' of 'The Greeting' will be held harmless in this life and the next, including all issuing posterity both now and forever. 'The Greeting' may be made by a licensed 'greetor' and any liability assumed or created by the 'greetee' shall be the sole responsibility of said 'greetor.' If you have been aggrieved, offended, waylaid, parlayed, filleted, or delayed in any way, either real, imagined, or perceived by said 'Greeting' and/or by 'greetor' as the result of receiving said 'Greeting' you can call toll free 1-800-CHRISTMAS to speak with legal counsel." *(December 2004)*

❧ I am asked, "How did the Princeton conference go?" A nice thing about growing older is that there are more anniversaries to celebrate. The twentieth anniversary of *The Naked Public Square: Religion and Democracy in America* was observed with a session at the American Political Science Association meeting in Chicago last September. Some of those presentations were published in our November 2004 issue. In October 2004, there was a two-day conference on the book at Princeton University, sponsored by the James Madison Program in cooperation with Baylor University. I will not bore you with all the details. Not that I was bored, mind you. I'm discovering that being feted is rather pleasant. Many interesting things were said; the criticisms I will take to heart, the praise I will store up for the lean years. Arthur Schlesinger Jr. was there. He is getting old and frail but managed a feisty assault on George W. Bush as "the most aggressively religious president in American history." Jeanne Heffernan of Villanova and George McKenna of City College, New York, effectively countered that Bush is very much in the presidential mainstream of mixing transcendent and temporal themes in articulating American purpose and identity. Joseph Weiler of New York University addressed the contrast between America and Europe in their understanding of religion and morality in the public square. Weiler is an orthodox Jew whose book on "Christian Europe" and why it should remain Christian has stirred great interest across the Atlantic. It is hoped the book will soon be published here. William Galston of the University of Maryland argued that John Rawls and I are not so far apart in our understanding of what counts as "public reason," and there is something, albeit only a little something, to that. Galston spoke of his becoming more seriously Jewish, which has brought with it a new awareness of the incommensurability of religious prescription and public reason. One respondent, philosopher Michael Pakaluk of Clark University, was not buying, contending that every assertion, whether "religious" or "secular," is subject to the question, "Is it true?" This led to fascinating reflections on the difference between Jewish and Christian views of the relationship between faith and reason. In his presentation, Gerard Bradley of Notre Dame suggested that the problem of the naked public square was being redressed by the direction of recent Supreme Court decisions. That roseate view met with considerable skepticism. Philip Hamburger of the University of Chicago argued in response that the great contest on the Court was not between the religious and the secular but between the liberally religious and the orthodox, with the former rather consistently prevailing. Almost everyone agrees that the triumph of the skeptics and liberally religious on the Court began with the *Everson* decision of 1947, and Hamburger noted, in a wry aside, that almost all the Justices of that time were Masons and decidedly anti-Catholic. The second day began with John Finnis of Oxford and Notre Dame on "telling the truth about God and man in a pluralistic society." It was a tour de force, ending with the question of whether human dignity can be sustained without a transcendent, meaning religious, warrant. Eric Gregory of Princeton responded that Finnis and those of similarly doleful mind may be lacking an Augustinian appreciation of the grace of God. Gregory also suggested that we meet on the fiftieth anniversary of the book to see how things turn out. I rather doubt I will be able to make that meeting. In her presentation, Mary Ann Glendon of Harvard Law School offered much for our thought but naught for our comfort by observing that, while there is a lot more discussion of religion and public life than there was twenty years ago, the juggernaut of secularism rolls relentlessly on, especially in education. To which American historian Walter McDougall of the University of Pennsylvania countered that there was much more religious vitality in the society than most intellectuals are prepared to recognize, and that that vitality is gaining a more effective public voice. I did the final wrap-up, saying pretty much what readers of these pages would expect me to say. At the concluding dinner, Hadley Arkes of Amherst did a tragic-comical turn on what we would be discussing at a fiftieth anniversary conference on *The Naked Public Square,* if we were still permitted to hold such conferences. He left us laughing through our tears. There were many other striking interventions at this splendid conference (and I think I would call it that even if it wasn't about my book and me), but perhaps the above is enough in response to the question, "How did the Princeton conference go?" *(January 2005)*

❧ It was a festive dinner over at the Union League Club where we were giving Brian Lamb the annual History Award. On *Booknotes* and other C-Span programs he has for nearly twenty years run a national seminar on American history. In my few words I noted that my appearance on *Booknotes* to discuss *As I Lay Dying* had been scheduled originally for a week earlier, in which case it would have been episode number 666. That was a narrow escape. In his engagingly rambling remarks, Brian revealed that they received more orders for that tape than for any other program in the entire history of *Booknotes.* That was nice. He said it was because everybody knows they are going to die. I thought it was my telegenic charm and rapier-like wit. Maybe it was the combination of the dour and congenial. The dinner at the club was the week before Brian was taking *Booknotes* off the air. The final program the following Sunday evening was number 801, and the guest was a professor of English literature at a distinguished university, the University of Virginia I believe, who had just written a book on what it means to be an educated reader. Brian's genius as an interviewer, and it is genius, is in asking the right question and then stepping back to see what the guest does with it. Some people say he is laid back; I'd say he is incisively laconic. Brian never overtly agrees or disagrees with what is said, but sometimes there is the slightest smile of approval or twitch of the eyebrows indicating incredulity. Brian asked whether the professor was religious. No, he had been raised Catholic but at the age of twelve he had decided that none of that stuff could be scientifically proved and, anyway, it was too negative, so he chucked religion. He was not asked whether there was any other vast field of human inquiry, art, imagination, and literature about which the professor had definitively made up his mind at age twelve. What about, Brian asked, the complaint of liberal bias in the academy? That, said the professor reassuringly, was greatly exaggerated. He and his colleagues were open-minded, fair, compassionate, and interested only in respectfully trying to understand all viewpoints. Does he encounter resistance from students who are religious? Sometimes, he allowed, but they are often among the brightest, and he delights in liberating their repressed capacity to think for themselves. Many of them, he was pleased to report, end up being as wonderfully open-minded and caring as he is. The professor's big enthusiasms, not surprisingly, were Emerson and Walt Whitman, although he is also getting into Buddhist spirituality. During the program, Brian ran clips from past interviews with worthies such as Gertrude Himmelfarb, Paul Johnson, and Milton Friedman, and asked the professor what he thought about what they said. In one clip, Friedman was talking about Friedrich Hayek's *The Road to Serfdom.* The professor said he had never read *The Road to Serfdom.* In fact, said he, he had never heard of *The Road to Serfdom.* This is a man who had written a book on what it means to be an educated reader. Longtime Lamb watchers witnessed a pronounced twitching of the eyebrows as the last episode of *Booknotes* came to a close. Brian Lamb, who is also the CEO of C-Span, will be doing other interview programs that will not require him to prepare by reading a scheduled new book every week. Now he can read what he wants. In my experience, and the experience of a multitude of others, he is the only interviewer who obviously read the books to be discussed. In fact, and despite the final interview with the English literature professor from, as I recall, the University of Virginia, *Booknotes* was the only intellectually serious interview program on television. It will be much missed. And I do not say that because I wanted to be invited again. *Booknotes* had an unbendable rule: nobody appeared more than once. Brian Lamb has the idea that the 801 programs might serve as a kind of audio-visual history of the wisdom and nonsense that was the intellectual life of America at the turn of the millennium. I expect he is right about that. *(February 2005)*

❧ According to Reuters, gay and lesbian organizations are in an uproar. It seems that male penguins in the zoo of Bremerhaven, Germany, have been attempting to mate with one another and to hatch offspring out of stones. The zoo has imported some female penguins from Scandinavia. In response to protests, the zoo's director, Heike Kueck, says, "Nobody here is trying to break up same-sex pairs by force. We don't know if the males are really gay or just got together because of a lack of females." The protesters are not appeased. Giving the penguins a choice would deprive them of the choice of being gay. And who knows whether, given time enough, the stones might hatch? *(May 2005)*

VI

September 11 — Before and After

September 11. This is written the day after, just under the deadline for this issue. For years to come, I expect, we will speak of "before" and "after" September 11. I was on my way to say the nine o'clock Mass at Immaculate Conception, on 14th Street and First Avenue, when the hijacked airline hit the first tower. There was a small crowd at the corner of 14th and I remarked that there seemed to be a fire at the World Trade Center and we should pray for the people there. But I could not stay or I would be late for Mass. Only after Mass did I discover what had happened. How strange beyond understanding, I thought, that as we were at the altar offering up, as Catholics believe, the sacrifice of Christ on the cross, only a little to the south of us was rising, in flames and mountains of smoke, a holocaust of suffering and death. That, too, was subsumed and offered on Calvary. It occurred to me that Friday, only three days away, is the feast called The Triumph of the Cross. Exactly.

The first commentary I heard was from a woman coming out of the church: "That's what we get for unconditionally supporting Israel." I wondered how many others would draw that lesson. Watching television during the day, the question was several times asked, "Why do they hate us so much?" And the answer given in one word was "Israel." The further question implied was, Is our support for Israel worth this? What justice requires us to do in order to punish the perpetrators and ward off even greater evil is done for Israel, of course, but it is done, much more comprehensively, for the civilization that Christians, Jews, and everyone else will now come to see more clearly as it is seen by others: the Christian West.

My part of Manhattan is a long string of hospitals, and I went to be of whatever help I could. After a couple of hours it became obvious that very few of the injured were coming into the hospitals. The doleful conclusion is that, except for the many who were able to get out and away, the people at ground zero are dead. Many thousands they are saying today; no doubt we will find out how many in the days ahead. It will be a city of funerals for weeks to come, as bodies and pieces of bodies are identified. The church, the residence, and our offices are all north of 14th Street. At the house and office, everyone is safe. I am sure the same is not true of all our parishioners. It is weird. We can look down the avenues and see the still billowing smoke, as though watching a foreign country under attack, but of course it is our city, and our country.

Before and after September 11, what difference will it make? That's the subject of endless chatter and nobody knows. For what it's worth, I anticipate five major changes. It will inaugurate a time of national unity and sobriety in a society that has been obsessed by fake pluralisms while on a long and hedonistic holiday from history. Second, there will be an understandable passion for retaliation and revenge that could easily veer into reckless bellicosity. That is a danger. The other danger is that fear of that danger will compromise the imperative to protect and punish. Third, a legitimate concern for increased security will spark a legitimate concern for personal freedoms. Many will warn that freedom cannot be protected by denying freedom, and such warnings should not be lightly dismissed, even as we know that the liberty we cherish is not unbridled license but ordered liberty. Without order there can be no liberty; it is for liberty that we surrender license. I expect that many Americans who never understood that will now be having long second thoughts.

Fourth, after some initial sortings out, America will identify itself even more closely with Israel. Disagreements over the justice of how Israel was founded and how it has maintained itself in existence will not disappear. But the diabolical face of the evil that threatens Israel, and us, is now unveiled. Among Americans and all who are part of our civilization, it will be understood that we must never surrender, or appear to be surrendering, to that evil. Finally, the question of "the West and the rest" will be powerfully sharpened, including a greatly heightened awareness of the global threats posed by militant Islam. Innocent Muslims in this country and Europe are undoubtedly in for some nastiness, and we must do our best to communicate the distinction between Islam and Islamism, knowing that the latter is the monistic fanaticism embraced by only a minority of Muslims. But almost inevitably, given the passions aroused and the difficulties of enforcing the law among people who are largely alien in their ways, such distinctions will sometimes get lost. We can only try to do our best by those Muslims who have truly chosen our side in "the clash of civilizations." It seems likely also that, after September 11, discussion about immigration policy will become more intense, and more candid.

That's a mixed bag of possible consequences, and, of course, I may be wrong about any or all of them. These are but first thoughts one day after. Only a little south of here thousands are buried under the rubble. So it is now to the tasks at hand. It will be the work of weeks, perhaps months, to give them a proper burial. The consolation of the living is a work without end. *(November 2001)*

Plain Talk about "Muslim Rage"

We are told by President Bush that the overthrow of the Taliban regime in Afghanistan is just the beginning of the war on terrorism. Yet I am struck by how many pundits and news reports give the impression that that was an isolated action; all that is left is a clean-up operation and then it's back to the world as usual. Our December 2001 editorial, "In a Time of War," asserted that, whatever happens next, power relationships in the world have already been dramatically reconfigured by September 11. At the center of that reconfiguration is Islam, as a religion and a culture. In that editorial, we cited Bernard Lewis, doyen of Western students of Islam, on how the resentment and rage of most of the billion Muslims in the world came to be targeted on the United States. Many Middle East "experts" and those who teach in Islamic studies departments in this country have been telling us for a long time, and continue to tell us, that the "Muslim problem" is really the "American problem"; that terrorism is, if not excusable, at least understandable in view of the nasty things we have done to Muslims, and especially to Arab Muslims.

Of course, it is always imperative to work at better understanding, to clear up misunderstandings, to build bridges, and even, if possible, replace conflict with peaceful dialogue. Such were the aims of Pope John Paul II with his January 24 gathering of world religious leaders at Assisi. Such efforts, no matter how futile they may sometimes seem, are to be wholeheartedly and prayerfully supported. It is absolutely necessary that de-politicized space be created for conversation about, and mutual recognition of, our common humanity and our accountability to a judgment that transcends our animosities and clashes. In no way should such efforts be dismissed as soft, idealistic, or utopian. "How many divisions does the pope have?" Stalin cynically asked. Those who did not know the answer before were amply instructed by the fall of Soviet communism. In politics among nations, as everywhere else, it is a crackpot "realism" that derides the importance of culture and ideas, and especially the commanding ideas associated with religion.

It is precisely in order to achieve peaceful understanding that we need plain talk about what stands in the way of such understanding. Victor Davis Hanson, a military historian and foreign policy analyst, provides such plain talk in "Why the Muslims Misjudged Us" (*City Journal,* Winter 2002). "The catastrophe of the Muslim world," he writes, is that its leadership recognizes the failure of their societies but then "seeks to fault others for its own self-created fiasco. Government spokesmen in the Middle East should ignore the nonsense of the cultural relativists and discredited Marxists and have the courage to say that they are poor because their populations are nearly half illiterate, that their governments are not free, that their economies are not open, and that their fundamentalists impede scientific inquiry, unpopular expression, and cultural exchange." Chances for better understanding are now much reduced. "Tragically, the immediate prospects for improvement are dismal, inasmuch as the war against terrorism has further isolated the Middle East. Travel, foreign education, and academic exchanges, the only sources of future hope for the Arab world, have screeched to a halt. All the conferences in Cairo about Western bias and media distortion cannot hide this self-inflicted catastrophe and the growing ostracism and suspicion of Middle Easterners in the West."

Muslim autocrats make threatening noises about the dire consequences for the West if they are provoked. Hanson writes: "There is an abyss between such rhetoric and the world we actually live in, an abyss called power. Out of politeness, we needn't crow over the relative military capability of one billion Muslims and 300 million Americans; but we should remember that the lethal 2,500-year Western way of war is the reflection of very different ideas about personal freedom, civic militarism, individuality on the battlefield, military technology, logistics, decisive battle, group discipline, civilian audit, and the dissemination and proliferation of knowledge." Hanson is undoubtedly right about that, although the potential destructive power of terrorism is, by definition, in its indifference to the "Western way of war."

One-Way Copying

Here is how he depicts the larger picture: "Values and traditions — not guns, germs, and steel — explain why a tiny Greece of fifty thousand square miles crushed a Persia twenty times larger; why Rome, not Carthage, created world government; why Cortes was in Tenochtitlán, and Montezuma not in Barcelona; why gunpowder in its home in China was a pastime for the elite while, when stolen and brought to Europe, it became a deadly and ever evolving weapon of the masses. Even at the nadir of Western power in the medieval ages, a Europe divided by religion and fragmented into feudal states could still send thousands of thugs into the Holy Land, while a supposedly ascendant Islam had neither the ships nor the skill nor the logistics to wage jihad in Scotland or Brittany. Much is made of five hundred years of Ottoman dominance over a feuding Orthodox, Christian, and Protestant West; but the sultans were powerful largely to the degree that they crafted alliances with a distrustful France and the warring Italian city-states, copied the Arsenal at Venice, turned out replicas of Italian and German cannon, and moved their capital to European Constantinople. Moreover, their dominance amounted only to a rough naval parity with the West on the old Roman Mediterranean; they never came close to the conquest of the heart of Western Europe." That rings true, except for their never coming close. At least at the time, both Christians and Muslims thought the confrontation leading up to Vienna 1683 was a very close-run thing.

Today, however, it is a matter, above all, of culture. "We are militarily strong, and the Arab world abjectly weak, not because of greater courage, superior numbers, higher IQs, more ores, or better weather, but because of our culture. When it comes to war, one billion people and the world's oil are not nearly as valuable military assets as MIT, West Point, the U.S. House of Representatives, C-Span, Bill O'Reilly, and the GI Bill. Between Xerxes on his peacock throne overlooking Salamis and Saddam on his balcony reviewing his troops, between the Greeks arguing and debating before they rowed out with Themistocles and the Americans haranguing one another on the eve of the Gulf War, lies a 2,500-year tradition that explains why the rest of the world copies its weapons, uniforms, and military organization from us, not vice versa."

If Israel Did Not Exist . . .

Also in this country, there are many who claim that Israel is at the heart of this confrontation. Much more is that the claim in the Middle East. "Millions in the Middle East are obsessed with Israel, whether they live in sight of Tel Aviv or thousands of miles away. Their fury doesn't spring solely from genuine dismay over the hundreds of Muslims Israel has killed on the West Bank; after all, Saddam Hussein butchered hundreds of thousands of Shiites, Kurds, and Iranians, while few in Cairo or Damascus said a word. Syria's Assad liquidated perhaps twenty thousand in sight of Israel, without a single demonstration in any Arab capital. The murder of some 100,000 Muslims in Algeria and 40,000 in Chechnya in the last decade provoked few intellectuals in the Middle East to call for a pan-Islamic protest. Clearly, the anger derives not from the tragic tally of the fallen but from Islamic rage that Israelis have defeated Muslims on the battlefield repeatedly, decisively, at will, and without modesty. If Israel were not so successful, free, and haughty, if it were beleaguered and tottering on the verge of ruin, perhaps it would be tolerated. But in a sea of totalitarianism and government-induced poverty, a relatively successful economy and a stable culture arising out of scrub and desert clearly irks its less successful neighbors. Envy, as the historian Thucydides reminds us, is a powerful emotion and has caused not a few wars.

"If Israel did not exist, the Arab world, in its current fit of denial, would have to invent something like it to vent its frustrations. That is not to say there may not be legitimate concerns in the struggle over Palestine, but merely that for millions of Muslims the fight over such small real estate stems from a deep psychological wound. It isn't about lebensraum or some actual physical threat. Israel is a constant reminder that it is a nation's culture — not its geography or size or magnitude of its oil reserves — that determines its wealth or freedom. For the Middle East to make peace with Israel would be to declare war on itself, to admit that its own fundamental way of doing business — not the Jews — makes it poor, sick, and weak."

As for the U.S., its financial aid to Israel has to be weighed against the many billions of dollars that go to the Palestinians, Egypt, Jordan, and other Muslim countries. In addition, there is this: "Far from egging on Israel, the United States actually restrains the Israeli military, whose organization and discipline, along with the sophisticated Israeli arms industry, make it quite capable of annihilating nearly all its bellicose neighbors without American aid. Should the United States withdraw from active participation in the Middle East and let the contestants settle their differences on the battlefield, Israel, not the Arab world, would win. The military record of four previous conflicts does not lie. Arafat should remember who saved him in Lebanon; it was no power in the Middle East that brokered his exodus and parted the waves of Israeli planes and tanks for his safe passage to the desert."

We will remember what too many Muslims forget, writes Hanson. "The Muslim world suffers from political amnesia, we now have learned, and so has forgotten not only Arafat's resurrection but also American help to beleaguered Afghanis, terrified Kuwaitis, helpless Kurds and Shiites, starving Somalis, and defenseless Bosnians — direct intervention that has cost the United States much more treasure and lives than mere economic aid for Israel ever did. They forget; but we remember the Palestinians cheering in Nablus hours after thousands of our innocents were incinerated in New York and the hagiographic posters of a mass murderer in the streets of Muslim capitals."

"Even in the crucible of war," Hanson writes, "we have discovered that our worst critics love us in the concrete as much as they hate us in the abstract." The concrete evidence of their love, if that is what it is, is that they want to come here and to send their children here. Hanson asks, "Why do so many of these anti-Americans, who profess hatred of the West and reverence for the purity of an energized Islam or a fiery Palestine, enroll in Chico State or UCLA instead of *madrassas* in Pakistan or military academies in Iraq? The embarrassing answer would explain nearly everything, from bin Laden to the intifada. Dads and moms who watch Al-Jazeera and scream in the street at the Great Satan really would prefer that their children have dollars, an annual CAT scan, a good lawyer, air conditioning, and Levis in American hell than be without toilet paper, suffer from intestinal parasites, deal with the secret police, and squint with uncorrected vision in the Islamic paradise of Cairo, Teheran, and Gaza. Such a fundamental and intolerable paradox in the very core of a man's heart — multiplied millions of times over — is not a healthy thing either for them or for us."

Hanson ends on the note of friendly counsel: "So a neighborly bit of advice for our Islamic friends and their spokesmen abroad: topple your pillars of ignorance and the edifice of your anti-Americanism. Try to seek difficult answers from within to even more difficult questions without. Do not blame others for problems that are largely self-created or seek solutions over here when your answers are mostly at home. Please, think hard about what you are saying and writing about the deaths of thousands of Americans and your relationship with the United States. America has been a friend more often than not to you. But now you are on the verge of turning its people — who create, not follow, government — into an enemy: a very angry and powerful enemy that may be yours for a long, long time to come."

I'm sure that some might complain that Hanson's critique of Muslim venting is but another form of venting. I don't think so. I am reminded, rather, of Dr. Johnson's observation that clear thinking begins with clearing the mind of cant. The reconfiguration of world politics since September 11 offers nought for our comfort. Almost unbelievable has been the obtuseness and mendacity of Muslim organizations in this country. They continue to act as though nothing fundamental has changed; they are just another poor minority being picked on by a prejudiced majority. Because of the incorrigible niceness of Americans, they can get away with that most of the time. But continued denials and evasions about the evils perpetrated in the name of Islam and of Muslims seem almost suicidal. Again and again, one wants to cry out, "Please, please do not say that." They keep digging themselves into an ever deeper hole. We must continue to hope that voices of candor and correction will emerge from the Muslim world, both here and abroad. Meanwhile, I think Hanson got it about right in explaining why they misjudge us, and why we must brace ourselves for the duration, which is likely to be very, very long. *(April 2002)*

After Israel

I remember many years ago being taken aback when at a dinner party a friend concluded her vigorous defense of Israeli policy with the seemingly off-hand remark, "But of course, in the long run, Israel won't survive." When I pressed her, she explained that the Arabs, with such overwhelming numbers, will never be reconciled to the existence of Israel on "their" land. In other words, demography is destiny. It is true that the twenty-two nations of the Arab League have a fast-growing population of 300 million, compared with less than six million in Israel, with more than a million of those being Arabs. The population imbalance will become ever more dramatic, and Israel is such a small sliver of territory in such a vast region. I am no longer surprised when I hear people, including some in positions of considerable influence, say, usually sotto voce, that Israel will not survive "in the long run."

In this connection, I took note of a *Commentary* article by Norman Podhoretz — a more hawkish hawk on Israel than whom is not to be found — in which he argues that there is, in fact, no "peace process" between Israel and the Palestinians. Responding to Podhoretz, Ron Unz, the prominent California businessman and political activist, wrote: "As someone whose grandparents helped found Israel, I felt immense sadness after reading Norman Podhoretz's powerful analysis. There appear to be only two possible outcomes to this conflict. Israel may eventually choose to . . . exterminate or expel Palestinians from Israel and the West Bank. Or the endless bloodshed will produce an accelerating exodus of Israeli Jews to America and other more peaceful and affluent places, eventually leading to a collapse of the Jewish state. Since I doubt that Israel will ever develop a consensus for killing or expelling millions of Palestinians, I expect the country's trajectory to follow that of the Crusader kingdoms, surviving for seventy or eighty years after its establishment in

1948 and then collapsing under continual Muslim pressure and flagging ideological commitment."

I was even more impressed by Podhoretz's response to Unz: "I do not accept that Israel will wind up as another Crusader kingdom. . . . It would be foolish to dismiss this possibility altogether. . . . But I am still convinced that, if the Israelis can hold on tight against the forces [Unz] specifies, the day may yet come when the Arab world will call off the war it has been waging against the Jewish state since 1948." He agrees that killing or expelling millions of Palestinians is simply not an option. He then goes on to say that much depends on whether the U.S., in its current war against terrorism, treats Israel as a partner rather than an obstacle to its purposes in the Middle East. But there is a wan note to Podhoretz's response to Unz's prognosis: "I do not *accept* . . . I am *still* convinced . . . *if* the Israelis can . . . the day *may* yet come." And this from the archenemy of any hint of defeatism. I do not say this in criticism of Podhoretz. But it does seem to me that, for the first time in a very long time, there is now an explicitness about — and in some quarters an openness to — the possibility that Israel will not make it, and I find this profoundly troubling.

In Patrick Buchanan's new book, *The Death of the West,* he reports a conversation with former President Richard Nixon, known as a strong supporter of Israel. Buchanan's wife Shelley asked Nixon if Israel will survive. In the long run? he responded. He then turned his hand and put his thumb down. The answer was No.

What would it mean for the future of Judaism and world Jewry (the two are not separable) were the state of Israel to disappear? Of course I do not know. Nobody does. I don't mean what would happen if Israel was obliterated by an Arab atomic bomb, as some Arabs contemplate with relish. I mean, rather, the prospect of Israel being abandoned by Jews as a noble but failed Zionist dream. I suppose it is possible that five million Jews could go elsewhere, mainly to America, and flourish in security. It seems more than possible that a substantial number would, remembering Masada, be determined to die with the dream.

These are grim and unwelcome thoughts. As too many people are eager to remind us, Israel is doing bad things to the Palestinians. And, as too many fail to say, Palestinians are doing bad things to Israelis, and it is not always easy to sort out which is action and which reaction, which is aggression and which defense. There should be no difficulty, however, in sorting out the difference between the one party that has the declared purpose of destroying or expelling the other party, and the other party that wants only to live in security and peace. This, I think, we know for sure: there could be a real peace process and a real peace if the Arabs believably accepted a sovereign Jewish state in their midst. This, sadly, does not seem to be in the offing. So maybe the present conflict will go on for another five years. Ten years? Sixty years? How long is "the long run"? I may be wrong, but it seems to me that more supporters of Israel are asking that question, and asking it out loud. I'm not sure what should be made of that, but I am sure it is not unimportant. *(April 2002)*

While We're At It

❧ A seriously Catholic friend whose line of work has him hanging out with equally serious evangelical Protestants has a problem. "I'm not very good," he says, "at giving the kind of formulaic 'personal testimony' that they seem to expect." I know what he means. For many years I've been responding to evangelical friends who want to know when I was born again or, as it is commonly put, when I became a Christian. "I don't remember it at all," I say, "but I know precisely the time and place. It was at 357 Miller St., Pembroke, Ontario, on Sunday, June 2, 1936, when twelve days after my birth I was born again in the sacrament of Holy Baptism." (I was baptized at home because the chicken pox was going around.) That usually elicits a wry smile, and then the question, "Yes, but when did you *really* become a Christian?" In sober truth, there have been not one but several moments in my life that would no doubt qualify as what most evangelicals mean by a conversion experience. In circumstances appropriate to the disclosure of intensely personal experiences, I have told others about these moments. And some day, in pathetically pale imitation of Augustine and other greats, I might write about them in detail. My public testimony, however, is not to my experience but to Christ. It is not upon my experience but upon Christ that I rest my confidence that I am a child of God. The same set of questions is addressed from a Calvinist viewpoint in a recent issue of that mordant publication, *Nicotine Theological Journal.* The article includes this from the 1902 *Heidelberg Catechism, Twentieth-Century Edition:* "Nor need you doubt your conversion, your change of heart, because you cannot tell the day when it took place, as many profess to do. It did not take place in a day, or you might tell it. It is the growth of years (Mark 4:26-28), and therefore all the more reliable. You cannot tell when you learned to walk, talk, think, and work. You do not know when you learned to love your earthly father, much less the heavenly." The editors add, "This is the Reformed doctrine of 'getting religion.' We get religion, not in bulk but little by little. Just as we get natural life and strength, so spiritual life and strength, day by day." Of course, some do get it in bulk, and with a bang. One thinks, for instance, of the zealot from Tarsus on his way to Damascus. *(April 2000)*

❦ "A world trading system already exists; a world government does not, and in many quarters the very concept evokes resistance." So say the editors of *America,* the Jesuit weekly. "Christians believe that neither this nor any other hope for the future can be realized without grace, and so until the end of the ages they will continue to pray: 'Thy kingdom come.'" To think that all this time we've been praying for a world government. *(June/July 2000)*

❧ "New Age" has been around for more than thirty years now, and is still a very big and growing item in the publishing world, according to *Publishers Weekly*. The story quotes Carl Weschke, a Minneapolis book man, who says there really is a New Age. "It's all for the purpose of giving us a higher perspective, so we can save ourselves and save the planet," says Weschke. Another bookseller, however, says, "There is an odd change going on right now. The words 'New Age' are stigmatized by society, but what New Age stands for is embraced by the mainstream more every day." The story concludes that more and more publishers and sellers are expanding their New Age output, but they are also "calling it by different names." Although *PW* doesn't say so, a good many of those books by different names can be found in Catholic and evangelical bookstores, not to mention parish libraries. A Presbyterian pastor tells me one of his parishioners is writing a book on crystal decoding — i.e., discerning the meanings of crystals and using them to influence the future — "from a Presbyterian viewpoint." He told his parishioner that this might not be entirely consonant with a Christian understanding of the sovereignty of God, to which he received the response, "I know. We have to rethink the sovereignty of God." According to the studies, only a tiny percentage of Americans identify their religion as New Age. So who do you suppose is buying those millions of books each year? Answer: people who are very sure that they are Lutheran, Catholic, Baptist, or Presbyterian but are also "into alternative spiritualities." For most of them, the real alternative spirituality would be orthodox Christianity. *(October 2001)*

❧ The way in which some Catholics have internalized anti-Catholic stereotypes never ceases to amaze. Father James

Heft, Chancellor of the University of Dayton and prominent opponent of the bishops' efforts to implement *Ex Corde Ecclesiae,* writes in the *Chronicle of Higher Education* that the proposal that teachers of Catholic theology should be recognized as such by the bishops "runs the risk of diminishing academe's already shaky confidence in the compatibility of Catholicism and serious intellectual work." Oh dear. In view of the Catholic intellectual tradition and the innumerable Catholics who are distinguished in every field of scholarship, those who even hint at such an incompatibility should not be pandered to but clearly labeled as the bigots they are. The most durable anti-Catholic canard is that there is a tension or conflict between being authentically Catholic and authentically American. Heft writes: "Pope John Paul II's apostolic statement on higher education says that Catholic colleges and universities are *ex corde ecclesiae* — from the heart of the Church. In biblical thought, the image of the heart combines the capacities of a believer both to think and to love. Catholic colleges and universities are also *ex corde patriae* — from the heart of the nation. . . . Learning how to maintain that duality without division requires vision, humility, and courage." Paul Blanshard *(American Freedom and Catholic Power)* would agree. What requires vision, humility, and courage is to enrich the pluralism of American intellectual and academic life with colleges and universities that are, without apology or embarrassment, Catholic. The real embarrassment is Catholic educators, hat in hand, poignantly eager to be accepted by their presumed academic betters. *(April 2000)*

❦ So who, do you suppose, is the most influential evangelical Protestant of the last quarter century? Billy Graham? Bill Bright? James Dobson? Pat Robertson? Charles Colson? The answer is none of the above, according to the *Evangelical Studies Bulletin* that comes out of Wheaton College. Tim LaHaye, co-author of the zillion-selling "Left Behind" series, launched creationism in the 1970s, then went on to writing books that incorporated therapeutic and sex-fulfillment ideas into evangelical piety, and then with his wife Beverly (head of Concerned Women for America) was key to putting together what came to be known as the religious right. The *Bulletin* concludes that LaHaye was "influenced by all the changes swirling around evangelicalism, rose out of the ranks of the movement, and then in turn played a strategic role at key points that have cemented — for good or ill — the direction evangelicalism will be taking in the next few decades." Tim LaHaye, the most influential evangelical of the last quarter century? A plausible, if not conclusive, argument can be made for it. *(October 2001)*

❦ For almost two hundred years, liberal theology has been haunted by the question of the connection, if any, between the Jesus of history and the Christ of faith. B. A. Gerrish, a distinguished Reformation theologian, takes another crack at it in a two-part article in the *Christian Century*. Even if historical scholarship determined that Jesus never lived, it does not necessarily mean the end of faith in Christ. "Is faith really at the mercy of the latest report on the quest for the historical Jesus?" Gerrish asks. "The Christian assertion that saving faith is the gift of God in Christ Jesus is not a claim to know more about the past than historians can know. . . . It is the outward attestation of an inner conviction nurtured in the communion of saints." This is, finally, another variation on Rudolf Bultmann's affirmation of the resurrection gospel without the resurrection. Of course faith is not at the mercy of the latest report on the quest for the historical Jesus. The truly remarkable thing is that, apart from academic mavericks who are always coming up with a newly imagined Jesus, the basic picture of Jesus, his teaching and his life, presented by serious scholarship is pretty much what the Church held nineteen hundred years ago. Liberals believe they are boldly bracing themselves for the worst, but then console themselves with the thought that the worst isn't all that bad. But, if there was no Jesus, faith in Jesus the Christ is just another way of whistling in the dark. Much bolder is the orthodox acknowledgment, with St. Paul (1 Corinthians 15), that if Christ is not risen our faith is in vain. That is the radically historical nature of Christian faith that awaits its final and certain vindication from the future, when every knee shall bow and every tongue confess that Jesus Christ is Lord (Philippians 2). Contra the easy consolations of liberalism, if it is not true, be it ever so meaningful, it is not true. And if, as Christians believe, it is true, there will never be compelling evidence to the contrary. *(May 2000)*

❦ Remember the new painting of the epicene Jesus touted by the *National Catholic Reporter* as "someone who celebrates our differences"? In the revised version of Mark 1, the man with an unclean spirit cries out, "What have you to do with us, Jesus of Nazareth? Have you come to destroy us? I know who you are — the Holy One of God!" and Jesus reassures him saying, "Relax, I have come to celebrate our differences." As is so often the case, life beggars parody. Here is the comment on the same passage in *Celebrating the Eucharist*, the Mass guide published by Liturgical Press and used by thousands of Catholic parishes. After Jesus cast out the unclean spirit, we read in Mark that "All were amazed and asked one another, 'What is this? A new teaching with authority. He commands even the unclean spirits and they obey him.'" *Celebrating the Eucharist* comments: "Jesus' authority is not a 'power over' but a truth that calls forth life. His is an authority that derives from modeling how a true servant of God lives." If I get this right, the problem with the evil spirits is that they wanted to serve God but lacked an adequate role model until Jesus came along. In Mark it is said, "The unclean spirit convulsed the man and with a loud cry came out of him." In the psychobabbled Mass guide, one infers that the unclean spirit said something like, "Thanks, Jesus, I needed that." There are no convulsions or loud cries, although one imagines there might be some gagging in the pews. *(June/July 2000)*

❦ Now let's see if I get this straight. Father Richard McBrien of Notre Dame comments on a new report on Catholic seminarians and sees some very real problems. First, many of them "feel quite free to defy the faculty." Second, "approximately half are either converts to Catholicism or Catholics who had not practiced their faith since childhood." Third, "for a growing proportion of seminarians (25 percent), English is their second language." In other words, they think for themselves, their vocations emerge not from "the system" but from personal conversion and decision, and they are multicultural. One might think that this would cheer the cockles of Fr. McBrien's heart, for he is the most liberal of liberals. Not at all. The problem is that these seminarians are "conservative." Or, as Fr. McBrien puts it, they are "resistant to the renewal brought about by Vatican II [and] distract faculty and other students from the work at hand." In short, they disrupt business as usual. So says Fr. McBrien, the most establishment of establishmentarians. *(August/September 2000)*

❦ I recently spoke at the University of Pennsylvania at a conference titled "Extended Life, Eternal Life" and funded by the Templeton Foundation. It was, all in all, a chilling experience, with the "humanists" being greatly outnumbered by the "hard scientists" who made no secret of their enthusiasm for the revived eugenics project and the supposed inevitability of the eventual "conquest of mortality." The conference featured a debate between that font of moral wisdom, Leon Kass of the University of Chicago, and Lee Silver, a Princeton professor of molecular biology who is a leading propagandist for the manipulation of the genetic code in which venture capitalists and biologists have invested hopes of wealth beyond the dreams of avarice. It was a wondrous thing at the conference to listen to academics with life histories of support for leftist causes insouciantly proclaiming that decisions about the reconstruction of the *humanum* should be left to the forces of the free market. At a later date, I will return to that conference and the larger questions about the return of eugenics. Meanwhile, I note that a few days after the conference, Prof. Silver had an op-ed piece in the *Times* that concludes with this: "The public is understandably nervous about the idea of companies profiting from our genetic code. But if the goal is to make this genetic information useful as soon as possible, the debate should be focused on fair business practices and regulatory issues, not on ethics." Forget ethics. That at least has the merit of candor. *(August/September 2000)*

❦ On the website of the United Ministry at Harvard and Radcliffe there is posted a warning to new students about "certain destructive religious groups" that are not part of the United Ministry. Such groups are proselytizing, sometimes claim "a special relationship to God," and lead to "ego destruction, mind control, manipulation of a member's relationships with family and friends." "All the members of the United Ministry," on the other hand, "are committed to mutual respect and non-proselytization. We affirm the roles of personal freedom, doubt, and open critical reflection in healthy spiritual growth. . . . We're here to help you have a healthy, happy experience of your own spiritual journey while you're here at Harvard." And Jesus said, "I have come to help you have a healthy, happy experience of your own spiritual journey." *(August/September 2000)*

❦ There was that marvelous moment at Cardinal O'Connor's funeral when Bernard Cardinal Law declared from the pulpit that "the Church must always be unambiguously prolife." This was met by three minutes of standing applause by the thousands in the cathedral, while the Clintons and Gores squirmed. Reporting the event in the next day's *New York Times,* Adam Nagourney wrote, "In politics, the phrase 'pro-life' is shorthand for opposition to abortion." Really? In most other venues, such an explanation would seem condescending and unnecessary, but the *Times* never uses the term "pro-life," and the self-importance of the *Times* is such that it is assumed that, if a term is not used by the *Times,* it is unknown. Thus, for instance, the paper has run hundreds of stories on the controversy over partial-birth abortion, each time explaining that "partial-birth abortion is a term employed by abortion opponents in referring to" etc. Many years ago I remarked in passing to a *Times* reporter that they should change their style in an item of ecclesiastical nomenclature. It was a minor point and I had quite forgotten about it until I received a three-page letter from the then managing editor that the suggestion had been relayed to him and, after thorough research, they had decided I was right and would change their style book. The last line of the letter explains it all: "And so, Pastor Neuhaus [I was then a Lutheran], you may have the satisfaction of knowing that, in some small way, you have changed history." *(August/September 2000)*

❧ Conservatives generally favor tradition, but from time to time a decision must be made that a cause is lost. Those who adamantly decline making that decision are commonly called reactionaries. Evelyn Waugh, for delightful instance. "Requested by a British journalist to comment on the upcoming elections of 1959, Waugh responded, 'I have never voted in a parliamentary election. I shall not vote this year. . . . In the last three hundred years, particularly in the last hundred, the Crown has adopted what seems to me a very hazardous process of choosing advisers: popular election. Many great evils have resulted. . . . I do not aspire to advise my Sovereign in her choice of servants.'" *(October 2000)*

❧ The argument has been called clever, and it is that, but it is also more than that. In his new book *Bobos in Paradise: The New Upper Class and How They Got There* (Simon & Schuster), David Brooks proves himself an acute analyst of society and culture. The Bobos (bourgeois bohemians) in question are the people who are sometimes called "the new class" — well-educated, hard-working, and achievement-oriented folk who more or less live by bourgeois values but do so with an ironic lacing of self-consciously sophisticated bohemianism. Brooks recognizes that he is himself a Bobo, and he offers in a humorous and sometimes self-deprecating vein a mass of details on the jargon, eating habits, dress, musical tastes, distinctive consumption, and domestic habits of the elite to which he belongs. This new upper class, he says, is probably secure for as far as we can see into the future because it is an intensely meritocratic elite that is self-critical and morally flexible enough to co-opt whatever might challenge its rule. All in all, says Brooks, this is a fairly happy state of affairs. The morality of Bobos "doesn't try to perch atop the high ground of divine revelation." They are interested in spirituality but "cautious of moral crusades and religious enthusiasms. . . . They tolerate a little lifestyle experimentation, so long as it is done safely and moderately. They are offended by concrete wrongs, like cruelty and racial injustice, but are relatively unmoved by lies or transgressions that don't seem to do anyone obvious harm." Mr. Brooks' conclusion is that "This is a good morality for building a decent society." Brooks writes regularly for the *Weekly Standard* and is usually thought to be a conservative. There is, in fact, something deeply conservative about not expecting too much from people, about recognizing the value of quotidian niceness. At the same time, in his depiction, Bobos are preciously self-referential beings, apparently attuned to the bargain basement utilitarianism of a pleasure/pain calculus that is hardly up to providing a reason for bearing the burdens of others, or even to coping with the inevitabilities of their own serious self-doubt, failure, fragility, and death. Like the denizens of Aldous Huxley's *Brave New World,* there are few intensities among these people amply supplied with the soma of their smugly mutual approbation. It is difficult to know what the phrase "decent society" means in this case, absent the awareness of evil or transcendent good. Brooks provides a clever and sometimes insightful analysis, but we have to hope that, as a generalization about our new ruling class, it is wrong. In his telling, the Bobos are philistines. Affluent, talented, and fashionably ironic philistines, to be sure, but philistines nonetheless. Their "paradise" is purchased at too high a cost to their humanity. *(August/September 2000)*

❦ Charles Murray, author, with Richard Herrnstein, of *The Bell Curve,* says he is still puzzled by the outrage of the left against their claim that there are inherent differences between the races in IQ and other factors bearing on one's chances in life. After all, such a claim can be employed to advocate an expanded government role in equalizing life outcomes. Now Murray writes in "Deeper into the Brain" that we are facing a "neurogenetic revolution" in which biological factors will be discovered and made manipulatable not only relative to race and sex but also to many other group differences, such as those distinguishing "the English from the French, employed Swedes from unemployed Swedes, observant Christians from lapsed ones, and people who collect stamps from people who backpack." Eugenics, he says, "is in disrepute because of Nazism," but an older left — such as that of the Fabians and, he might have added, the Rockefeller Foundation — made no bones about the need for government policies that would encourage the lower classes to have fewer children and the better classes more. "The only difference," he writes, "will be that the old eugenicists had to rely on a rough statement ('the lower classes') whereas eugenicists of the future will be able to be more precise ('people with the following genetic profiles')." In response to Mr. Murray's puzzlement about the left, it might be noted that the utopian left must assume a literal and inherent equality among people if unhappy inequalities are to be blamed upon "the system," thereby justifying the ambition to revolutionize the system. But, as Murray notes, there has been another stream of the left — abetted by many who think of themselves as conservatives — that despairs of the "inferior" and "defective" and believes they must be contained, reduced in number, or eliminated. This touches on what Murray has elsewhere called the growth of "custodial democracy," and on the much-discussed question of whether Nazism was a phenomenon of the left or the right. "I confess to a certain optimism," says Murray, about the neurogenetic revolution and the prospect of our deciding to redesign Homo sapiens. "One of the main reasons that couples have babies is to produce *their* baby, the product of their combined genes. . . . The popular voluntary uses of gene manipulation are likely to be ones that avoid birth defects and ones that lead to improved overall physical and mental abilities. I find it hard to get upset about that prospect." That may well be true of the popular and voluntary aspects of the revolution, but Murray wisely acknowledges that his thoughts "are the ruminations of a twentieth-century man, destined to look as myopic a century from now as the predictions of nineteenth-century men about the twentieth." Some who have thought about these matters in the past were not so very myopic. See, for instance, Aldous Huxley's *Brave New World,* as discussed by Leon Kass in the March issue. *(October 2000)*

❦ Bill Mahan of Harrisburg, Pennsylvania, sent this item along and says it represents the decline from "Christian granite to social service gravel." That's not a bad way of putting it. The item is the newsletter of the YWCA of Greater Harrisburg. On the back page it carries the organization's mission statement of 1900 under the heading THAT WAS THEN (in old English type). The statement reads: "We, the Young Women's Christian Association of Harrisburg, a member of the Young Women's Christian Association of the United States of America, declare our purpose to be: To build a fellowship of women and girls devoted to the task of realizing in our common life those ideals of personal and social living to which we are committed by our faith as Christians. In this endeavor we seek to understand Jesus, to share his love for all people, and to grow in the knowledge and love of God." Then, under the heading THIS IS NOW (modern sans serif), there is the mission statement of 2000: "The YWCA of Greater Harrisburg emphasizes the empowerment of women and children by providing quality services designed to maximize their spiritual, emotional, educational, and physical development. It is committed to eliminating racism, sexism, and any other barrier or prejudice that impedes personal growth. It actively serves as an advocate and a resource to the community on issues that impact women and children." The poignant fact is that the people who write such stuff are almost certainly sincere in believing that it represents progress. *(October 2000)*

❦ The municipal council of Gamle in Oslo, Norway, has authorized the Islamic muezzin's public call to prayer for three minutes at noon on Fridays. In response, the "Norwegian Association of Pagans" has requested permission to make the public call, "God does not exist. Come to our meetings." Having once agreed upon the premise, to do what? *(November 2000)*

❦ On March 25, the Feast of the Annunciation, Mary Ann Glendon of Harvard Law School spoke at a Jubilee Day for Women in Washington. She reflected on the life of Dorothy Day, who died in 1980 and is now a candidate for beatification. It is no secret that many Catholics have a deep ambivalence toward Dorothy Day, admiring her orthodoxy and personal piety while deploring her doctrine of economics, or vice versa. As Joseph Pearce reports in his recent *Literary Converts* (Ignatius), Evelyn Waugh visited Day in the 1950s, finding her to be "an imperious woman who thinks we would be better off if we were all poor." Waugh was not persuaded. Professor Glendon, however, directs our attention to why many others think Dorothy Day should be raised to the honor of the altar. "In the roaring '20s, when Dorothy Day was in *her* 20s, she lived a life that she later described as 'drifting.' She had numerous love affairs; a short marriage; a longer cohabitation; a child born out of wedlock; and an abortion followed by the pain of being abandoned by the father of the child she had aborted.

Significantly, she titled her autobiographical account of those years *The Long Loneliness.* Not long after the birth of her daughter Tamar, Dorothy became a Catholic. Thereafter, she lived a life of voluntary poverty, devoting herself to raising her child and to caring for the poor and homeless. Together with Peter Maurin, she founded the Catholic Worker movement. What accounted for the dramatic change in Dorothy's life? The grace of God to be sure. But Dorothy Day was prompted to open her heart to that grace by the witness of other human beings — especially by the religious sisters whom she saw day in and day out feeding the poor in the depths of the Depression era. Dorothy began lending a hand to these women, and she began to question them. Throughout her life, she did 'not cease to put questions to Christ.' In the film based on her life, *Entertaining Angels,* one moving scene shows Dorothy storming into church after a day of dreadful disappointments, standing before the crucifix and asking, 'What do you want from me?' The answer, she comes to understand, is 'Everything.' Whatever the outcome of the proceedings in Rome, Dorothy's story speaks powerfully to young women today. For, unfortunately, the bohemian lifestyle of artists and intellectuals in the 1920s has spread to all corners of our society. It has taken a terrible toll, especially on women and children. How fortunate we are this morning, then, to be sustained by our shared faith and fellowship. As we thank God for the inestimable privilege of those gifts, let us give thanks for the life of Dorothy Day and pray that her example will lead ever more women out of their 'long loneliness' into the love of God. And let us not forget to give thanks for those wonderful sisters whose Christian witness helped to open Dorothy's heart to grace. I would like to think that perhaps we here might even follow their example. Could not each one of us resolve to reach out to the Dorothys we may know who are still lonely and drifting — that their voices too may be heard in a mighty chorus of yes to God." *(November 2000)*

❧ This is in the great ripostes department. I was speaking to Lutheran educators in Minneapolis a while back. One could not help but notice that the fellow giving the invocation was very small. He could hardly see over the podium. "I am often asked," he said, "'Were your parents very short?' To which I respond, 'Were your parents very obnoxious?'" *(November 2000)*

❧ The charges and counter-charges go on and on over what Pius XII did or did not do, should have done or should not have done, during World War II. One of the least persuasive claims is that the Holocaust, and maybe the war, would have ended if he had threatened to excommunicate Hitler and Mussolini, both of whom had long since excommunicated themselves. (An official statement of excommunication simply confirms what people have done to themselves.) This is brought to mind in reading a very useful little book by Joel S. Panzer, *The Popes and Slavery* (Alba House). Beginning with Pope Eugene IV in 1435, when the Portuguese launched the modern slave trade in the Canary Islands, popes condemned slavery in no uncertain terms, decreeing excommunication for all who participated in the practice. Similar condemnations, typically citing earlier papal precedents, were issued by Paul III, Gregory XIV, Urban VIII, and on up through Pius IX and Leo XIII in the nineteenth century. Prior to the Civil War, in what Father Panzer aptly calls a form of American Gallicanism, bishops in the U.S., to their shame, claimed that the papal condemnations of slavery did not apply to the "peculiar circumstances" in this country. Whether in Germany in 1939 or America in 1850 and 2000, the threat of excommunication is only as powerful as is the priority that people accord to being in full communion with the Church. Yet it may be argued that the integrity of the Church and her teaching requires imposing the censure, even if it is not effective in changing what people do. That is an argument that some make today in connection with Catholic politicians who, in direct contradiction of magisterial teaching, support the unlimited abortion license of *Roe v. Wade*. It is an argument that needs to be engaged more forthrightly than it has been to date. At the same time, however, historical experience with, inter alia, slavery, anti-Semitism, and abortion lends little support to the stereotype that, when the Church speaks authoritatively, the Catholic people fall into line. Worth noting also is the fact that those who, in the case of Pius XII, claim that he should have fiercely wielded the supposed sword of excommunication are usually the same people who condemn what they view as papal authoritarianism. The reality is that, in the words of John Paul II in the 1990 encyclical *Redemptoris Missio* (The Mission of the Redeemer), "The Church imposes nothing, she only proposes." That being said, she can also, as in the instance of abortion, publicly censure those who claim to accept the proposal that she teaches God's truth but manifestly have not. *(November 2000)*

❧ At Harvard University, Jack Kevorkian, who is serving a 10-to-25-year sentence for second degree murder, received in absentia a Citizen Activist Award, sponsored by the Gleitsman Foundation. The panel that selected Kevorkian included actor Ted Danson, feminist Gloria Steinem, and Candace Lightner, founder of Mothers Against Drunk Driving. Harvard psychiatrist Robert Coles was also on the panel but says he disagreed with the decision. Kevorkian will share the $100,000 award with Alabama attorney Bryan Stevenson, a crusader against the death penalty. Kevorkian has long advocated execution by lethal experiments or by removal of a prisoner's vital organs. Also on the embrace of death front, Derek Humphry's "how to" film on suicide, based on his book *Final Exit,* was shown on Hawaiian television, and was promptly followed by two people with a history of depression successfully following its instructions. Contacted in Eugene, Oregon, Humphry issued a statement: "The death of any person is deeply tragic, but if these people are intent on suicide and released themselves in a nonviolent way from their troubles, then I can live with that." Well, that's the important thing. Although one wonders about the notion of "nonviolent" killing, and whether Mr. Humphry has changed his mind and now believes that a desired exit from life is "tragic." The embrace of death confounds both mind and language. *(November 2000)*

❧ "I am a Christian because Christianity makes more sense of more facts than any other way of thinking I know of." I first ran across that statement many years ago, I believe in something by Reinhold Niebuhr, and it greatly impressed me. That's not the whole reason for being a Christian by any means, but it is a supporting consideration. Thoughtful human beings look for a total explanation, a "theory of everything," as it is sometimes called. On religion more generally, practitioners of evolutionary sociobiology, which is the soft underbelly of evolutionary biology, are today claiming that people are religious because religion has a strong survival value. Thus E. O. Wilson in *Consilience:* "There is a hereditary selective advantage to membership in a powerful group united by devout belief and purpose. . . . Much if not all religious behavior could have arisen by natural selection." Lionel Tiger in *Optimism: The Biology of Hope* writes that religion is universal and is fundamentally about hope. "Optimism is a biological phenomenon. Since religion is deeply intertwined with optimism, religion is a biological phenomenon rooted in our genes." So it is that evolutionary theory, which led many to believe there is no God, now purports to explain why we believe there is. In the absence of something that makes more sense, it makes a kind of sense. Fortunately, explanations that make more sense are not absent. *(December 2000)*

❧ *Publishers Weekly* says that Peter Singer's *Writings on an Ethical Life* may be his "break-out" book. All the usual media outlets, we are told, are lining up to interview Princeton's peddler of bargain-basement utilitarianism, which should be good for sales. And some of the unusuals. Nat Hentoff, for instance, interviewed Singer and strongly disagrees with him, saying that the gist of his message is that some lives are not worth living — e.g., severely disabled children and the expendable elderly — and should therefore be terminated. Noting that Nazi atrocities stemmed from "small beginnings," Hentoff says Singer's book is dangerous. *PW* quotes a bookseller who scoffed, "The alternative to writing that is dangerous is writing that is safe, and that, to a bookseller, is writing that doesn't sell." So neat is the fit between intellectual courage and capitalist greed. Dan Halpern, Singer's publisher at HarperCollins, says Singer gets a bum rap from his critics. "The sore points for people are his writings on euthanasia and impaired infants. They imagine he is trying to mandate killing without cause." Not at all. It is simply that he is so productive of new causes for killing. *(March 2001)*

❦ Coming soon from Germany! *Koerperwelten*! The word means body works, and refers to an exhibition in Berlin in which mummified corpses are used as works of art. The "artist" is Gunter von Hagen, an anatomy professor, and he preserves human tissue by replacing body fluids with synthetic resin. The corpses look like anatomical models with muscles, organs, the nervous system, and blood vessels clearly visible. There is a sectioned body of a pregnant woman with her unborn child. The exhibits are of people who gave their consent before dying. It is reported that museums in London and New York have expressed an interest in hosting *Koerperwelten*. One recalls reports a few years ago that Germans were no longer placing obituary notices in newspapers. Funerals were also in decline. People wanted simply to depart with no public notice taken. Between nothing and exhibitionism there used to be something called civilization. *(June/July 2001)*

❦ We have the word of *catholic eye* that this appeared in a London church bulletin: "The ladies of the church have cast off clothing of every kind and they may be seen in the church basement on Friday." *(February 2002)*

VII

Civil Religion or Public Philosophy

Traditional language about "Christian America" — which once served both liberal and conservative purposes, as those terms are used today — was vigorously attacked by the school of "Christian realism" associated with Reinhold Niebuhr and his brother, H. Richard Niebuhr. From the late 1930s through the 1960s, Reinhold in particular assumed a "prophetic" mode in debunking any idea of the "chosenness" of America. This was part and parcel of his attack on the idea of moral progress (see "The Idea of Moral Progress," FT, August/September 1999). In the regnant liberalism of the time, three ideas came together: the idea of moral progress, the idea of American chosenness, and the idea of a socialist utopia. This made for a heady mix that Niebuhr condemned as a snare and delusion. He employed his impressive polemical powers against the notion that history can be understood in terms of a conflict between "the children of light and the children of darkness." With almost mantra-like repetition, he underscored the "ironies" and "ambiguities" of history.

The Niebuhrs did their job well, perhaps too well in some quarters. While a Niebuhrian sensibility of skepticism toward historical delusions is to be cultivated, it was essentially a corrective against the excesses of the "Redeemer Nation" theme. In mainline Protestantism and in the liberal culture more generally, that skepticism was employed in a polemic against what was perceived as an anti-Communist crusade during the Cold War years. From the 1950s through the end of Soviet Communism in 1991, that crusade was portrayed as a contest between "the free world" and "godless communism." In other words, the children of light against the children of darkness. The attempt to check that exaggeration, an exaggeration frequently freighted with hubris and self-righteousness, reinforced an attitude aptly described as anti-anticommunism. In this view, the great evil was not communism but anticommunism, a cause presumably discredited by the excesses of Senator Joseph McCarthy. The anti-anticommunism that McCarthy did so much to abet lived on long after his censure by the Senate and his pitiful death in 1957.

The story of American religion during the Cold War years, so closely connected with the idea of Christian America, still awaits historians who can untangle its knotted complexities. In retrospect, it is generally recognized, also by those who scoffed at the notion at the time, that there really was something very much like a free world that stood in sharp contrast to the tyranny of a communism that was "godless" in its aggressive atheism. Except in the most diehard circles of the left, it is not controversial today to refer to Soviet Communism as an "evil empire." That was not the case in oldline Protestantism — meaning, roughly, those churches belonging to the once influential National Council of Churches — only a few years ago. From the mid-1960s until very recently, the Vietnam War was in these quarters taken as definitive proof that talk about a free world was a lie, and a good many religious leaders frankly believed that, for all its faults, communism was "the wave of the future." In this view, as it was conventionally asserted, the United States was "on the wrong side of history."

Even more common — indeed so common as to constitute a secure liberal consensus — was the belief that communism was a permanent feature of world history, or at least it would endure as far as we could see into the future. Many expected and encouraged a "convergence" between communism and the free world (the latter being defined as capitalism). All who participated in this consensus were committed to "peaceful coexistence" with communism. Figures such as Pope John Paul II, Ronald Reagan, and British Prime Minister Margaret Thatcher, who made no secret of their belief that Soviet Communism was a temporary and unsustainable aberration, were routinely criticized for threatening that peaceful coexistence.

As I say, American religion during the Cold War is a fascinating story that is yet to be told adequately. For present purposes, I simply note that the period resulted in an emphatic repudiation — and not only among oldline Protestants — of the last remnants of the idea of Christian America. Other factors contributed to that repudiation, notably the convergence of the civil rights movement with anti-anticommunism, and the passions surrounding the Vietnam War. Under the leadership of Dr. Martin Luther King, Jr., the civil rights movement was typically an affirmation of the American experiment, as most memorably articulated in his great "I Have a Dream" speech of August 28, 1963. His argument was that slavery and racial segregation contradicted the essential creed and character of that experiment. That was the liberal position. The later and more "radicalized" argument of the "new politics" would be that slavery and segregation, far from contradicting America, convicted America of being essentially racist, in addition to its inherent sins of militarism, imperialism, and propensity for the capitalist exploitation of the world's poor. It followed that only the enemies of Christianity would want to call such a country Christian.

A Replacement Religion

Prior to what many perceive as the anti-American turn of what is comprehensively (perhaps too comprehensively) called The Sixties, the idea of Christian America had been sharply modified, and in some ways replaced by, the idea of an American "civil religion." This was influentially set forth in Will Herberg's book of 1955, *Protestant, Catholic, Jew: An Essay in American Religious Sociology.* Herberg, a Jew and a great admirer of Reinhold Niebuhr, spoke of the American way of life as "the characteristic American religion, undergirding life and overarching American society despite indubitable differences of religion, section, culture, and class." During those years and up to this day, a statement presumably made by President Dwight D. Eisenhower in 1954 is frequently quoted: "Our government makes no sense unless it is founded on a deeply felt religious faith — and I don't care what it is." While it has never been documented that the statement, first cited in the *Christian Century,* was ever made by Eisenhower, the sentiment fit perfectly Herberg's thesis. As Sydney Ahlstrom wrote in his monumental *A Religious History of the American People,* "The postwar form of civil religion debased the older tradition which had reverenced [America] as a bearer of transcendent values and summoned citizens to stewardship of a sacred trust."

Now even that debased form of the American Way of Life as a civil religion has little currency in our public discourse. Beginning in the late 1960s, sociologist Robert N. Bellah and others tried to revive the civil religion argument, adapting it to the stringent critique of America favored by the left, but their efforts never caught on beyond students of religion in the academy. By the 1970s the doctrine, assuming dogmatic status, had been firmly established that America is a secular society. At least it appeared to be firmly established. When in 1984 I published *The Naked Public Square: Religion and Democracy in America,* it was generally viewed as a provocative — some thought eccentric and even dangerous — challenge to what "everybody knew" about the secularity of America. Still today there are those who contend that the dangerous argument of that book is that the naked public square should be replaced by the sacred public square. My argument then and now, however, is that the naked public square — meaning public life stripped of religion and religiously grounded morality — should give way not to a sacred public square but to a civil public square.

Writing in the *New York Review of Books,* the late J. M. Cameron was sympathetic to the argument of the book but suggested that the kind of religiously legitimated public philosophy that I called for required a credal form of Christianity with rich intellectual resources, such as Catholicism, rather than the revivalistic Protestantism now insurgent in American public life. The latter form of "fundamentalism," he believed, had long since been bagged and stuffed by H. L. Mencken and was of no possible use in public moral discourse. It is a point that should not be dismissed lightly. At the same time, Cameron's view does not take into account the degree of credal seriousness, albeit confusingly articulated, among Baptists and others, or the richer intellectual resources of the minority Calvinist tradition within evangelical Protestantism. Equally important, it fails to reckon with initiatives such as "Evangelicals and Catholics Together," launched in the early 1990s, which give expression to a growing convergence in both cooperative action and theology. In this convergence, Catholic social doctrine, and particularly the power of natural law philosophy, are challenging conventionally secular habits of public debate.

Civil Religion Untethered

The reconstructed public philosophy that is required could provide a secure foundation for the civil public square. The civil public square is one in which different convictions about the common good are engaged within the bonds of civility. The "common good" is — and we can never tire of making this point — unavoidably a moral concept, and that means the religiously grounded moral convictions of the American people cannot be excluded from the public square. Given the role of religion in American culture, both historically and at present, a religion-free public square is a formula for the end of democracy. To exclude the deepest convictions of the people from the deliberation of how we ought to order our life together is tantamount to excluding the people from that deliberation, and that is the end of democracy. We need not be delayed here by the old debate, still pressed by many conservatives, over whether our constitutional order is that of a democracy or a republic. Suffice it that the Constitution itself, as unanimously asserted by the Founders, is that of a republic, but it rests on the democratic premise that political sovereignty rests with the people. The Declaration of Independence declares that "just government is derived from the consent of the governed." As the political sovereign, the people are authorized to name a sovereignty that they acknowledge to be higher than their own; for instance, "the laws of Nature and of Nature's God." This is not, as some claim, a formula for theocracy. It is an exercise of democratic authority through republican or representative means by which the people place a check upon their own power by designating the higher authority to which they hold themselves accountable.

The civil public square requires something not entirely unlike Herberg's civil religion. The problem with calling it a civil religion is that most Americans think they already have a religion and are not interested in exchanging it for another. For this reason among others, it is better to say that the civil public square requires a public philosophy attuned to the Judeo-Christian moral tradition. A Judeo-Christian moral tradition is not a Judeo-Christian religion. A moral tradition is part of religion but by no means the whole of it; nor, especially in Christianity, is it the most important part. But it is a necessary part. Sustaining the Judeo-Christian moral tradition in public requires that Americans who are Christians recognize that tradition as theirs, and recognize that it is necessarily dependent upon Judaism, both historically and at present. Here, too, it becomes apparent that cultivating the Jewish-Christian relationship is much more than a matter of interfaith politesse; it is essential to reconstituting the moral basis of our common life.

Civil religion, when it is untethered from biblical religion, can become a rival religion. Some Christian thinkers would go further and say that civil religion is by definition a rival religion. Such was surely the case with, for example, the religion of America's "manifest destiny" mentioned earlier in this series on Christian America. In that instance, Christians succumb to a notion of the "Redeemer Nation" that is disengaged from, and becomes a competitor to, their Redeemer. The perennial attempts, commonly called "Wilsonian," to assert some grand national purpose within the world-historical scheme of things are usually Christian in inspiration but end by aspiring to take the place of Christianity. If I am right in thinking that Henry Luce of *Time* was premature, that it is the twenty-first century that is "the American century," it is certain that America will be safe neither for itself nor for the world without a guiding public philosophy. And it is, I believe, equally certain that any public philosophy that might be constructed will not be democratically sustainable unless it engages in a fresh way the idea of Christian America. *(December 2000)*

Velvet Glove, Iron Fist, and Irony

It has been said in these pages and elsewhere that, looking back now, it is apparent that Aldous Huxley's *Brave New World,* written at the beginning of the thirties, has turned out to be more prophetic than George Orwell's *Nineteen Eighty-Four,* written at the end of the forties. I did not know, however, until I read Jeffrey Meyers' new biography, *Orwell: Wintry Conscience of a Generation* (Norton), that Huxley expected things to turn out this way, and delicately explained why to Orwell in a letter of October 1949. Huxley praised *Nineteen Eighty-Four* very highly: "Agreeing with all that the critics have written of it, I need not tell you, yet once more, how fine and how profoundly important the book is." He then went on to say:

> The philosophy of the ruling minority in *Nineteen Eighty-Four* is a sadism which has been carried to its logical conclusion by going beyond sex and denying it. Whether in actual fact the policy of the boot-on-the-face can go on indefinitely seems doubtful. My own belief is that the ruling oligarchy will find less arduous and wasteful ways of governing and of satisfying its lust for power, and that these ways will resemble those which I described in *Brave New World*. . . . Within the next generation I believe that the world's rulers will discover that infant conditioning and narco-hypnosis are more efficient, as instruments of government, than clubs and prisons, and the lust for power can be just as completely satisfied by suggesting people into loving their servitude as by flogging and kicking them into obedience. . . . The change will be brought about as a result of a felt need for increased efficiency.

Nineteen Eighty-Four, like *Animal Farm* before it (Meyers reports that Orwell rushed around London bookshops taking *Animal Farm* out of the children's section and putting it in the adult section), was of inestimable importance during the Cold War in alerting people to the reality of Soviet totalitarianism. Our debt to Orwell on that score can never be fully repaid. But Huxley recognized a half century ago what is now evident to all, that the brutal boot-on-the-face tyranny of communism was terribly inefficient. There are still in the world plenty of tyrants who rule by the boot, machete, club, and machine gun, and there likely will be for a long time. But the more sophisticated who want the total control that is *totalitarian* tyranny will resort to means more like those depicted in *Brave New World* — baby hatcheries, cloning, the elimination of the unfit, and the exclusion of moral and historical reasoning by a uniform sense of therapeutic well-being induced by what Huxley called *soma* and is today chillingly similar to multiple variations on Prozac. It will be a softer, and therefore more efficient, totalitarianism.

In his 1991 encyclical *Centesimus Annus,* John Paul II speaks of what can happen when moral reasoning is eliminated from public life and politics is reduced to the manipulation of desires and images in order to secure the acquiescence of a compliant majority. The result he calls "thinly disguised totalitarianism." The danger at present and in the future is more Huxley's velvet glove than Orwell's iron fist, although, to be sure, the velvet glove is not entirely absent in *Nineteen Eighty-Four,* and the compassionate and gentle manipulations of *Brave New World* only thinly disguise the iron fist.

Meyers' *Orwell* is, by the way, a very good read. One does wish, however, that he had not tried to explain Orwell's relentless truth-telling and life of self-deprivation in pop psychology terms of guilt feelings. It is more convincing that Orwell's determination to tell the truth was just that, a determination to tell the truth because he hated brutal and self-serving lies, and because he believed that decent people should counter lies with truth. Then too, Meyers' claim that Orwell was the greatest and most popular writer of his time leads him to exaggerations that undermine his otherwise admirable defense of Orwell's achievement.

Particularly egregious is his citing, among many others, spy novelist John le Carré in praise of Orwell. Le Carré says, "Orwell's hatred of greed, cant, and the 'me' society is as much needed today as it was in his own time — probably more so. He remains an ideal for me — of clarity, anger, and perfectly aimed irony." That is a self-serving statement of a very low order. Le Carré's novels of the Cold War all too often were almost perfect exemplifications of the "moral symmetry" that denied any real moral difference between the free world and the Soviet Union's evil empire, or at least any real moral difference in their struggle to prevail. Orwell wrote not against the "me" society but against the totalitarian "them" who denied the possibility of "I." As for perfectly aimed irony, there is not a hint of irony in Orwell's depiction of the difference between human freedom and dignity, on the one hand, and a regime of oppression and debasement, on the other. Orwell's perfectly aimed anger is directed, then and now, at those whose playful irony makes light of the murderously inverted rules of the animal farm. *(March 2001)*

Caught Out and Catching Up

Everybody knows by now Irving Kristol's definition of a neoconservative: a liberal who has been mugged by reality. Actually, the term "neoconservative" is not much used now, and I use it almost never. But in some circles the neoconservatives are still a lively topic of conversation, as witness William Dean of Iliff School of Theology, Denver, writing in a symposium in *Religion and American Culture.* He takes his liberal academic colleagues to task for letting the neoconservatives — meaning mainly the usual suspects, Michael Novak, George Weigel, and your writer — monopolize the field of public theology. Public theology in this context means theology that has something to say about the *res publica.*

"The neoconservatives overtook the academic public intellectuals for three reasons," Dean writes. "First, because the neoconservatives were shaken to their foundations, they were forced to rethink their positions, while the academics were unshaken; second, the neoconservatives remained classical, small 'r' republicans, and the academics did not; third, the neoconservatives developed a basic cultural, sometimes even theological, interpretation of America, and the academics did not." The liberal and mostly Protestant academics, Dean observes, smugly continued on in the tradition of Walter Rauschenbusch, Reinhold Niebuhr, and Paul Tillich, failing to appreciate that these figures in their lifetimes underwent a shaking of the foundations comparable to today's neoconservatives.

From the late 1960s on, he writes, "this small band of intellectuals grew strong enough to provide much of the intellectual ballast for the Reagan Administration," to found journals of influence such as *Public Interest* and *First Things*, and, in general, to dominate the discussion of religion, ethics, and public life. "As they moved from the far left to the right wing of the left and then to the antiliberal wing of the right, they endured the outrage of liberal intellectuals who had once been their friends and colleagues." Dean clearly includes himself among those liberal intellectuals, but he has some pointed advice for his friends: "The academic public theologians need to develop a distinct theological interpretation of America, one that gives context and impetus to their particular and often admirable political, economic, gender, racial, and ecological arguments. But to do this, they must get within mugging range of reality."

There are several things that might be said about this, apart from the fact that those of us who are called neoconservatives are, contra Dean, the champions of the liberal tradition. First, William Dean considerably overestimates our influence. Second, the arguments of his liberal friends are, in substance and temperament, generally hostile to the American experiment, both past and present. People will not buy their self-understanding from those who are perceived to be, and often declare themselves to be, their enemies. Third, the liberal academics he has in mind are, with exceptions, Protestant, as is the tradition of Rauschenbusch, Niebuhr, and Tillich to which they adhere. The leading "neocons," on the other hand, are Catholic, determined to advance the vision of John Paul II, and energetic in embracing the best in the Protestant tradition of public theology, notably the work of Reinhold Niebuhr. Moreover, they are assiduous in cultivating a close relationship with evangelical Protestants, who are anathema to most of Dean's oldline liberal academics, not least because evangelicals are favorably disposed toward a theological interpretation of America. (In the same symposium, Mark Noll of Wheaton College suggests, with some justice, that the most influential public theology today is being advanced by evangelicals.) Conclusion: Dean and his friends do need to get "within mugging range of reality," and his essay is a sign that this may be happening. But, once sufficiently mugged, it is not evident that they have an alternative vision to propose. But then, who could have predicted that, to cite but one example, the author of the 1969 *Theology of Radical Politics* (Michael Novak) would have so much to contribute? *(June/July 2001)*

At the Origins of the Culture War

One of the many contributions of Gertrude Himmelfarb's new book, *One Nation, Two Cultures* (Knopf), is to remind us that the phenomenon now called the culture wars is not all that new. She begins with this passage from Adam Smith's *The Wealth of Nations,* published in 1776: "In every civilized society, in every society where the distinction of ranks has once been completely established, there have been always two different schemes or systems of morality current at the same time; of which the one may be called the strict or austere; the other the liberal, or, if you will, the loose system. The former is generally admired and revered by the common people; the latter is commonly more esteemed and adopted by what are called people of fashion."

I was recently reading Sam Tanenhaus' splendid biography, *Whittaker Chambers* (Random House), and was reminiscing over dinner about my own brief brush with a vestige of that tumultuous period. The Hiss-Chambers trials of 1949-1950 happened long before I came of political age, and I had no firm views on the contentions surrounding those events. Years later, however, in the mid-seventies, I was connected with an organization that routinely invited the then elderly Alger Hiss to its receptions and other occasions. He was something of a celebrity and seemed very much the gentleman. I never raised with him awkward questions about the past, but after one such occasion I asked an older colleague whether he thought Hiss was guilty of the crimes for which he had spent more than three years in federal prison. I was taken aback by the insouciance of the answer, "Oh, of course, he was a perjurer and Soviet spy." If that is the case, I naively asked, why on earth did we invite him to our affairs? The response came in the tones of a self-evident truth: "He insists he is innocent and to publicly disagree is to lend aid and comfort to McCarthyism." The reference, of course, was to Senator Joe McCarthy, who contributed so powerfully to the anti-anticommunism that was then regnant among "what are called people of fashion." What is a little perjury and treason, or even a lot of perjury and treason, among friends who agree on the important questions?

Later I would read Whittaker Chambers' *Witness* and come to reckon it one of the most important books of the century. There Chambers wrote: "No feature of the Hiss case is more obvious, or more troubling as history, than the jagged fissure, which it did not so much open as reveal, between the plain men and women of the nation, and those who affected to act, think, and speak for them. It was, not invariably, but in general, the 'best people' who were for Alger Hiss and who were prepared to go to any length for him. It was the enlightened and the powerful, the clamorous proponents of the open mind and the common man, who snapped their minds shut in a pro-Hiss psychosis, of a kind which, in an individual patient, means the simple failure of the ability to distinguish between reality and unreality, and, in a nation, is a warning of the end."

On the basis of what is now known from the files of Soviet intelligence and other sources — all helpfully summarized by Tanenhaus — nobody but the willfully obtuse believes that Hiss was innocent. Among people of a certain age, however, and until quite recently, whether one sided with Hiss or Chambers divided the liberal *bien-pensant* from the ignorant peasantry. But the larger divide between the "strict" and the "loose" described by Adam Smith has not always been the case. Perhaps it has always been the case that many among the wealthy and aristocratic, along with the riff-raff and criminal elements of society, have deemed themselves largely exempt from general moral norms. (This is what I have described as a culture caught between the overclass and the underclass, a locution subsequently picked up by the prolific Michael Lind and turned to quite different purposes.) In the modern period artists and intellectuals typically certify themselves to be such by their defiance of what they take to be established norms. Lionel Trilling called this the "adversary culture," and a decade and more ago the phenomenon was much discussed in terms of the "new knowledge class."

A Deeper Divide

Whittaker Chambers, among others, thought the phenomenon not so universal as did Smith nor so new as do more recent thinkers. As he wrote in *Witness* and in earlier days when he was a major voice in Henry Luce's empire of Time Inc., the phenomenon is to be traced to modernity's decision against God and the human soul. Chambers frequently wrote in the mode of the prophetic jeremiad, a mode that found a readier audience in the 1950s when figures such as Reinhold Niebuhr, Hannah Arendt, and even the Arthur Schlesinger

Jr. of *The Vital Center* also spoke in urgent tones about the crisis of the West. Less than twenty years later, the once lionized Aleksandr Solzhenitsyn would lose most of his audience in the West when he, like Chambers, traced the problem to the origins of modernity. For instance, in *A World Split Apart* (1978): "The mistake must be at the root, at the very foundation of thought in modern times. I refer to the prevailing Western view of the world which was born in the Renaissance and has found political expression since the Age of Enlightenment. It became the basis for political and social doctrine and could be called rationalistic humanism or humanistic autonomy. . . . The West has finally achieved the rights of man, and even to excess, but man's sense of responsibility to God and society has grown dimmer."

In the Hiss-Chambers period and up through the fall of the evil empire a decade ago, the divide between the two cultures of the one nation was, at least among intellectuals and the politically engaged, the divide between anticommunism and anti-anticommunism. Behind that and deeper than that, according to thinkers such as Chambers and Solzhenitsyn, is the chasm opened by modernity's divorce of the human project from its source and end in God. That chasm created the space for the growth of modernity's children, of which communism was perhaps the most destructive in its deformity. The future of the culture war in this nation will depend in large part upon whether we come to think that the American experiment is another deformed child of modernity — a view increasingly urged by some religious conservatives — or whether we engage its capacities to be corrected and renewed by the prophetic critique of the modernity of which it is undoubtedly, but by no means exclusively, the product. Put differently, the American experiment — as the word "experiment" suggests — is a work in progress. The culture war is about, inter alia, how the experiment is to be defined. It would be a great pity were conservative thinkers to join with "what are called people of fashion" in so defining it that it must be rejected by the morally and religiously serious. That, too, would be a kind of treason. *(April 2000)*

While We're At It

❦ Robert Craft on Igor Stravinsky is a subject almost as endless as other writers on Robert Craft and Igor Stravinsky. But here is an aspect I had not come across before. Craft is commenting in the *Times Literary Supplement* on John Warrack's review of a new Stravinsky biography: "Warrack has perceived that the book's discussion of Stravinsky's 'indebtedness' to [Jacques] Maritain is exaggerated. But it is a mistaken argument that Stravinsky's 'sudden assemblage of icons, votary candles, and so forth [was no] more than a symptom of an exile's nostalgia.' Every morning before he composed, Stravinsky prayed to an icon that he had brought from Russia. Superstition was undoubtedly a large element in Stravinsky's religion — as in other people's — but the drawing of the Crucifixion on the flyleaf of the *Symphony of Psalms* sketchbook, and the Church calendar dates found in his scores — 'I. Stravinsky after Friday confession, April 9, 1926' on the cover of the *Sérénade en la* — are indications of a profound religious belief, and we know for certain that he wanted his uncommissioned Mass to be used liturgically; when it was, in a Los Angeles church for a Thursday noon Holy Day of Obligation service, he knelt throughout." *(April 2001)*

❦ Megachurches, as they are called, require mega-solutions. When it was communion Sunday at Southeast Christian Church in Louisville, Kentucky, it took seven volunteers thirty hours to fill the 350 trays of individual shot glasses, as they are somewhat irreverently called, with grape juice. Until, that is, inventor Wilfred Greenlee joined the church and cut the preparation time down to an hour and a half. I quote: "The Greenlee Communion Dispensing Machine is made of a stainless steel bucket with forty plastic tubes that run through a sheet of Plexiglas into the cups of a communion tray. A push of a lever on the side allows just enough juice to fill each cup half full." A communion dispensing machine. The phrase has possibilities. Mr. Greenlee's invention, however, takes second place to a news story from Denmark a couple of years ago reporting that a church was mailing communion in little plastic containers, thus both dispensing communion and dispensing with the troublesome community of believers that is the Church. In two thousand years we have learned a thing or two about efficiency. *(November 2001)*

❧ Much like almost everything else in life, literacy is a mixed bag. During the cold war, Communist regimes boasted of the high literacy rate they had achieved, but, even if true, it was a limited good since people could not read anything deviating from the party line. It may also be that more Americans are reading books, but then consider what they choose to read. According to *Publishers Weekly*, here are the authors of books that were on the top ten best-sellers list during the 1940s (asterisk indicates several times): Ernest Hemingway,* John Steinbeck,* Van Wyck Brooks, William L. Shirer, John Gunther,* Winston Churchill, Pearl S. Buck, William Saroyan, W. Somerset Maugham, John Hersey,* Sinclair Lewis, James Hilton, Richard Wright, James Thurber, Daphne du Maurier, Erich Maria Remarque, Norman Mailer, John O'Hara. Here is the list for the 1970s: Ernest Hemingway, Graham Greene, John Updike, Alexander Solzhenitsyn, Chaim Potok, Gore Vidal, Kurt Vonnegut, E. L. Doctorow, Saul Bellow, J. R. R. Tolkien, John Le Carré,* Anaïs Nin, William Styron. As for the years 1990-1998? Here are the best-selling authors: John Grisham, Stephen King, Danielle Steel, Michael Crichton, Tom Clancy, Mary Higgins Clark. Of the fifty best-selling books of the decade, forty-one were written by these six authors. No, of course I'm not against literacy, but much like everything else in life . . . *(November 2001)*

❧ Here's an unusual advertisement: "CELEBRANTS for weddings at hotel churches, bridal halls, and restaurants. Ordained pastors welcomed. Experienced religious Christians are also acceptable. Daily Japanese conversation ability required." It's not all that unusual in Japan, however, where the ad appeared in *Japan Times,* the major English-language newspaper. Reader Charles de Wolf of Keio University sent it along, noting that over the thirty years he has been in Japan "Christian-style" weddings have become the norm, with family members and guests who have never been in a church stumbling over the Japanese version of "What a Friend We Have in Jesus." The ceremonies typically take place in "hotel churches," and it is preferred that the person dressed up as the pastor should be an Occidental male. An American priest friend who is a missionary in Japan puzzled a hotel manager by turning down the suggestion that, since he was a "professional" and already had his own "costume," he could make a lot of money presiding at such ceremonies. The fact that he, as an "experienced religious Christian," had some problems with the deal appeared to be quite beyond the manager's ken. Professor de Wolf adds, "The public square in secular Japan is not naked. It is filled with myriad monuments to the eclectic worship of kitsch." *(May 2001)*

❧ Among more theologically conservative Protestants, one frequently encounters a declared determination to "keep faith" with the sixteenth-century reformers such as Luther, Calvin, or Zwingli. It is a matter of defending a tradition, including the tradition of positing *sola scriptura* (Scripture alone) against tradition. David C. Steinmetz, church historian at Duke Divinity School, discusses in *Theology Today,* the journal of Princeton Theological Seminary, the ironic twists by which a later Protestant identity became something very different from the self-understanding of the original reformers. By the middle of the sixteenth century, a permanent and self-perpetuating Protestant culture was developing. "The older ex-Catholic leadership of former priests, nuns, friars, and monks was slowly replaced by a new leadership that had never attended Mass, much less said one, and by a laity that had never confessed its sins to a priest, gone on pilgrimage, invoked patron saints, made a binding vow, or purchased an indulgence." In truth, some of the first generation did not think of themselves as ex-Catholics. It is probably the case, for instance, that when Philip Melanchthon, Luther's friend and chief aide, died in 1560 he understood himself to be a Catholic, despite what he viewed as the temporary rupture with Rome. Steinmetz nicely summarizes the general situation: "While Protestants continued to write anti-Catholic polemics, their treatises lacked the passion and sense of betrayal of the polemics written by the first generation. Protestants were permanent outsiders with their own fixed institutions, parishes, confessions, catechisms, and settled sense of identity. They harbored no illusions about reunion and felt no twinges of nostalgia for a church that had never been their home. Unlike their grandparents, they cherished no hope for an evangelical reformation of the Catholic Church and settled into a mode of permanent opposition. In all these respects, the third generation of Protestants differed from the first. The Reformation began as an argument among Catholic insiders; it continued as an argument between Catholics and former Catholics until well past the middle of the century. The transformation of a movement led by former Catholics into a movement led by traditional Protestants took two generations to effect. Unless we understand the Catholic background, context, and character of the early Protestant Reformation, we shall inevitably misunderstand it. Luther, Zwingli, Calvin, Hubmaier, Hooper, and Melanchthon were not Protestants in the way Voetius, Ames, Turrettini, Perkins, Wollebius, and Spener were. In the nature of the case, they could not be." *(May 2001)*

❧ This, I suppose, comes under the heading of closing loopholes. After the Netherlands became the first nation to legalize the killing of the old and not so old who would — in their judgment or in the judgment of a properly authorized party — be better off dead, the minister of health, Mrs. Els Borst-Eilers, has a further proposal. There are some people, she notes, who would prefer to kill themselves rather than depend upon a doctor. She suggests that such people should be provided with a suicide pill. She adds that the provision of the pill should be carefully regulated to ensure that those asking for it really are "tired of life and desperate to die." So how tired are you of life, really? Perhaps some kind of measuring instrument could be devised. One imagines the health minister, eager to share death benefits as equitably as possible, asking herself, "Now, let's see. Have we left anyone out?" *(November 2001)*

❧ She smoked cigars, had seven children, did the definitive translation of Wittengenstein's major work, succeeded to his chair at Cambridge, publicly protested Truman's use of atomic bombs, was arrested as a pro-life activist, possessed one of the great philosophical minds of the century, and was an upfront Christian. How I wish I had known her personally. The tributes to G. E. M. (Elizabeth) Anscombe (including John M. Dolan's in these pages [May]) have me going back to read her works. Christopher Howse in the *London Daily Telegraph* observes: "Elizabeth Anscombe was no fundamentalist, but nor did she use philosophy to explain away the creed in which she believed. To an essay on the Eucharist, republished in the third volume of her collected philosophical papers (1981), she gave the title 'On Transubstantiation,' even though the term *substance* was not one that her contemporaries or mentors used in their cosmology. The essay begins with the problem of explaining to a child the Real Presence of Christ in the Sacrament. 'When one says "transubstantiation," one is saying exactly what one teaches the child in teaching it that Christ's words, by the divine power given to the priest who uses them in his place, have changed the bread so that it isn't there any more (nor the stuff of which it is made), but instead there is the body of Christ. I knew a child,' she continues, 'close upon three years old and only then beginning to talk, but taught as I have described, who was in the free space at the back of the church when the mother went to communion. "Is he in you?" the child asked when the mother came back. "Yes," she said, and to her amazement the child prostrated itself before her. I can testify to this, for I saw it happen. I once told the story to one of those theologians who unhappily (as it seems) strive to alter and water down our faith, and he deplored it.' The story no doubt shocked, even if that paper was delivered to a Catholic audience. And, of course, Elizabeth Anscombe knew, as she went on to mention, that Christ is not present 'dimensively' (nor does transubstantiation imply that he is). She was only exemplifying what Dr. Johnson noted: 'Sir, there is no idolatry in the Mass. They believe God to be there and they adore him.' And now Elizabeth Anscombe has moved from the shadows and metaphors of philosophy into Reality, *ex umbris et imaginibus in veritatem* [out of shadows and images into the truth]." *(June/July 2001)*

❧ This from the *Seattle Times:* "Seattle has the smallest percentage of children of any big city in the country except for San Francisco." Seattle is truly Bobo paradise, "a sanctuary for professionals too busy to raise families." The report says that otherwise thriving neighborhoods "have become virtual child-free zones where kids make up less than 10 percent of the population." San Francisco at least has an excuse, of sorts. *(November 2001)*

❧ This year is the bicentenary of the birth of John Henry Cardinal Newman. John Paul II has written a letter on the occasion, in which he says: "Newman was born in troubled times which knew not only political and military upheaval but also turbulence of soul. Old certitudes were shaken, and believers were faced with the threat of rationalism on the one hand and fideism on the other. Rationalism brought with it a rejection of both authority and transcendence, while fideism turned from the challenges of history and the tasks of this world to a distorted dependence upon authority and the supernatural. In such a world, Newman came eventually to a remarkable synthesis of faith and reason which were for him 'like two wings on which the human spirit rises to the contemplation of the truth' *(Fides et Ratio).* It was the passionate contemplation of truth which also led him to a liberating acceptance of the authority which has its roots in Christ, and to the sense of the supernatural which opens the human mind and heart to the full range of possibilities revealed in Christ. 'Lead kindly light, amid the encircling gloom, lead Thou me on,' Newman wrote in *The Pillar of the Cloud;* and for him Christ was the light at the heart of every kind of darkness. For his tomb he chose the inscription: *Ex umbris et imaginibus in veritatem;* and it was clear at the end of his life's journey that Christ was the truth he had found." The Pope adds that he hopes the time is near when the Church, having already declared Newman "venerable," will "publicly proclaim the exemplary holiness of one of the most distinguished and versatile champions of English spirituality." *(June/July 2001)*

❧ The G-7 leaders met in Genoa, with Russia, the wannabe eighth, invited to drop by afterwards. An estimated fifty thousand protestors rioted for sundry causes under the banner "Smash Capitalism!" The second day of the meeting, the lead story in the *New York Times* is under the heading, "Leaders Continue Meeting, Despite Death of Protester." How heartless. Presumably the world leaders should have called off the meeting after a young man was shot in the act of attacking an Italian police car. The next day the *Times* report continued to fret that the nations of the world were not letting the rioters set their agenda. "But in private, several of Mr. Bush's aides conceded that the imagery of the leaders meeting in the splendor of a thirteenth-century medieval palace, while smoke and tear gas wafted over the hills nearby, seemed only to highlight the gulf between the leaders and the protestors." Oh, dear. In fact, Mr. Bush did his best to "highlight the gulf" between his determination to include, and the rioters' desire to exclude, poor nations from what the encyclical *Centesimus Annus* calls the circle of productivity and exchange. For the *Times,* however, radical chic is still chic, even when dressed in the tattered rags of socialisms past. It is not that the editors have a love affair with socialism, although some do, but they are in the grip of their (usually inflated) memories of their own youthful rambunctiousness. Remember Chicago '68! Remember the Catonsville Nine! Remember whatever. Show them a picture of a young thug throwing a firebomb at the pigs, and they're off on their Wordsworthian reverie, "Bliss was it in that dawn to be alive, / But to be young was very heaven!" What with arthritis and one's membership in the AARP, reporting for the *Times* is not quite the same as marching again, but it's the next best thing. *(October 2001)*

❦ Excommunication is a matter of the Church's determination that a person has excommunicated himself. This comes up again in the response of Patriarch Alexis II of Moscow to demands that the Church revoke the excommunication of Leo Tolstoy more than a hundred years ago. "We do not have the right," said the Patriarch, "to force a person who died a hundred years ago to return to the Church he rejected." Rome has made a similar response to suggestions that the excommunication of, for example, Martin Luther be revoked. Presumably both cases have already been disposed of by higher authority. *(June/July 2001)*

❦ Peter Singer of Princeton is back, this time with an essay on bestiality. "One by one, the taboos have fallen," he writes, but people still have this hang-up about doing it with animals. Singer's view seems to be that there is nothing wrong in having sex with animals, so long as no cruelty is involved. For instance, some men do it with chickens, sometimes killing the chicken in the process. Singer disapproves of that, although he notes that "it is no worse than what egg producers do to their hens all the time." His chief complaint is against "the Judeo-Christian tradition" that imagines there is "a wide, unbridgeable gulf" separating us from animals. He goes on to cite many examples of this mistaken view. He might have, but does not, cite the fact that only human beings get appointed to tenured chairs of ethics at Ivy League universities. Given his argument, that would seem to be profoundly unfair. I have no doubt that in such a position my dog Sammy would perpetrate less intellectual and moral confusion than some who are unjustly privileged by virtue of the speciesism that is rampant in our institutions of higher learning. The fact that we too are animals, Singer concludes, "does not make sex across the species barrier normal or natural, whatever those much misused words may mean, but it does imply that it ceases to be an offense to our status and dignity as human beings." The fact that Peter Singer promotes such views does not necessarily make him lunatic or perverse, whatever those much misused words may mean, but it does not do much for his status and dignity as a professor of ethics, nor for that of the university that honors him. *(June/July 2001)*

❧ Recall Ronald Reagan's formula for negotiating arms agreements with the Soviets: "Trust, but verify." In similar vein is a new book by Arlene G. Dubin, *Prenups for Lovers: A Romantic Guide to Prenuptial Agreements* (Villard). It's described this way: "This step-by-step handbook shows how to create a fair, balanced, and loving prenuptial agreement. Legal, financial, and psychological sources contribute to the discussion of finances, future goals, and what each partner should expect from marriage." Building a house of romance on a foundation of suspicion. *(November 2001)*

❧ You want to make the argument that most people agree with you. One way to do it is to get some research assistants to go out and do interviews with "ordinary" people, preferably middle class and fairly articulate. Twenty interviews will do, although a hundred makes it sound like really serious research. Then you excerpt from the interview transcripts what you want people to say and, voila! they say pretty much what you want them to say. Such was the "methodology" employed by Alan Wolfe, who heads Boston College's Center for Religion and American Life, to produce his book *One Nation After All.* Both the methodology and Wolfe's hostility to religion in public — the latter making his appointment by Boston College even curiouser — came in for scathing criticism in Gertrude Himmelfarb's *One Nation, Two Cultures.* Now Wolfe has a new book, *Moral Freedom.* The combination of fraudulence and fatuity is stunning. Wolfe's argument is that, having achieved political and economic freedom, Americans are now achieving moral freedom. He writes: "The ultimate implication of the idea of moral freedom . . . is that any form of higher authority has to tailor its commandments to the needs of real people." As Adam and Eve agreed. Or this: "Morality has long been treated as if it were a fixed star, sitting there far removed from the earthly concerns of real people. . . . In the contemporary world, however, people experience in their own lives many situations for which traditional conceptions of morality offer little guidance: What do you do when the pursuit of one virtue conflicts with another?" Homer, Augustine, Aquinas, Shakespeare, MacIntyre — and, yes, you too, Charlie Brown — call your offices immediately! *(June/July 2001)*

❦ Speaking in North Dakota, President Bush told an audience, "My job is to say to the moms and dads of America, 'Your most important job is to love your children with all your heart and all your soul.'" The Associated Press smelled a story in Bush's "controversial" statement and quotes three academics (from New York, Boston, and the University of Missouri) who say there is nothing in the Constitution that gives the President that job. *National Review Online* comments, "The AP should get credit for enterprise. Finding three people to criticize the President for saying parents should love their children can't have been easy." Actually, there is a story here. The only one we are to love with *all* our heart and *all* our soul is the Lord God. But that nuance — well, really more than a nuance — apparently escaped both the AP and *NRO. (June/July 2001)*

❧ It would be a very good thing, writes Bruce Bawer in the *New York Times Book Review,* were there a revival of interest in Sigrid Undset, and I warmly agree. Undset was a Norwegian convert to Catholicism who won the Nobel Prize in literature in 1928. If you have not read the saga *Kristen Lavransdatter* (be sure to get the T. Nunnally translation), yours is the prospect of delight in a great discovery. Unfortunately, Bawer, author of *A Place at the Table* and apologist for a "conservative" version of the homosexual movement, has to get in some swipes at Undset's alleged views on sexual differences. Already at age nineteen, she wrote to a friend that "most marriages run aground because the two people have tried to know each other too well." Those who have had to deal with marriages running aground may think that an acute observation. But not Bawer, who writes, "What to make of this trailblazing contrarian who, recoiling from what she saw as groupthink, expressed her fierce individuality by sneering at women's rights and preaching the gospel of male as protector?" He thinks the answer may be in one biographer's judgment that Undset was "nearly filled with hate for her own sex." As any reader of *Kristen* or *The Master of Hestviken* will recognize, that is preposterous. I confess that I am influenced on this by no less an authority than my late mother. Undset was probably the last major reading project she undertook a few years before her death at age ninety-four. Never, she declared, had she met an author who so perfectly understood women, marriage, and sex. Of these subjects my mother was no mean student, being married for almost fifty years to a greatly difficult man and rearing eight children. But others with more literary credentials, if not more life credentials, have recognized Undset's courage in clearing her mind of the cant that has, for more than a hundred years, confused the discussion of the sexes. Bawer notes in a parenthesis that Undset became a Catholic in 1924, but her Catholicism was anything but parenthetical. This has been underscored in more recent books, such as J. C. Whitehouse's *Vertical Man: The Human Being in the Catholic Novels of Graham Greene, Sigrid Undset, and Georges Bernanos* (St. Augustine's Press), and *Sigrid Undset: On Saints and Sinners,* edited by Deal Hudson (Ignatius). The place to start, however, is with *Kristen Lavransdatter.* Let the Sigrid Undset revival begin. *(November 2001)*

❧ *America* magazine on a statement by the Congregation for the Doctrine of the Faith: "The statement of doctrinal principles drew heavily from the recent controversial document, *Dominus Iesus,* which strongly emphasized Christ as the unique savior and rejected the idea that 'one religion is as good as another.'" How controversial can you get? *(June/July 2001)*

❧ This is a beautiful book — beautifully conceived, beautifully executed, and rare in the beauty of its pastoral and theological sensibilities. It is by Richard Lischer, professor of homiletics at Duke Divinity School, and is titled *Open Secrets* (Doubleday, 256 pp., $23.95). There has not appeared for a very long time such a compelling story of Christian ministry. Do not be put off by the occasionally too breezy style or the PC opinions on this and that; the former is only occasional and the latter are strictly by-the-way asides that have no bearing on the tale that Lischer tells. The tale is about his three years as pastor of Cana Lutheran Church in a little German no-place hamlet near Alton, Illinois. He and his wife Tracy (he with his newly minted Ph.D. from England, and thinking himself quite God's gift to the Church) could not have been more disappointed or more out of place with this rustic congregation so drearily set in its ways. Slowly, awkwardly, and with many a misstep, Lischer came to see in these people the face of Christ. The last phrase is, of course, from Georges Bernanos' *Diary of a Country Priest,* and I can offer no higher praise of this book than to say that at times it explores heights and depths of Christian ministry in a manner worthy of Bernanos. With a literary grace that never loses touch with the thus and so-ness of everyday lives, Lischer reveals to the reader, as was revealed to him, the presence of Christ in his body. It is not the whole of the truth, but it is a too easily forgotten part of the truth, to say that all Christianity is local. This people, this place, these wounds, these healings, these questions left, it seems, forever hanging. The book caught my attention because Lischer was a pastor in the Lutheran Church–Missouri Synod, which I also once was, and graduated from Concordia Theological Seminary in St. Louis, which is my alma mater as well. But these personal connections, interesting though they are to me, are not the reason for my strong recommendation of *Open Secrets.* I could only feel sorry for a Catholic priest or a minister of any denomination who does not resonate to Lischer's discovery of the mystery of Christ in the ordinary. And it is far from being a book for clergy alone. Every Christian who, looking honestly at the ragtag company of disciples that is every local church, has ever asked, "Is that all there is?" should read this book and be opened to the wonder of the One who meets us in others who are — in the words of Mother Teresa — Christ in distressing disguise. *Open Secrets* is a rare achievement. *(June/July 2001)*

❦ "Do Poles, along with Germans, bear guilt for the Holocaust? It is hard to imagine a more absurd claim." So writes Adam Michnik, a Jew and editor of Poland's largest daily, *Gazeta Wyborcza,* in the *New York Times.* "Not a single Polish family was spared by Hitler and Stalin. The two totalitarian dictatorships obliterated three million Poles and three million Polish citizens classified as Jews by the Nazis." Of course some Poles did terrible things. He cites this from a letter written about a wartime incident on a Warsaw bridge: "Another time, on the Kierbedz bridge, a German saw a Pole giving alms to a starving Jewish urchin. He pounced and ordered the Pole to throw the child into the river or else he would be shot along with the young beggar. 'There is nothing you can do to help him. I will kill him anyway; he is not allowed to be here. You can go free, if you drown him, or I will kill you, too. Drown him or die. I will count . . . 1, 2 — ' The Pole could not take it. He broke down and threw the child over the rail into the river. The German gave him a pat on the shoulder. '*Braver Kerl.*' They went their separate ways. Two days later, the Pole hanged himself." Michnik does not deny the anti-Semitism in Polish culture. "The anti-Semitic tradition compels the Poles to perceive the Jews as aliens while the Polish heroic tradition compels them to save them." And many thousands did engage in heroic actions to save Jews, even at the risk of their own lives and the lives of their families, during the time of Hitler. "I feel guilty," he writes, "when I read so often in Polish and foreign newspapers about the murderers who killed Jews, and note the deep silence about those who rescued Jews. Do the murderers deserve more recognition than the righteous?" *(August/September 2001)*

❦ As has been frequently pointed out, the right to die almost inevitably morphs into the obligation to die. The Oregon Health Division (OHD) reports that in the third year of that state's euthanasia law 63 percent of those who sought and received physician-assisted suicide gave as their reason that they feared being a burden to family, friends, and other caregivers. That compares with 23 percent in the second year. In 1999 37 percent were referred for psychiatric evaluation before being euthanized, compared with 19 percent in 2000. The process is also speeding up. It was on average eighty-three days from first request to killing in 1999, compared with a much more efficient thirty days last year. Our Gilbert Meilaender might suggest that it is the family and friends who need to be referred for evaluation. See his "I Want to Burden My Loved Ones" (October 1991), also included in *The Eternal Pity* (University of Notre Dame Press), edited by Richard John Neuhaus. *(August/September 2001)*

❧ You may recall that a few years ago there was much media hype about a rash of burnings of black churches across the South. It turned out to be just that, hype. But the National Council of Churches and others raised about a million dollars for rebuilding churches that were not burned. The money was spent, of course, on "fighting racism." Now in Canada, the federal Multiculturalism Minister (yes, they have such an office), Hedy Fry, raised an alarm about racist cross-burnings. That, too, turned out to be fictional. But Lorne Gunter of the *Edmonton Journal* notes there really was an instance of cross-burning a year earlier in Montreal, when feminists stormed the Catholic cathedral on International Women's Day, an observance much encouraged by Multiculturalism Minister Fry. "The feminists, hiding behind ski masks, set alight homemade crosses, then stormed the cathedral. They vandalized the walls and altar with spray paint proclaiming No God, no masters. They knocked down elderly nuns, destroyed hymnals and prayer books, smeared the walls with used sanitary napkins, and strewed condoms around, all in the name of tolerance. It seems these protesters could not bear any views on abortion or women's rights that disagreed with their own. And since the Catholic Church believes all abortion is sin and chooses not to ordain women as priests, well then, its cathedrals were fair game for a good ransacking." You will probably not be surprised to learn that the Ministry of Multiculturalism had nothing, as in absolutely nothing, to say about what happened in Montreal. *(August/September 2001)*

❧ A medieval monk, it is said, worked all day on a manuscript, finally writing in the margin, *Nunc scripsi totum, pro*

Christo da mihi potum — I have now written everything, for the sake of Christ give me a drink. That I was told by an author whom I invited over for a drink at the house when he delivered his article. It may be true. At the end of some days it is certainly apt. *(May 2001)*